BROADCASTING AND POLITICS IN WESTERN EUROPE

BROADCASTING AND POLITICS IN WESTERN EUROPE

Edited by
RAYMOND KUHN

FRANK CASS

First published in 1985 in Great Britain by
FRANK CASS AND COMPANY LIMITED
Gainsborough House, 11 Gainsborough Road,
London, E11 1RS

and in the United States of America by
FRANK CASS AND COMPANY LIMITED
c/o Biblio Distribution Centre
81 Adams Drive, P.O. Box 327, Totowa, NJ 07511

Copyright © 1985 Frank Cass & Co. Ltd

British Library Cataloguing in Publication Data
Broadcasting and politics in Western Europe.—
 (West European politics, ISSN 0140-2382; v.8; no.2)
 1. Broadcasting—Political aspects—Europe
 I. Kuhn, Raymond   II. Series
 384.5'4'094   HE8689.E9

ISBN 0-7146-3274-0

This group of studies first appeared in a Special Issue on *Broadcasting and Politics in Western Europe* of *West European Politics*, Vol. 8, No. 2 published by Frank Cass and Co. Ltd.

All rights reserved. No part of this publication may be reproduced, stored in a retrieval system, or transmitted in any form, or by any means, electronic, mechanical, photocopying, recording, or otherwise, without the prior permission of Frank Cass and Company Limited.

Printed in Great Britain by
John Wright & Sons (Printing) Ltd. at The Stonebridge Press, Bristol

Contents

Notes on the Contributors		vii
Introduction	Raymond Kuhn	1
Politics, Parties and the Media in Britain	Jean Seaton	9
Proclaiming the Republic: Broadcasting Policy and the Corporate State in Ireland	Desmond Bell	27
France and the 'New Media'	Raymond Kuhn	50
Political and Market Forces in Italian Broadcasting	Donald Sassoon	67
Pluralism in the West German Media: The Press, Broadcasting and Cable	Arthur Williams	84
Broadcasting and Politics in the Netherlands: From Pillar to Post	Kees Brants	104
Broadcasting in Spain: A History of Heavy-handed State Control	Esteban López-Escobar and Ángel Faus-Belau	122
Greece: A Politically Controlled State Monopoly Broadcasting System	Dimitrios Katsoudas	137
The Politics of Cable and Satellite Broadcasting: Some West European Comparisons	Kenneth Dyson	152
Abstracts		172

FOR ANNE
WITH LOVE AND AFFECTION

Notes on Contributors

Desmond Bell lectures in the School of Communications at the National Institute for Higher Education, Dublin. He has published a number of articles on social theory and communication practice and is currently researching in the area of the political economy of the media.

Kees Brants is a lecturer in politics and mass communication at the University of Amsterdam. He has published widely (mainly in Dutch) on media policy-making, the media and elections, and racism in the Netherlands.

Kenneth Dyson is Professor of European Studies at the University of Bradford as well as Chairman of its Postgraduate School of Languages and European Studies. He is author of *The State Tradition in Western Europe* (1981), *Party, State and Bureaucracy in West Germany* (1977), *Industrial Crisis* (with S. Wilks, 1983), as well as of numerous articles on comparative public policy and the history of political ideas and institutions. At present he has an ESRC grant for research on satellite and cable broadcasting.

Dimitrios Katsoudas is a senior researcher at the Centre for Political Research and Information in Athens. He is also assistant editor of, as well as a regular contributor to, the Centre's bi-monthly journal, *Epikentra*. He is the author of numerous publications on Greek politics, including a recent article (with Kevin Featherstone) on Greek voting behaviour published in the *European Journal of Political Research*.

Raymond Kuhn is a lecturer in the Department of Political Studies at Queen Mary College, University of London. He has written several articles on the media in France and is editor of *The Politics of Broadcasting* (1985).

Esteban López-Escobar teaches in the Faculty of Information Sciences at the University of Navarra, Pamplona. He is author of *Análisis del 'nuevo orden' internacional de la información* (1978) and co-author of *La televisión por cable en Europa y América* (forthcoming).

Angel Faus-Belau teaches in the Faculty of Information Sciences at the University of Navarra, Pamplona. He is author of *La radio: introducción a un medio desconocido* (1981) and *La información televisiva y su tecnología* (1979).

Donald Sassoon lectures in History at Westfield College, University of

London. He is the author of *The Strategy of the Italian Communist Party* (1981) and of a forthcoming book on post-war Italy.

Jean Seaton lectures in Sociology at the Polytechnic of the South Bank, London. She is co-author of *Power Without Responsibility: The Press and Broadcasting in Britain* (1981), the second edition of which is to be published in the spring of 1985.

Arthur Williams is a senior lecturer in German Studies in the Modern Languages Centre at the University of Bradford. He is the author of *Broadcasting and Democracy in West Germany* (1976) and of various articles on West German broadcasting and social policy. He is currently involved in an ESRC funded project which is investigating regulatory policies for cable television in Great Britain, France and West Germany.

Introduction

Raymond Kuhn

The changing face of Western European broadcasting provides a fascinating subject of study for the contemporary observer. In part this is because the structures of different national broadcasting systems have altered over the past few years with the growth of new radio stations and television channels. A by-no-means exhaustive checklist of such developments would include *inter alia* the creation of Channel 4 in Britain, the recent launching of *Canal plus* in France, the *de facto* establishment of private television networks in Italy, the introduction of a second channel in Ireland, the beginnings of regional television in Spain, the introduction of cable television in West Germany and its expansion in the Netherlands, as well as the legalisation of private local radio in France, Italy and Spain among others. The general trend is towards an increase in the number and type of radio and television outlets, with previously excluded political and economic actors actively seeking, and in some cases gaining, a foothold in the broadcasting field.

Impressive as these structural changes undoubtedly are, however, they seem relatively small beer when set against *potential* developments. The introduction of fibre-optic cable networks and of direct broadcasting by satellite (DBS) may be about to usher in a new audiovisual era in which American-style multi-channel television comprising local, regional, national and supranational transmissions is regarded as the norm. In the more developed Western European countries governments are at present encouraging or directly participating in the development of cable and the launching of broadcast satellites for largely industrial and commercial reasons. The objective is to ensure that the countries concerned will not miss out on the assumed benefits of the communications revolution as their economies progress from manufacturing-based to service- and information-orientated activities.

Of particular interest to political scientists is the fact that in many cases the contemporary debate on broadcasting, as it affects both the 'old' and 'new' media, is taking place in a different political/ideological environment as well as a changing technological one. In various Western European countries changes of government have helped focus attention on to the broadcasting issue as new policies are formulated and legislation introduced, often quite radical in principle if not always in practice. France, Greece and Spain are obvious examples with, in each instance, the recent advent to power of a Socialist government after a prolonged period of right-wing rule (democratic or authoritarian) stimulating political interest in the media as these governments strive, not always very valiantly, still successfully, to implement reforms and overturn traditional practices of partisan control of news output.

Even in those countries where there has been a notable continuity in governing elites, such as Italy, or where alternation in government is a well-established feature of political behaviour, such as Britain and West Germany, the debate on broadcasting is frequently taking place in a new political/ideological climate. Nowhere is this more the case than in Great Britain, where the present Thatcher government's antipathy to state intervention in the economy and welfare provision marks a break with the postwar elite consensus shared by Conservative *and* Labour governments alike. This espousal of neo-liberalism has had obvious consequences for the government's policies on communications (for example, the privatisation of British Telecom) and broadcasting.[1] A general hostility has been shown towards the BBC, the flag-bearer of public service broadcasting in Britain, while the installation and operation of the nascent cable networks has been deliberately left to the *private* sector.[2] In other Western European countries too there has been a move, more or less pronounced, towards greater private control of broadcasting. In Italy and France, for example, the state monopoly in radio and television has been dismantled, while in West Germany and the Netherlands commercial interests are making inroads into broadcasting areas from which they were excluded previously.

For a combination of reasons, therefore, now is an opportune moment to provide an up-to-date survey of broadcasting and politics in Western Europe. This is the objective of this special issue of *West European Politics*, which consists of eight single country studies and one cross-national comparative article. For reasons of space, not every Western European country has been included. Regrettably some countries with fascinating broadcasting systems have had to be omitted, notably Belgium, Switzerland and the Scandinavian democracies. On the other hand, the present volume does cover the four main states – Great Britain, France, Italy and West Germany – as well as Spain and Greece, in both of which the broadcasting media have had to accommodate themselves to dictatorship, the establishment of democracy and, most recently, the electoral victory of their respective Socialist parties. There is also an article on the Netherlands which, with its pillarised broadcasting system, has traditionally provided a contrast with other Western European radio and television organisations, as well as an article on Ireland, a country much neglected in many studies of Western Europe but which may play an increasingly important role in the broadcasting field if its plans for satellite transmissions come to fruition. Finally, there is a comparative article on cable and satellite broadcasting which may well act as a pointer to the future of television in Western Europe – more transmissions at the local and regional level, but also more programmes penetrating previously well-defended national boundaries.

Although all the articles (with one exception) are single countryorientated, it is evident that certain themes and issues cut across national boundaries and are relevant to all, or at least some, of the countries covered in this volume. One obvious issue is *the independence of broadcasting from partisan political control*, which focuses attention on the relationship between governments and political parties on the one hand and radio and television on the other. Many of the articles are concerned wholly or in part with the ways in which politicians, particularly in the executive branch, seek

INTRODUCTION 3

to control the broadcast product, most notably, but by no means exclusively, news and current affairs output, for partisan political ends, ranging from short-term electoral manipulation to long-term ideological indoctrination. Such control may be exercised in a very overt, direct way, through ministerial censorship, for example, or more usually in a covert, indirect fashion, by means of appointments or through recourse to financial constraints. Attempts to control broadcast output by these methods generally contradict the prevailing statutory obligations which call for balanced and impartial political coverage.

As the articles on France, Italy, Spain and Greece make clear, broadcasting in these countries has traditionally been, and to a large extent remains, subordinate to a high degree of frequently overt, partisan political control. In practice, the objective of balance and impartiality in political output has rarely, if ever, been pursued, far less achieved. The conflict between the broadcasters and the politicians has been as one-sided as much of the resultant output.

In the other four countries studied in this volume, political control over broadcasting appears to be less nakedly partisan and political coverage somewhat more balanced, either because traditions of editorial autonomy and political independence are more strongly entrenched (Great Britain and, to some extent, Ireland) or because the structure of the broadcasting system allows *different* political forces, deliberately or otherwise, to exert some control over output (West Germany and the Netherlands). Yet it would be naïve in the extreme to believe that these last four countries have somehow satisfactorily resolved the tensions between broadcasters and politicians inherent in a liberal democratic polity. The articles on Britain, Ireland, West Germany and the Netherlands show that neither the BBC public service approach (imitated by the Irish and the West Germans among others), nor the Dutch pluralist model has escaped criticism and censure from a variety of quarters for allegedly biased, narrow and superficial coverage of politics.

The recent combination of political and academic attacks on the BBC, for so long regarded by many politicians and commentators on the continent of Europe as the embodiment of a broadcasting organisation whose political output could generally be regarded as fair and balanced, is particularly noteworthy in this respect. In the last few years, critics of the BBC have become more numerous and strident in their attacks on the Corporation's political coverage. Various factors have helped contribute to the decline in the credibility of the BBC as a medium of political information. For example, the fragmentation of the British party system as new political forces, notably the nationalist parties and the SDP, stake their claim for coverage has upset one of the traditional 'balances' between Conservative and Labour. One symptom of the contemporary failings of the BBC approach is the extent to which a middle-of-the-road party, indeed *the* middle-of-the-road party *par excellence* – the SDP, has felt itself obliged to complain about its allocation of broadcast time.

The SDP is not alone among the established political forces in registering a complaint. To long-standing distrust by the Labour Party has been added dissatisfaction on the part of many Conservatives, most evidently manifested at the time of the Falklands crisis.[3] For defenders of the BBC it is unfortunate that the present Conservative leadership is antipathetic to the public sector generally, and to the pragmatic, compromise approach to politics which the BBC espouses (at least superficially). Thatcher's stance in support of the free market and her ideological commitment to 'conviction politics' both make her a natural enemy of the BBC.

A final element in the critique of the BBC's political coverage stems from the flourishing academic interest in radio and television, as media studies become one of the latest growth areas in the social sciences. As a result of this academic development, broadcasting structures, work practices and content have come under closer empirical examination than ever before. Mass media research, which previously concentrated overwhelmingly on the effects of the message upon the audience, now also focuses on issues such as the relationship between broadcasting and the state, the role of broadcasters in the news production process and the content of news programmes.[4] Much of this research has been critical of the BBC. As a result, broadcasters have been forced to respond to the attacks of many media academics as best they can, while some politicians, especially on the left, have seized upon the research findings for their own political purposes. Almost every major political issue covered by the broadcasters is now, or so it seems, the object of detailed content analysis: election campaigns, Northern Ireland, the Falklands conflict, the nuclear defence controversy, industrial relations and, most recently, the coal dispute. The broadcasters may, and usually do, dispute those findings which are directed against them, but they can no longer ignore them. They have been drawn into the controversy, defending assumptions and work practices previously esoteric but now made public.

In my view some of the criticisms of British broadcasting's political coverage are valid.[5] Yet, while there is no room for smug complacency, it is not immediately apparent how the structures of British broadcasting can be organised so as to achieve a wider and deeper coverage of political and social questions on the one hand *and* still retain the viewers' interest on the other. To argue that 'far-reaching changes ... could only occur through a restructuring of the place of broadcasting in British society',[6] or that 'broadcasting will not change until the population ... demand instead *truly democratic media*'[7] (my italics), or that

> ... anything coming closer to a genuine 'balance' would, as a preliminary, require a drastic change in the balance of forces in society itself, and a labour movement sufficiently strong politically, intellectually and organizationally, to create a broadcasting system in which it would have its own stations transmitting programmes alongside other stations representing other social and political forces and interests, and competing in *a genuinely pluralistic situation* (my italics) ...'[8]

is to combine unhelpful platitudes with utopian daydreaming. These are not practical proposals for action.

In this regard, the creation of Channel 4 shows what might be achieved even within the confines and constraints of the present broadcasting arrangements. Its main evening news programme has consistently been more innovative, wide-ranging and analytical than its BBC and ITV counterparts. It has sought to provide access for previously excluded or marginalised social groupings. It has taken its information function seriously, refusing to trivialise the dramatic or dramatise the trivial. Although not a perfect 'solution' to the problem of political broadcasting (no such solution exists), it is certainly a welcome step in the right direction.

As Jean Seaton points out in her article on Britain, some commentators look to the arrival of 'new media' technology and, hence, additional broadcasting outlets for any radical amelioration in the range, depth and pluralistic nature of political coverage. *The introduction of new media* is the second theme which cuts across the national boundaries of most of the articles in this volume. The ramifications of these 'new media' technologies for broadcasting are not yet fully apparent. Utopian predictions and doom-laden prophecies compete against each other and with more balanced analyses for dominance in the marketplace of ideas and opinions. No one knows for certain whether the 'new media' will be commercially successful and, if so, how they will affect the range and quality of programming, viewing habits and leisure patterns. Their development may drastically alter certain established structures, long-standing practices and traditional expectations. On the other hand, their impact may well be less than some have feared and others predicted.

The prevailing climate of uncertainty is due to the fact that despite all the projections, plans and policies, the vast majority of viewers in most of Western Europe continue to depend on the programme output of the old media, albeit with some incremental increase in the number of outlets. The relatively stable post-war picture in Western European broadcasting may be on the point of changing, perhaps radically, but the reality is that it has not yet done so.

As a result, there may be a natural tendency on the part of some to argue that the communications revolution, like the Trojan war, will not take place. This is especially the case in Britain as discussions about direct broadcasting by satellite drag on interminably and some of the consortia-granted cable franchises get cold feet in the light of low levels of market demand and the high capital investment costs of installing the networks.[9] As various launch dates are put back, prognostications of only a few months' standing now look wildly optimistic. Academics, politicians, entrepreneurs and, not least, conference organisers with a vested interest in hyping up the introduction of the new media would appear to have cried wolf too early and too often.

Yet there are dangers in pursuing the anti-revolutionary argument too far and concluding that the wolf will never come. One is that outside Britain change may take place more quickly, especially in those countries, such as France, where the state is playing a more interventionist role in promoting the 'new media' technology. Demand for new sources of programming may also be greater in continental Europe, particularly in those countries where there is a high level of dissatisfaction with the quality of the existing output. Even in Britain some areas will be cabled over the next few years and direct broadcasting by satellite is still more likely than not to become operational.

In any case, the anticipated development of the new technology has already influenced the political debate on broadcasting in several Western European states. The main outlines of that debate are covered in several articles in this volume and it would be foolish to confuse the information and speculation contained in them with mere wishful thinking.

The third and final concern common to many of the contributions that follows on from the previous two themes, but also transcends them, is *the ethos of broadcasting as a public service*. While there is no universally accepted definition of the term 'public service broadcasting', the concept certainly embraces 'a commitment to quality, to providing the same level of service to the entire country irrespective of geographical location or social and economic circumstance and to presenting issues impartially and in a balanced manner'.[10] The overwhelming majority of the broadcasting organisations of Western Europe have public service obligations and duties laid down in their charters and operating conditions, with the classic model being the BBC, much of whose corporate ethos can still be traced back to its early days under the management of John Reith.[11] The BBC model, which secured its reputation on the Continent during the Second World War, was consciously imitated by many Western European states, although rarely very successfully, as their own broadcasting systems were reconstructed after the war.

The ethos of broadcasting as a public service is now under attack for a variety of reasons. Partly, as we have seen, this is because the feasibility of one broadcasting organisation giving balanced and impartial political output is severely open to question. Second, the introduction of 'new media' technology is undermining one of the foundations upon which the public service ethos rests: the technical shortage of airwave space for transmissions. If a multiplicity of broadcast outlets is now practicable, then the necessity to have balanced scheduling *within* a single organisation is reduced and, some would argue, eliminated altogether. This applies both to news output and general programming. The situation in broadcasting following the introduction of cable and satellite transmissions will be, some argue, more analagous to the situation of the press than to traditional broadcasting. At the same time, if the introduction of the new media leads to extensive audience fragmentation, then the legitimacy of the established public service institutions will be increasingly called into question.

Third, public service broadcasting across Western Europe is in a serious financial position. As many of the institutions are dependent, wholly or in part, on licence revenue for their income and since the television market is saturated in most Western European countries, the public service organisations are largely reliant on government increases in the cost of each individual licence to augment their budget. For political reasons, governments are generally unwilling to raise the cost of the licence in line with the broadcasters' demands. A drop in audience ratings as some viewers switch to the new media (including video cassette recorders) may also make the case for licence increases even less defensible to governments. Moreover, in some countries licence evasion is in any case fairly common practice. Simultaneously, television production costs are escalating while many public service organisations are increasing their output via new television channels, additional radio stations (especially local ones) and extended programming hours, including breakfast television. The likely consequence of these developments for television is more repeats, greater recourse to cheap, 'talking heads' programmes and more imports, especially from the United States. It would seem, therefore, that the public service broadcasters are caught in a double bind: they feel obliged to extend programming hours to maintain their ratings (and their own sense of self-importance), while one result of such a strategy is almost inevitably a greater emphasis on television purely as a medium of entertainment. A possible scenario is that while the public service *institutions* may survive, to a considerable extent it will be at the cost of the *ethos* they represent.

One perhaps ought not to overestimate the contemporary problems of public service broadcasting. In some countries, such as France and Italy, the public service organisations have rarely lived up to the ideals laid down in their statutes. The decline in their importance *vis-à-vis* other broadcast outlets may not be mourned by many. One could also argue that public service broadcasting has never been static and that it has in the past evolved in response to changing needs and tastes. In Britain, for example, the BBC in the 1920s was a very different animal from the BBC in the 1960s. The spread of television as a mass medium, the introduction of Independent Television and changes in British social mores all affected (and continue to affect) the Corporation's output, in terms of both content and style. One might even add that the public service ethos is remarkably resilient and adaptive: Channel 4 may be a good example of the capacity of the public service to expand its role into relatively unexplored areas.

It might also be contended that although the values of public service broadcasting are under threat, this in itself is not a cause for concern. The liberal marketeer might suggest that in an era of multi-channel television the viewer should be allowed to choose his own programming 'menu', not be compelled to swallow a 'balanced diet' decided on by others: the consumer should be sovereign in the television programme market-place. In this analysis the paternalistic, Reithian concerns about educating, informing and seeking to raise audience tastes are as anachronistic as the television valve. The logical thrust of this argument is towards greater de-regulation of television output: a trend visible in many Western European countries, including Britain (the reforms governing cable), France (*Canal plus*) and Italy (the private television channels).

However, there are counter-arguments. As some of the contributors to this volume point out, an increase in the number of outlets does not necessarily lead to greater choice in *programming*. Fragmentation of the audience may result in certain diseconomies of scale, with the result that some types of programme are less frequently produced because no single channel is guaranteed a large enough audience to cover production costs. Competition between channels may lead to a policy of playing safe rather than taking risks, with channels 'competing' within a very narrow spectrum of output. Finally, the viewer may have to exercise his/her consumer preferences in a market increasingly dominated by US-made or American-style programmes, with possible costs for the preservation and dissemination of indigenous cultures.[12]

Broadcasting in Western Europe is then at a crossroads, with tremendous opportunities for new types of service and programming on the horizon, but also clearly visible risks. The aim of those involved in the debate about the future of broadcasting, whether they be politicians, entrepreneurs, academics or broadcasters themselves, should be to preserve the best of the public service tradition, while at the same time not being resistant to ameliorative change. In the various countries covered in this volume this will require different emphases in policy formulation and implementation. The following articles make clear the difficulties involved in achieving such an objective. They also reveal the extent to which this remains a real possibility.

NOTES

1. T. Hollins, *Beyond Broadcasting: Into the Cable Age* (London: BFI, 1984), pp. 31–2.
2. D. Green, 'Cable TV in France: A Non-Market Approach to Industrial Development', *National Westminster Bank Quarterly Review*, Aug. 1984.
3. See R. Kuhn, 'Government and Broadcasting in the 1980s: A Cross-Channel Perspective, *The Political Quarterly*, Vol. 53, No. 4 (Oct.–Dec. 1982).
4. Some examples of recent mass media studies on such topics include: The Glasgow University Media Group, *Bad News* (London: Routledge & Kegan Paul, 1976); Philip Schlesinger, *Putting 'Reality' Together* (London: Constable, 1978); Michael Tracey, *The Production of Political Television* (London: Routledge & Kegan Paul, 1977); and J. Curran and J. Seaton, *Power Without Responsibility: The Press and Broadcasting in Britain* (London: Fontana, 1981).
5. See, for example, R. Kuhn, 'Ballot Box: Television Coverage of the 1983 General Election', *Stills*, No. 8 (Sept.–Oct. 1983) and R. Kuhn, 'Television's Coal War', *Stills*, No. 13 (Oct. 1984).
6. Schlesinger, op. cit., p. 272.
7. Glasgow University Media Group, *Really Bad News* (London: Writers and Readers, 1982), p. 168.
8. R. Miliband, *Capitalist Democracy in Britain* (Oxford: Oxford University Press, 1982), p. 84.
9. See T. Forester, 'The Cable That Snapped', *New Society*, Vol. 71, No. 1152 (24 Jan. 1985).
10. Hollins, op. cit., p. 3.
11. See J. Curran and J. Seaton, op. cit., Chs. 8–13 and 16.
12. In this connection it is interesting to note that the French state television service has recently launched a French equivalent of the highly popular American soap opera *Dallas*. See *The Guardian*, 31 Dec. 1984.

Politics, Parties and the Media in Britain

Jean Seaton

Broadcasting and the press are in the news. Mrs Thatcher's media campaign is widely believed to have contributed to the 1983 Conservative victory; Labour, on the other hand, is unhappy about what it sees as bias in reporting, while the Alliance first basked in the overwhelmingly favourable media attention it received, then diminished in influence and authority when it moved out of the limelight. As a result the political role of the media has never been more contentious or had a greater prominence in British political life, while the miners' strike of 1984–85 has once again highlighted the directly *political* dangers and possibilities of media manipulation.

In particular, the political consequences of electoral change need to be considered with reference to the role of the media: certainly, a high degree of electoral volatility provides more scope for a possible 'catalytic' effect. For example, during the 1983 Bermondsey by-election, large numbers of voters continued to be uncertain, even to switch allegiances on polling day. A survey conducted for BBC Newsnight showed that an increasing proportion of electors were switching votes as the day wore on.[1] In this case news conveyed through the media of how 'everyone else' was voting appears to have had an immediate impact.

Electoral turbulence creates problems for political parties. If volatility accurately reflects a new 'end of ideology' in the electorate, as some academic writers suggest, this may, or may not, indicate a maturation of attitudes and a trend towards rational, informed political behaviour. What it does mean is a series of new anxieties for politicians and their clients.

The classic example of extreme volatility is a frightening one: the last years of the Weimar Republic.[2] There is, of course, no equivalent of the Nationalist Socialist Party in Britain. Nevertheless, changes in national 'mood' – something different from issues themselves – which caused rapid changes in support for Hitler, may also provide an important element in British electoral change. Such changes of mood are, arguably, particularly susceptible to media influence.

A number of questions present themselves. Does political broadcasting make people more, or less, interested in politics? Does television, in particular, have more influence on parties and party leaders than on voters? Or is it the whole flow of television, the massive hours of entertainment, that have a greater influence on activists and voters alike? Does the shift to the right of the popular press affect political opinion, or are the recent changes in the style, content and values of the quality press more significant? Are leaders using the media more effectively than in the past, or are politics and politicians misrepresented and distorted by the media? None of these questions has yet to receive an adequate answer. For a long time the results of research have pointed away from common sense assumptions, suggesting that the media have little effect on political behaviour. Perhaps all this has ever meant is that the effects are complex and not easily measurable; or that researchers were looking for the wrong effects in the wrong places. In addition, it is not just the political climate of the media which is changing. There have also been rapid changes in the pattern of media ownership and in media technology. This article aims to examine some of these areas of inquiry with regard to recent developments in politics and the media in Britain.

THE MEDIA AND ELECTORAL VOLATILITY

Research between the 1950s and 1970s, which seemed to indicate that the media had little or no independent political effects, largely concentrated on the effects on public opinion – rather than on any possible impact, more indirectly, on institutions. This was the period of what Richard Rose called 'Trench Warfare' elections.[3] That the role of the media was itself a variable, having a specific role in periods of electoral stability, but one which might change under other conditions, was not on the whole recognised.

Along with this minimalist theory of the media went a series of assumptions about politics. Governments, it seemed, lost elections; oppositions hardly ever actively won them. As voting was determined by broad identification with parties, all that parties had to do was to assert their image in order to bring out their supporters. Implicit in much of the work on broadcasting and political behaviour was a model of the rationality or irrationality of voters. The apparent willingness of voters to vote in accordance with barely articulated senses of 'solidarity' with various class and generational groups was seen as 'irrational', although the word itself was evaded or even rejected. Voters were not informed calculators, according to the received wisdom, but unconscious followers of feelings. The role of the media in this process was potentially dangerous, but in practice small.

During the 1970s the image of the voter seemed to change radically. Since 1964 there has been a marked decline in the intensity rather than the extent of identification with parties. In 1964, 79 per cent of voters felt very strongly committed to one party; by 1974 this figure had declined to 46 per cent. Such a dilution of commitment was a general phenomenon, spread evenly between the parties, and across barriers of class, age and sex.[4] In addition, as has now become familiar, identification with parties and actual voting behaviour became more loosely connected, and the floating voter, formerly (according to the widely accepted view) a particle of lumpen ignorance and apathy, began to take on his new form as the informed discriminator between policies.

The main effect of psephological change was to reduce still further the capacity to predict voting behaviour. As Himmelweit *et al.* argued:

> When the party becomes less of a guide to the future, where the influence of group membership becomes less pervasive, and where trust in the parties' wisdom and competence is at a low ebb, it is not surprising that the commonly held assumption that voters stay loyal to a party turns out to be the exception rather than the rule.[5]

But Himmelweit and her colleagues were also surprised by the wide variety of voting patterns that developed during the careers of their panel of voters. Political behaviour and party choice began to appear more complex and sophisticated than before, with consequences for perceptions of the political role of the media.

As early as 1974, Blumler and McLeod pointed out that the 'limited effects model' of the influence of the media was in decline.[6] Chaffee and Dennis went further and argued, 'It may be that selectivity is less an empirical reality and more an artifact of researchers who have organized studies around their own expectations'.[7] In 1960 the US presidential debates on television appeared to have no effect on the amount of political information held by voters; in contrast, the 1976 debates were seen to be enormously influential. Whether this difference was a consequence of changes in voters, candidates or researchers was not, however, clear.

Researchers, quite as much as teenagers or voters, are creatures of fashion. Social scientists tend today to be suspicious of attempts to relate attitudes too clearly to class, or to see 'class' in itself as a basic indicator of political behaviour. Yet it is as well to remember that class has suffered similar fashionable declines before (particularly at the end of the 1950s and in the early 1960s) only to be rediscovered later, alive, well and determining people's tastes, habits and views.[8] Hence we need to be cautious when looking at the supposed decline in class solidarity. If, however, some traditionally class-based attitudes appear diluted, is it possible that the media are at least partly responsible?

There is a British sociological tradition which has always been concerned with the supposed deleterious effects of consumer industries and the media on the working class. This tradition, given prominence by Richard Hoggart and still evident in Raymond Williams's and Stuart Hall's work, has characterised the mass media as in some sense 'eroding' genuinely working-class forms of entertainment and consciousness, and replacing them with commercialised and mass-produced substitutes, which in turn affect the capacity of the working class to perceive its group interests. Another more recent strand of research has suggested, by contrast, that the working class builds its own cultural forms from what commerce offers.[9] However, this broad tradition influenced the 'Affluent Worker' debate in the 1960s, and more recently Goldthorpe, in his work on mobility, indicates the extent to which, in his view, mass education and mass leisure have homogenised class experience.

The tradition has given rise to two arguments: first, that the media, and in particular broadcasting, affected working class habits by replacing communalistic leisure patterns with atomistic ones; and second, that broadcasting eroded communitarian class values, replacing them with pseudo wants and needs. One inheritor of that tradition, Jeremy Seabrook, blames broadcasting and all that is most 'popular' about television for 'emptying the rich system of working class experience of meaning'.[10] He suggests that 'lineages of wealth and abundance' pour from the media with no concession to failure and imperfection. Capitalism, he argues, continues to be projected from every television screen as the provider of abundance and fulfilment;

and this is overtly at odds with the way it was perceived in the depressed working-class areas of the 1930s.[11] The role of the media is to isolate, privatise, and act as the long-term inculcator of materialist values.[12]

Seabrook's romantic and maudlin attitude towards forms of working-class association hardly provide an analysis. Nevertheless, it may well be worth considering the social and political effects of fantasy. On average, of the 26 hours' television seen by adults per week in Britain, over 17 hours consist of fiction of one kind or another. Sport and TV games come a close second.[13] Various studies have suggested that within broadcast fiction, resolutions to conflicts are typically individualistic and that television restricts social perspectives – to those of the family or very small community. Other writers have suggested how entertainment in general supports the *status quo*, by producing material which celebrates 'spontaneous forms of existence',[14] in which structural features like class, race and sex are absent. Some have discussed the role, particularly of television, in re-working ideas of nationhood – and have pointed out that indeed images of nationality are an important aspect of all television programming.[15] Certainly television images played an important, though probably complex, part in establishing views about the nature, limits and possibilities of the Falklands war.[16]

This kind of work at least highlights the problem of the effects of political values which form the unacknowledged background to overtly non-political programmes. The political importance of this kind of programme may well be exacerbated by the increasing dominance of 'entertainment' in the broadcasting schedules – unaffected of course by any statutory obligation concerning 'balance' or fairness – and indeed largely perceived as 'non-political'.

A major problem with this kind of (mainly content-based) study, however, is that it assumes that its reading of the meaning of television entertainment is also an analysis of effects on the audience. Another problem is that general political attitudes, and attitudes towards political parties, do not seem to have exhibited a parallel change. Although there has been a steady decline in the firmness of allegiance to parties since the 1950s, attitudes towards the welfare state, and expectations of government, have changed only recently, and far more suddenly. In particular, attitudes towards the market showed a swift alteration in the late 1970s.[17]

In resisting the claims of those who assert an erosion of working-class morality caused by television, we need not, of course, dismiss the growing importance of television in working-class lives. Whether or not television is corrupting, it would be surprising if it had no effect on attitudes. Hence it is important to consider the context of, and assumptions behind, the programmes people watch.

Difficulties arise, however, in assessing the nature of the political bias of entertainment television and even more in assessing its impact. Hypotheses about political balance and bias are more securely based, therefore, on programmes with an explicitly political content. Here, the increasing readiness of voters to desert traditional loyalties also becomes relevant. First, 'volatility' has often been linked by researchers to a supposed rise in 'issue' voting. Second, one common conclusion has been that although they may not determine political values or even opinion, the media and especially television do set the agenda of what people think about.

Thus Maxwell McCombs and his colleagues argued, on the basis of research conducted during American presidential elections, that

> Unmistakably the issues our panel thought were important were all derived directly from the press and broadcasting. As election campaigns proceed, the fit between the agenda of the media and the public agenda becomes increasingly tight. By the end they were identical.[18]

Television is the dominant source of information on issues. The public sense of what issues are important frequently comes from television. Public opinion is then backed up with media-derived evidence. If voters pay more attention to issues than in the past, then it seems likely that the electoral influence of television has increased – because of the influence of television in determining current fashion in issues – by providing the agenda for debate.

TELEVISION'S AGENDA

If television plays a part in setting the political agenda, who sets the agenda for television? This question becomes of immediate importance. The first constraint on the media is 'news value'. As Colin Seymour-Ure points out, early coverage of the Social Democratic Party was largely explicable in these terms. 'Even if the SDP enjoyed no sympathy among journalists at all, it fitted conventional news values so well that extensive coverage would be assured.'[19] The SDP received attention partly because it was a personality, not policy, based party. There was also another factor: the SDP had a great advantage because its definition of the 'middle ground' of political 'common sense' and compromise was extremely close to the prejudices of broadcasters themselves. Indeed, the long-term agenda of broadcast politics has clearly been affected by the conventions of broadcasting. The development of style and habits for dealing with broadcast television politics took place in the heyday of the two-party system. In this context a relatively simple political strategy of 'balancing' two opposing views was sustainable. The reduction of politics to a continuum between left and right has always misrepresented political reality. Yet such an approach solved many problems for broadcasters. As one television producer put it, 'It used to be easy. Broadcasters sat on the fence. Things have been more difficult since the SDP joined us there.'

At the same time, the agenda of 'legitimate politics' has been set by particular conventions which emphasise the desirability of debate, opposition and 'balance' rather than explanation or illumination. Thus the agenda of broadcasting has been determined by concern with issues that demonstrate opposition and conflict in a simple form.

Meanwhile, television may also be influenced by the agenda of the press. Thus it has been argued on the basis of American election campaigns that newspapers establish the issues television later takes up, and these in turn determine electors' views on priorities.[20] As the date of the election grows closer, the 'take up' by broadcasters of newspaper issues becomes faster.

But only by the last day or two of the campaign are broadcasters finally setting the pace themselves.

In Britain, it is possible to see a similar process. Chibnall has shown how broadcast news of crime is both thematically and, in detail, dependent on the press. Similarly, Murdoch and Middleton have shown that stories about 'welfare scroungers' originating in the press have taken, on average, one to two weeks to percolate through to television. Broadcast news about trade union and industrial affairs is also dependent for its stories on the press.[21] The press is not, of course, limited by the constraints of balance which affect broadcasters. Television justifies its use of press stories on the grounds that what appears in newspapers is news. But what appears in newspapers is not neutral news.

There have, however, been important changes in the British press which have undoubtedly affected its news values. Not only has the general 'tabloidisation' of the majority of newspapers occurred, a movement which obviously favours those parties best able to produce tabloid, personality based copy. In addition, the ownership of the press has recently taken a new and dramatic turn. In the 1960s and 1970s the press was being bought up by international conglomerates with little interest in newspapers except for their profits. Since then, newspapers have increasingly come to be owned as 'loss leaders' to give respectability to other parts of organisations by owners with very clear interests in the *political* rather than economic value of newspaper ownership. Men like Rupert Murdoch, Tiny Rowlands and Robert Maxwell are as interested in the political role of the papers they own as in the money they make.[22] Thus the pace setting role of the press has changed in its tone and political values.

Politicians, of course, try to manage and use news values to their own advantage. One successful tactic employed during elections (where the parties have more capacity to command attention) is to ignore the media's own sense of news priorities. Thus, during the 1983 election campaign, the Conservative Party held its press conference later in the day than other parties, and simply refused to respond to the issues raised at earlier press conferences. Similarly, the Australian Labour Party, in its successful campaign in 1980 against the background of even more hostile broadcasting and press networks, controlled the issues that were raised by refusing to hold press conferences at all. Instead, the party issued one brief statement each day, thereby forcing television to report what was done by party leaders. These tactics may demonstrate a greater political preoccupation with controlling news values than in the past.

One particularly favoured kind of news story, the public opinion poll, may be more influential in a period of volatility. Certainly the 1983 election was dominated by polls. Stories about poll results made the headlines in all three quality papers on seven days, and the remaining tabloid papers on 11 days during the campaign. The dominant news story is always the supposed public reaction to what the polls say. Indeed, as we have seen, at least in the case of by-elections like Bermondsey, one result of massive exposure to public opinion polls may be that some voters make up their minds on the basis of them. Of course, the influence of the polls may on occasion be related to 'tactical voting' – something much emphasised and publicised in the press during the 1979–83 period, when there were many articles telling people how to do it.

PACKAGING VERSUS ISSUES

There is a paradox. On the one hand, we are told that voters are more volatile, and that volatile voters, far from being apathetic as had been believed, are, in reality, closest to the model of how voters ought to behave, shopping around for their best political buy and not merely herded together or determined by class, age and sex. On the other hand, we are also told that politicians are increasingly packaged and concerned with their image. In this view, election results have more to do with manipulation than with any rational assessment by voters. Common to both interpretations of current trends is the supposed increased role of the media. In the first version, the media are the main source of all the new information needed by rational voters. In the second, the media are the critical tool in managing the voter-sheep.

That politicians attempt to manage their image is, of course, not a new idea. Some of the means employed today are described by de Tocqueville and even by Machiavelli. To be a politician is to manipulate symbols, to attempt to control how your actions are 'read' and to simplify complex problems into clichés. Political rhetoric is often boring to read, because it is intended to associate problems of state with the lowest common denominator of what people understand.

Ideas about the effects of advertising, and the impact of all pervasive propaganda, originally developed as part of the radical critique of consumerism in the 1960s, have been revived in the wake of the Reagan and Thatcher campaigns. Many of the techniques were described by Joe McGinniss in his book about the 1968 Nixon campaign, *The Selling of the President*.[23] Nixon believed he had lost to Kennedy in 1960 because of too much sweat and beard on TV. He had what one associate called, 'an advertising man's approach to his work, he acted as if he believed policies were products to be sold to the public – this one today, that one tomorrow, depending on the discounts and the state of the market'.[24] Nixon's campaign was concerned about camera angles, dress, and the composition of the audiences which would 'spontaneously' applaud, greet, and question the prospective leader. 'The family', according to one White House memo, 'should always be seen present in the audience. They *always* should look as if they are enjoying themselves.'[25]

Of course, there are many differences in the communication opportunities and expectations between a President who is a head of state as well as chief executive, and a Prime Minister who does not have the same opportunities as a President. The head of state has the advantage of being able to hide executive power behind the myths and dignity of office. Thus Seymour-Ure writes, 'Whenever he plays the head of state, he can speak (not quite) the truth, (not quite) the whole truth and (not quite) nothing but the truth. He benefits from the little lies made possible for that office by the willing suspension of journalistic disbelief.'[26] 'Presidentialism' is, of course, a growing feature of British political campaigns – and never more so than in the 1983 election. The sincerity machine – which allowed Mrs Thatcher to look at her audience directly without putting her head down; the tasteful decor of the Conservative press conference room; the careful arrangement of meetings where members of the unemployed were unlikely to attend or heckle – were all aspects of this new development. Mrs Thatcher constantly appeared against jolly and active visual backgrounds, micro-chip factories, fish and chip lunches, and mud in real English fields. Her campaign would, indeed, have made a good case study for McGinniss: the aim was not to sell the public policies, but rather a style of government.

Avoiding potentially embarrassing discussion of policies and problems, the Conservatives skilfully moved the debate on to a 'moral' plane. Here television once again proved the ideal medium: far better at projecting gut reactions than at investigating policy claims. Television, feeding off itself, accepted the government's own definition of the campaign.

The obverse of Conservative efficiency was Labour incompetence. Labour's 1983 campaign was, to be sure, an object lesson in how not to run an election. At the same time, it was symptomatic of a deeper, long-term malaise and failure to come to terms with the reality of modern communication media. Here it is notable that Labour has used opinion polls both between and during elections far less than the Conservatives or the Alliance. The Labour NEC has been consistently hostile to spending money on advertising. This is a long-standing prejudice. Thus the man who ran Labour's 1979 campaign has complained of 'the hypocrisy of the Labour Party towards advertising agencies'.[27]

On the other hand, the Labour Party's ambiguity about grooming itself cannot simply be dismissed as incompetent or old-fashioned. Indeed – it should not be forgotten – Labour's lack of 'efficient' organisation for elections is not only part of its tradition; it has also not in the past prevented the party from winning elections. As Peter Pulzer points out, Labour's lack of instinct for public relations reflects its own radical temperament. This temperament is 'distrustful of paternalism, distrustful of efficiency for efficiency's sake, distrustful of the mechanisation of any aspect of human life, but particularly of government and the formation of public opinion'.[28]

Such distrust does not necessarily or inevitably work to the party's disadvantage. In 1983, however, it did so, and by the third week of the campaign Labour's lack of co-ordination – its failure to 'get its act together' – had become the story implicit in most reporting. Once established (and in many respects it had been well established long before the campaign began), the story was, in practice, immutable. Part of the routine of journalism, especially television, is finding a groove and sticking to it; reports which involve breaking out of it are less likely to be recognised.

Those who think politicians not only attempt to create, but also succeed in creating, their own media 'package' tend to downgrade the significance of what it is that politicians are trying to sell. What they stress is the extent to which politics is concerned with codes and symbols and the way in which political behaviour is determined by moods, emotions and images.

Indeed, it is significant that in a period of apparent increase in public cynicism about politicians, one of the images politicians have themselves become increasingly concerned about is their 'sincerity'. That is what all the looking straight into the camera unflinchingly on party political broadcasts is supposed to communicate. It was what Oswald Mosley tried to impress his newsreel viewers with, when he made film interviews in the 1930s – which now look so surreal and unconvincing. Perhaps the visual mode of 'being sincere' has changed more than is usually recognised. Certainly political performance is more stylised and mannered in the 1980s than it was previously. Indeed, there is another paradox. Politicians, to be successful, have to *seem* to be sincere. Actually *being* sincere, as in the case of Michael Foot, may be a considerable disadvantage in mass communication.

Another problem with the packaging model is that it assumes there is a pure 'unpackaged' politics and that there is some politically unmanipulated style of true politics. This is fallacious. 'Packaging' and 'politics rationally presented' are not alternatives in the real world. Rather, all political presentation is packaging, which comes in different forms. The 'non-packaging' of the Labour Party in the past, at least, may have been as effective a communicator of a message as packaging. Parties communicate images, even when they appear not to.

EMOTIONS, SYMBOLS AND VOLATILITY

An unconsidered consequence of increased voting volatility is the scope it gives to 'symbolic' influences. One example is the curious persistence of the 'Falklands Factor' in political opinion. Peter Kellner has pointed out that the Falklands war raised Mrs Thatcher's opinion poll ratings for a far longer period than might have been expected.[29] Here, emotional rather than 'policy' influences were involved, with repercussions for domestic politics because of the fluid nature of electoral behaviour.

Similarly, some analysts have suggested that the level of unemployment has declined as a determinant of government popularity, and has been replaced by 'the level of real wages, a more privatized yardstick – whose adoption especially during the time of a Labour government – eroded some of the ideological credibility of the collectivist elements of Labour's appeal'.[30] Thus it has repeatedly been suggested that the working class has become less altruistic and more individualistic (and materialistic) in its voting behaviour.[31]

Many studies assume that at the level of the individual the pattern of determination remains the same. This is not necessarily so. As Rose and McAllister argue, 'By definition a turbulent electoral environment is not deterministic. The influence of issues is variable, not constant.'[32] This has a variety of consequences. The media – in a period when electorally relevant issues develop swiftly – are more likely to be prominent in their communication. But also, in a period of turbulence, emotive and symbolic communication may also increase.

If this is the case, then the influence of the media may have altered in two ways. First, the short-term impact may be greater. Yet we have very few studies of the role of the media in periods of sudden crisis or dramatic change. As Kurt and Gladys Lang in their work on the Watergate story argue, 'the media helped transform what began as a campaign issue into a legal-judicial issue .... But the salience of Watergate developed long after most people knew what had happened. The role of the media may be particularly crucial in periods of crisis of confidence.'[33] It is not that in these situations the media determine public opinion, but that they may be more influential. More significantly, the long-term influence of the media may become more powerful. Thus long-term changes in the structure, ownership, direction and political balance of the media may become more important predisposers to certain kinds of view than before.

LEADERS, ACTIVISTS, VOTERS – AND TELEVISION

One of the long-term anxieties about television is the opportunities it appears to provide for politicians to impress the public directly, without the mediation of party organisations. Seymour-Ure, in a paper for the 1977 Royal Commission on the Press, suggested that this direct communication has emphasised the role of the party leader at the expense of local party organisation.[34] But it may also be that it has changed the meaning of belonging to a party. It has become a cliché of political journalism that, in the Labour Party, genuinely representative members of the working class have been supplanted by left-wing activists.

Of course, active members of political parties have always been rather odd people, and not necessarily representative of the class in whose interest the party operates. Changes in party allegiance, however, pose new problems of communication for party leaders. In one sense, Tony Benn's acrimonious relationship with the media demonstrates this. The 'bad' image of Benn conveyed in the press and television probably did him little harm, and may have done him much good, among his followers within the Labour Party. Arguably, indeed, there is a category of 'non consensus' political leaders (especially, though not exclusively, on the left) who are able to exploit media hostility to their own advantage: not least because their supposedly outrageous behaviour becomes newsworthy in itself, thereby earning far more attention than respectable politicians usually receive, and also because extensive coverage enables them to talk directly to the select group of activists on which they depend. Not only can this section of the audience 'read' their message through media coverage, but the hostility of the media becomes a reason in itself for popularity among those who regard the media with suspicion, providing a stamp of out-group legitimacy. This is not to say that 'press victim' politicians deliberately create media hostility: only that the relationship between politicians and the media remains more complex than the simple imagery of distortion and bias imply.

NEW TECHNOLOGY AND POLITICS

Politics, however, is entertainment, and entertainment as politics is likely to become more, not less, prominent under the impact of the new technological developments of cable, satellite, and video. Just as the introduction of radio had far-reaching consequences for politics and politicians, the dramatic changes now occurring in television are also likely to have profound effects.

Until recently, broadcasting, and especially television, had been a vehicle of political integration, establishing what Denis McQuail has called the 'common coin of values, ideas, information and cultural expression'.[35] Television has monitored and set a general political agenda – ordering public priorities and arousing public concern for good or ill.

Essential to this process has been the national audience. The power of television has been based, to a considerable extent, on lack of choices: almost any nationally networked programme is certain to count its viewers in millions. Cable, satellite and video increase the range of 'choice'. Without necessarily increasing variety or quality of subject matter (perhaps, as has been argued, reducing it), a larger number of highly competitive commercial stations will fragment and atomise. The national audience will vanish. In the 1920s public service broadcasting developed, in part, out of anxieties about broadcasting's capacity to educate the listener-voter of the new mass electorate. Broadcasting was seen as one means of producing a 'responsible' voting public. With the fragmentation of the mass audience, perceptions of the political functions of broadcasting are bound to change. Such changes may have beneficial results or bad ones. Given the centrality of broadcasting to modern politics, however, it is virtually certain to alter the nature of the political game.

The problems posed by the development of cable, satellite and video broadcasting are common to all countries. Few countries, however, have such strong broadcasting traditions as Britain, or such determined neophiliacs at the helm. When the Conservative government came to power in 1979, an official ideology of non-interference in the market was buttressed by a vigorously optimistic view of information technology. A key Cabinet Information Technology Advisory Panel (ITAP), including experts in electronics and industrialists (but nobody with any broadcasting experience), concluded that industrial revival was to be stimulated by 'cabling up' the nation. The necessary condition for this economic miracle (a high proportion of homes linked to high quality cable networks) would best be created, it was argued, by providing an alluring range of television channels for the eager public. That these would inevitably (because only economically feasible if they did so) offer a consistent diet of old films, sport, American soap opera and light entertainment was regarded as incidental.

The nation was to be lured into the new infrastructure by stealth: having paid for cabling in order to receive more entertainment, television users would find themselves linked to a variety of multipurpose networks with opportunities for computerised shopping, working and learning. 'It is as if', one commentator has suggested, 'the Roman Senate had sanctioned, without debate, the proposition that improvements to the supply system of the Roman legions should first be introduced by speeding up the chariots in the hippodrome'.[36]

More viewing opportunities will mean a more thinly spread audience. In the new hyper-competitive climate, funds will be in short supply. As the 1982 White Paper (*The Development of Cable Systems and Services*)[37] pointed out, one hour of home-grown documentary can cost £20,000 and one hour of high quality drama as much as £200,000. By contrast, an hour of American soap opera can be bought for as little as £2,000. We may expect, therefore, a trend similar to that in the cinema in the 1940s and 1950s: fewer programmes made in Britain and an ever-expanding proportion of imports.

If this analysis is correct, following the collapse of network audiences, a shift of power within the networks is also likely to follow. Where broadcasting is protected through subsidy or monopoly, producers can be given their head; where commercial pressures necessitate a heavy reliance on imported package deals and low budget formula programming, producers will be reduced, in effect, to corporation men: executives carrying out company policy. With less money available, making fewer 'original' programmes, initiative will be at a low premium. In particular, there will be little incentive to make programmes about British subjects – political, social or cultural – purely for domestic consumption.

Another consequence of the erosion of the mass audience may be the reduction of national political coverage and the emergence, through the proliferation of regional broadcasting opportunities, of more concern with local issues. Such a development might be positive. It might provide citizens with a greater awareness of what affects them directly and give more scope to local campaigns and pressure groups. On the other hand, the example of the existing local press gives little ground for optimism. Lack of initiative, cost and the fear of writs have discouraged the vast majority of newspapers, including the big-circulation regional dailies, from acting as anything more than publishing houses for politicians' handouts.

If, therefore, a diversity of stations produces an increase in local political reporting, the benefits remain uncertain. What does seem likely is that the present 'privileged' status of news and documentary, which has been a prominent feature of public service television, will be threatened. Political coverage at least held its own as inter-channel competition increased: between 1956 and 1976 the time devoted to politics quadrupled on average.[38] But this tendency may have already begun to be reversed. During the 1983 election, campaign coverage on the two major channels (BBC 1 and ITV) was restricted to little more than a series of interviews with leading personalities: examination of campaign issues was relegated to BBC 2 and Channel 4[39] and the 'minority' audiences. Cable stations with small budgets and instant commercial targets are scarcely likely to widen the range or deepen the level of discussion. Indeed, for all its failings, television coverage of politics in Britain has in the past been serious and sustained. Indeed it could be argued that political programmes with the depth of reporting of the quality press (although with its narrow definition of the limits of political debate) are served out, for largely historical reasons, to a *Sun-* and *Star-* buying public. It seems likely that the commercial pressures of cable and video may ensure that, instead of deriving political information from television, large numbers of people will be deprived, in effect, of any reliable political information at all.

Even if there is no reduction in the time allotted to current affairs and documentary programmes, cuts in budgeting are bound to have a deleterious effect on quality, and in particular, originality. National reporting all too easily becomes a collaborative exposure of the point of view of the spokesman for a particular interest, provided that the interest in question has Establishment approval. The reason is cost as much as bias: investigative journalism, digging beneath the surface and asking uncomfortable questions, involves more time, resources and financial risk. Here, competitive pressures may be the enemy of imagination, professionalism, and the controversial.

Clearly, under these new competitive pressures, politicians are more likely to have to 'win' their audiences than in the past. Blumler and Ives suggested that in the face of declining interest in party political broadcasts, responsibility for political broadcasting should be handed over to the journalists.[40] Brian Walden has argued that although the broadcasting authorities

> should be enjoined to seek balance over a period, they should give prime consideration to their estimation of the value or interest of the programme ideas .... The onus would be thrown upon politicians to come forward with interesting and valuable programmes rather than dull repetitious propaganda.[41]

Indeed, as early as 1983 many people were apparently 'videoing' their way out of exposure to political broadcasting altogether.

Other observers have pointed to contradictions in recent analyses, especially those of the left. It is hardly, both Kuhn and Connell suggest, as though public service broadcasting has in practice been particularly responsive to the whole range of political views – let alone socialist ones. Kuhn has pointed out that the existing public service system is increasingly subject to pressure 'to be *really* impartial, to give the working class and its representatives more favourable coverage, and to act as a support for the political views of the government'.[42] Connell argues that some critics, like Nicholas Garnham,[43] when they write about cable, imply the existence of some other 'ideal BBC'. For the left, Connell argues that the commercial sector is still often seen as the opposite of all that responsible and accountable broadcasting should be.

> In comparison then the BBC can seem positively wonderful. When set against this image of the commercial broadcasting companies or even worse, those transglobal corporations with a base in hardware, the BBC comes to appear as the flawed (biased or partial, a bit dull and snooty) but perfectible expression of the ideal of public service.[44]

Yet the most recent commercial development, Channel 4, is clearly based on a new (although possibly the last) elaboration of the public service ideal. Thus the increased range of channels offered by cable and video might be, these writers imply, more responsive to a wider range of political views.

Indeed, the collapse of the national audience is seen by some as liberating new opportunities for political broadcasting. David Elstein, a controversial television producer, has suggested that, 'there is one overwhelming advantage for producers in audience fragmentation: the more programmes there are, the less exposed any individual programme is to political interference'.[45] Certainly, since the crisis produced by the Falklands war, there has been a period of increased tension and insecurity in the relations between broadcasters and the government. One of the organisational failures of the war was that, without a structure like the Ministry of Information of the Second World War to stand between the media and the politicians, government interference and control was felt to be purely political. However, whether a multiplicity of stations will produce more current affairs programmes, yet alone more independent and politically critical ones, is debatable.

CENSORSHIP, CONTROL AND LEAKS

Some political effects of the new technology are speculative. Others are already disturbingly apparent. One development in the second category is the closing of doors which many had regarded as permanently unlocked: the re-imposition of censorship in a new form.

Thus, there has been little opposition to the new video censorship bill[46] because no one wants to be caught out apparently defending pornography and violence. Indeed feminist campaigns about the commercial exploitation of images of women and the supposed effects of pornography have significantly altered the climate of opinion, so that there is now wide support for more stringent controls over sexual imagery. It is not necessary, however, to believe that there should be no control over films and videos to recognise the dangers inherent in the new legislation. The rejection of 'liberal' cultural ideals has political implications: for, like sex, politics is often 'offensive'.

The new bill sets aside the 'interpretative' view of film images developed by the British Board of Film Censors (BBFC).[47] This view was concerned with evaluating the meaning and intention of scenes, and emphasising that any given act had to be judged in context. The new legislation introduces what is, in effect, an index of prohibited acts. There are things, whatever their intention, that cannot be shown.

Ostensibly the new censorship is concerned with pornographic or violent videos. In practice its implications will be far wider. The definition of 'prohibited acts' is certainly sufficiently wide to include, for example, any realistic account of modern wars, let alone the effects of a nuclear attack. In addition the defence of a cultural product against prosecution for 'obscenity and the tendency to corrupt' on the grounds of its artistic or literary merit is likely, in the case of films and broadcasts, to be set aside and, in the case of novels and plays, to be seriously diminished. Indeed, as films and television programmes are increasingly made with the home video market in mind, the legislation introduces statutory controls into entirely new areas. No doubt the porn industry will soon be working very lucratively just inside the limits. But broadcasts and films which challenge conventions or those that intend to disturb their audience in any way seem likely to fall outside them.

Indeed, for the first time, the government is seeking to legislate about what people may and may not do in private. The bill is concerned primarily with controlling the 'sale, loan, leasing or gift' of videos for home consumption. Since 1959, and the decriminalisation of suicide, what has been called the 'Wolfenden strategy' has dominated legislation about personal freedom and expression. Although it has been criticised,[48] the concept that what you do in private (as long as it 'harms' no one else) is not a matter for the law has been the basis of the reforms dealing with prostitution, abortion and homosexuality, and has established the background for discussion of political and cultural expression. The Wolfenden strategy is now apparently being abandoned, and the notion of 'harm' dramatically extended.[49]

There are three important consequences of these developments. First, as has already been suggested, radical, oppositional and non-conventional material is most under threat and most likely to be inhibited under the combined influence of the new, more censorious nature of public policy. Second, general standards of 'acceptable' broadcasting are likely to be influenced quite extensively, not as much by direct prohibition as, all the more powerfully, by auto-censorship. This is simply because everyone assumes that it is acceptable and proper to be opposed to 'sexual offensiveness', although the right to offend in general is perceived, somewhat loosely at least, as some kind of political right. 'Sexual offensiveness' is, as it were, the acceptable campaigning position of those who are often, in practice, concerned with the limitation of a far more general category of 'offensive' acts and views. Third – and perhaps most significant – the campaigns around these measures create a new public and political mood: one which is politically and individually restrictive. The views which are 'allowable' at the extremes have a direct impact on the spectrum of conventional views. Thus the limits of broadcasting are likely to be narrowed and this in turn will influence the limits of political discussion.

LEAKS AND SECRECY

At the same time other developments in the relations between government and the media affect the range of information available for political discussion. The British political information machine is run, of course, on a closed system. Defenders of the lobby claim that this allows a few journalists to understand how government is actually operating (even if they do not reveal what they know). The accusers point to the supine dependence of the lobby on politicians. 'There stand the correspondents', wrote Anthony Howard, 'waiting, soliciting for the politicians to come out: . . . in some ways I think that lobby correspondents do become instruments for a politician's gratification'.[50] Of course, journalists are a group who are particularly likely to see politics in terms of conspiracies, but the lobby system does manage to obscure from the public how it operates. It is not necessarily good at exposing how government runs either. Thus, as Bruce Page has pointed out, during the Callaghan government one half of the Cabinet did not even know that the other half was sitting in a key economic policy-making committee.[51]

But the lobby is not only a system for withholding information. It is also a vast baroque bureaucracy for legitimating leaks as well. According to Michael Cockerell, 'As Bishops are against sin, so Prime Ministers are against leaks'.[52] The reality is, of course, that Prime Ministers like their own leaks, not other people's. It is through leaks and the lobby that Cabinet battles are re-fought. The reporting of these battles does not merely inform the public of the squabbles, but far more significantly ratifies the conclusions of the fights.

Prime Ministers may thus be divided into three kinds: those that are paranoid about the media; those that are obsessed and paranoid; and the rest, who are really hysterical. Harold Wilson was notoriously anxious about the way in which he was reported. 'Our morning prayer', commented Dick Crossman, developed into a long discussion 'because I found that the Prime Minister was obsessed about the problems of leaks . . . the discussion lasted 3 hours'.[53]

The Thatcher government has, of course, also been anxious about leaks, and far more prepared to use legislation to try and control them than other recent administrations. As Seymour-Ure has pointed out, no administration can make itself 'leak-proof', but 'the stricter the rules the deeper the throat'.[54] However, the degree of leaking is in itself an indication of the relative strengths and weaknesses of a government.

By this criterion, Mrs Thatcher so far seems to have created a comparatively non-leaky Cabinet (compared, that is, with recent predecessors), although this too may create problems. This government has also unleashed a powerful new morality of non-leaking and has been more prepared to use the law against leakers than its recent predecessors. Nevertheless, it has been plagued by non-Cabinet leaks – from the Belgrano to the Tisdall and Ponting affairs. This may have contributed to a climate of caution and uncertainty within the media. But it is clear that in a variety of ways the press and broadcasting are in a period of change. Traditional philosophies have been undermined and institutions are altering.

CONCLUSION

If voters are more volatile, then the effects of all the influences that determine voting, including the media, are also more variable than they used to be. Clearly the political role of broadcasting is likely to get more, rather than less, difficult.

Of course scepticism about the impact of the media is still in order. As Malory Wober *et al.* point out, people hardly gorged themselves on political information during the last election. On average, individuals saw rather less than one out of ten current affairs programmes, and 'the viewing intake of news, for the population as a whole, hardly held its ground during the election and continued on its seasonal reduction thereafter'.[55]

However, the relationship between political communication and the media remains complex. Broadcasting and newspapers do not create changes in mood and view; they are more important as elaborators and communicators of moods and views developed elsewhere. They also remain parasitic. Nor is it easy to define what their influence is. Over unemployment, for instance, the sources of information and influence, affecting perceptions of politicians and policy makers, will have been quite different to those influencing other workers, let alone the unemployed themselves. But in addition, the public 'trust' broadcasting less than they used to. Broadcasting remains the main source of political information for most people, but it has declined in authority since the early 1960s. In part, this decline in authority may reflect the more general collapse of consensus. Or it may simply reflect a greater sophistication on the part of the audience. But a decline in authority is not necessarily the same thing as a decline in power.

NOTES

The author would like to thank Julia Langdon, Peter Kellner and George Grace for interviews. The views expressed, of course, are entirely her own.

1. 'The Newsnight Poll: Bermondsey', *The Listener*, 7 April 1982.
2. See Thomas Childers, *The Nazi Voter: The Social Foundation of Fascism in Germany 1919–33* (Chapel Hill, NC: University of North Carolina Press, 1984).
3. Ian McAllister and Richard Rose, *The Nationwide Competition for Votes* (London: Frances Pinter, 1984), p. 47.
4. Martin Harrop, 'The Changing British Electorate', *Political Quarterly*, Vol. 53, No. 4 (Oct./Dec. 1982), pp. 385–402.
5. H. Himmelweit et al., *How Voters Decide* (London: Academic Press, 1981), p. 192.
6. J. Blumler and J. M. McLeod, 'Communication and Voter Turn Out in Britain', in A. T. Legett (ed.), *Sociological Theory and Survey Research* (London: Sage, 1974), pp. 265–313.
7. S. H. Chaffee and J. Dennis, 'Presidential Election Debates: An Empirical Assessment', in A. Ranney (ed.), *The Past and Future of Presidential Debates* (Washington: American Institute for Public Policy Research, 1979), p. 9.
8. See Ben Pimlott, 'New Politics', in Ben Pimlott (ed.), *Fabian Essays in Socialist Thought* (London: Heinemann Educational and Gower, 1984), pp. 1–13.
9. See, for example, Paul Willis, *Sacred and Profane Culture* (London: Routledge & Kegan Paul, 1977) and Richard Hebdidge, *Revolt into Style* (London: Paladin, 1979).
10. J. Seabrook, *Unemployment* (London: Paladin, 1983).
11. J. Seabrook, 'Unemployment Now and in the 1930s', in B. Crick (ed.), *Unemployment* (London: Methuen, 1981), p. 9.
12. In fact Seabrook seems to consider the material improvement in the conditions of the unemployed as the *cause* of a greater misery in comparison with the 1930s. See Seabrook, *Unemployment*, op. cit., pp. 105–7.
13. BBC/ITV Viewing Survey, 1983–84.
14. Charlotte Brunsden and David Morley, *Everyday Television* (London: British Film Institute, TV Monograph No. 10, 1978), p. 92.
15. See Tom Nairn, *The Break Up of Britain* (Harmondsworth: Penguin, 1980).
16. See Anthony Barnett, *Iron Britannia* (London: Allison & Busby, 1982) for a good chapter on the media, and Robert Harris, *Gotcha: The Media and the Falklands War* (London: Methuen, 1983).
17. See C. Husband, 'Government Popularity and the Unemployment Issue 1966–83', paper for the 1984 BSA conference.
18. Maxwell McCombs et al., *The Emergence of American Political Issues* (Chicago: University of Illinois Press, 1979), p. 78.
19. Colin Seymour-Ure, 'The SDP and the Media', *Political Quarterly*, Vol. 53, No. 4 (Oct./Dec. 1982), p. 433.
20. Maxwell McCombs et al., op. cit.
21. Steve Chibnall, *Law and Order News* (London: Constable, 1979); Graham Murdock and Sue Middleton, 'Welfare Scroungers and the Media', *Media Culture and Society*, Vol. 6 (1982), pp. 20–37; Jean Seaton, 'Trade Unions and the Media' in B. Pimlott and C. Cook

(eds.), *Trade Unions in British Politics* (London: Longman, 1982), pp. 32–102.
22. See Michael Leapman, *Barefaced Cheek: The Apotheosis of Rupert Murdoch* (London: Allen & Unwin, 1983).
23. Joe McGinniss, *The Selling of the President* (London: Andre Deutsch, 1970).
24. Ibid., p. 31.
25. Ibid., p. 75.
26. C. Seymour-Ure, op. cit.
27. Tim Delaney, 'Labour's Advertising Campaign', in R. Worcester and M. Harrop (eds.), *Political Communication: The 1979 General Election* (London: Allen & Unwin, 1982), p. 27.
28. Peter Pulzer, 'The Politicians' Decision', in R. Worcester and M. Harrop (eds.), op. cit., p. 53.
29. 'Mrs. Thatcher and the Falklands Factor', *New Statesman*, 15 June 1983.
30. See C. Husband, op. cit., p. 22.
31. J. Alt, *The Politics of Economic Decline* (Cambridge: Cambridge University Press, 1977).
32. Ian McAllister and Richard Rose, op. cit., p. 218.
33. Gladys and Kurt Lang, *The Battle for Public Opinion: the President, the Press and the Polls during Watergate* (New York: Columbia University Press, 1983), p. 305.
34. Colin Seymour-Ure, 'Political Parties and the Media', in *Studies on the Press*, Royal Commission on the Press, Working Paper No. 3 (London: HMSO, 1977).
35. Denis McQuail, 'The Mass Media and Privacy', in J. B. Young (ed.), *Privacy* (Chichester: John Wiley, 1978), p. 181.
36. S. Hearst, 'The Development of Cable Systems and Services', *Political Quarterly*, Vol. 54, No. 3 (July/Sept. 1983), p. 388.
37. *The Development of Cable Systems and Services* (London: HMSO, 1982).
38. BBC and ITV Handbooks, 1956–76.
39. P. Kellner, 'The Last Television Election?', *New Statesman*, 26 Aug. 1983.
40. J. Blumler and J. Ives, *Election Broadcasting* (1978).
41. Brian Walden, 'Broadcasting and Politics', IBA Lecture, 1983, *Independent Broadcasting* (March 1983), p. 15.
42. Raymond Kuhn, 'Government and Broadcasting in the 1980s: A Cross-Channel Perspective', *Political Quarterly*, Vol. 53, No. 4 (Oct./Dec. 1982), p. 445.
43. N. Garnham, 'Public Service Broadcasting', *Screen*, Vol. 23, No. 2 (July/Aug. 1982), pp. 24–37.
44. Ian Connell, 'Commercial Broadcasting and the British Left', *Screen*, Vol. 24, No. 6 (Nov./Dec. 1983), p. 73.
45. David Elstein, 'Smash the Regulators', *Stills*, No. 6 (May/June 1983).
46. Video Recordings Bill, Cmnd. 72410 (London: HMSO).
47. See Beverley Brown, 'An Interview with James Forman', *Screen*, Vol. 23, No. 5 (Nov./Dec. 1982).
48. See Jean Seaton, 'Private Faces in Public Places', *New Socialist*, (Sept./Oct. 1982), pp. 9–11.
49. *Report of the Committee on Obscenity and Film Censorship*, Cmnd. 7772 (London: (HMSO, 1980), can thus be seen as the final version of the 'Wolfenden Strategy'.
50. A. Howard, in A. King and A. Sloman (eds.), *The Westminster Lobby Correspondent* (London: Macmillan, 1979), p. 210.
51. Bruce Page, 'The Secret Committee', *New Statesman*, 21 July 1978.
52. Michael Cockerell, 'Sources Close to the Prime Minister', *The Listener*, 11 March 1982.
53. Richard Crossman, *The Diaries of a Cabinet Minister* (London: Jonathan Cape), Vol. 1, p. 120.
54. Colin Seymour-Ure, *The American President: Power and Communication* (London: Macmillan, 1982), p. 83.
55. M. Wober, M. Svennevig and B. Gunter, 'The Television Audience and the 1983 General Election', in M. Harrop and R. Worcester, *The 1983 Election* (forthcoming).

Proclaiming the Republic: Broadcasting Policy and the Corporate State in Ireland

Desmond Bell

BROADCASTING POLICY IN THE 'INFORMATION AGE'

We are, it is argued, now witnessing the end of the era of broadcasting. The new media technologies – video, cable, satellite and data transmission systems – with their technical capacity for 'narrow casting' and ability to overspill national boundaries are perceived by many commentators as challenging the hegemony of state broadcasting agencies.

Increasingly the 'footprints' of direct broadcasting satellites spread beyond political territorialities. The volume of transborder data-flows under the control of transnational corporations grows exponentially. Accordingly the capacity of individual nation states to regulate the 'free flow' of information and cultural commodities lessens. In so far as the integrity of nation states rests on a degree of cultural hegemony within their political boundaries, national sovereignty is potentially eroded. Moreover, the willingness of a number of European states to regulate the proliferating new media and information technologies seems to be diminishing. We are experiencing in Europe, as in the US and Japan, a series of rapid technological and commercial developments which are leading to the integration of previously discrete systems of telecommunications, information processing and broadcasting – the so-called 'tele-informatic revolution'.

The formulation of mass communications policy, traditionally an area characterised by a high degree of state regulation, is also being conditioned by a new *ideological* climate. Neo-liberal economic thinking has sustained a social market doctrine committed to 'rolling back the frontiers of the state': a cause which a significant number of western governments have enthusiastically espoused. Such thinking challenges the public service model which has guided state broadcasting policy in Western Europe since the 1920s. For the deregulatory stance as regards the new media services now being taken by the current US and British governments would seem to involve a wider ideological commitment to open up the entire field of the mass media to the 'discipline of the free market'.

Indeed, in the current debate on cable and satellite technologies, the larger issues of economic development and industrial policy seem to have replaced traditional concerns about the content and impartiality of broadcasting as the central focus of state interest in the media.

As the report of the British government Information Technology Advisory Panel declared in 1981, 'We believe cable to be an essential component of future communications systems, offering great opportunities for new forms of entrepreneurial activity and substantial direct and indirect industrial benefits'.[1] In Britain public broadcasting has taken a back seat in the formulation of mass communication policy by a government politically committed to privatising nationalised industries in the telecommunication and information processing sectors and facilitating a deregulatory climate in the new media field. In Western Europe generally, cable is seen as a potential electronic grid, facilitating the convergence of previously discrete telecommunication and information processing systems. It is being hailed by a number of Western governments as the biggest infrastructural revolution in Europe since the building of the railways. As such it is heralded as a source of economic rejuvenation for their crisis-torn economies. Together with the wider electronic industry, cable is seen as the core sector around which industrial restructuring will occur. The development of an electronic grid with application in 'tele-marketing' and in vastly expanding the productivity of the commercial service sector (banking, insurance, etc.) via data networking services and, in addition, the expansion of consumer demand for electronic hardware and software, are seen as opening up vast new areas of potentially profitable capital investment.[2] Cable, it would seem, is simply too big for broadcasters to have a monopoly over it.

Accordingly the debate on the new media technologies has much wider parameters than traditional policy discussions within broadcasting which focused on issues of cultural content, political bias and journalistic ethics. Broadcasting policy is now motivated by the wider concerns of *political economy*. Central to those wider concerns has been the growing scepticism of a number of western governments about the state's capacity to regulate the economy – and indeed about the desirability of state management of this area. Parallel to the intellectual crisis in Keynesianism and social democracy has occurred a crisis in confidence in public service broadcasting. This has been occasioned not only by the very real budgetary constraints now faced by state broadcasting agencies (RTE, the state broadcasting service of the Irish Republic, had a current account deficit of £2.8 million in 1982 with a total income of £56.4 million; long-term indebtedness was the equivalent of 80 per cent of total assets), but also by an increased questioning of the legitimacy of the monopoly, or at least priority, of state broadcasting over the air waves.

In Ireland, however, the nationalisation of the communication sector in general, and the state monopoly of broadcasting in particular, did *not* find its ideological legitimation during the period of post-war growth (somewhat later in Ireland from around 1958 onwards) by reference to a 'Keynesian' model of the economy and a social democratic conception of the state.[3] It is rather with reference to a nationalist political rhetoric, centring on issues of national sovereignty and cultural identity, that a statist approach to the management of the economy in general and the provision of public service broadcasting in particular has been justified. As the Broadcasting Review Committee, which reported in 1971, ten years after the introduction of the national television service, demanded:

> The broadcasting system should be effectively owned and controlled by bodies to be set up under statute with responsibility for safeguarding, enriching and strengthening the cultural, social and economic

fabric of Ireland .... The system should provide a service that is essentially Irish in character .... and provide for a continuing expression of Irish identity.[4]

Issues of national identity and control over national resources still remain at the top of the agenda in political debates about mass communication policy in a country which since the 1920s has had to compete with British broadcasting stations for the attention of the national audience. Indeed it could be argued that in so far as the case for public service broadcasting is popularly perceived as resting on fundamental issues of national sovereignty and cultural identity, it has proved more resilient to political criticism from those who espouse neo-liberal economic policy options than in Britain where the entire public sector growth in the post-war period found its legitimation in 'Keynesian' and social democratic rhetoric. In Britain since the mid-1970s, in the context of the ongoing fiscal crisis of the state and the political ascendancy of Thatcherism, the public service ideal and its attendant claims to the privilege of priority over the air waves has increasingly come under scrutiny from a government programmatically committed to a 'free market' doctrine in the communication as in other fields.[5] This has not been the case in Ireland.

THE IRISH SITUATION

In Ireland, despite the high degree of *personal* commitment to neo-liberal economic thinking on the part of members of the major political party in the current government coalition (Fine Gael), and indeed a consensus among all the three major parties (the Labour Party in the coalition and Fianna Fail in opposition) about the necessity to curtail public expenditure, there has been little serious political challenge to the corporate state in Ireland from the right. To date, RTE has been able to preserve its legal monopoly over the air waves, originally established for the pioneer radio service in 1926 and most recently confirmed for television and radio in the 1976 Broadcasting Authority (Amendment) Act.

1. Cable

That Act also incorporated a series of regulations passed in the 1974 Wireless Telegraphy Act which made RTE the beneficiary of a 15-per cent levy on the rentals paid by subscribers to wired relay, that is, cable, systems. To date this privileged position of RTE *vis-à-vis* private cable operators has not been legally challenged. And, to the ire of those entrepreneurs competing for franchises to provide relayed broadcast services and additional pay-as-you-view entertainment channels, the state services RTE and An Bord Telecom (formerly P & T) retain their legal monopoly over point-to-point microwave transmission. Indeed, as significantly, RTE, who have run their own cable operation since 1970 (RTE Relays), have recently bought out the remaining private-cable company operating in the Dublin area, after receiving permission to do so from the Monopolies Commission! This currently gives RTE a monopoly in cable provision and servicing in the area of the country which contains over a third of the total population of the Republic and with the highest level of cable penetration (some 200,000 subscribers or 60 per cent of television owners/renters as opposed to a penetration figure of 40 per cent for the country as a whole).

Responding to a wider European interest in cable's industrial implications, the Irish government has set up a 'Cable Television Committee' to advise on government policy for the development of cable in Ireland. The terms of reference of this committee are:

> To examine and make recommendations on a national strategy for the development – on the most cost-effective basis possible – of cable systems, and on the design and technical standards that should be applied, bearing in mind advances in technology and the additional services that may be available for relay in the future.[6]

The terms of reference, like those of the British ITAP committee, include not only entertainment functions of the new medium, but also interactive information services and networking links with telecommunication systems including satellite broadcast and data transmission services. Like the ITAP, the committee is drawn from the world of industry and, in particular, the private communication sector rather than from the world of broadcasting.

However, unlike the ITAP or the later Hunt Committee on Cable in the UK, it now seems likely that the Cable Committee will recommend that RTE's monopoly over broadcasting (including microwave relay) be *maintained* and envisages the state service having a major role in the development and regulation of cable services. Although the committee sees cable developing within a wider telecommunication context, it will apparently recommend that the semi-state Bord Telecom, rather than cable operators, should be the provider of data networking and interactive services as part and parcel of an integrated digital information system.[7] In this the committee seems to be following the French model of entrusting telematic developments to the semi-state PTT, a national policy very much against the world trend towards deregulation and privatisation.

2. Satellite Broadcasting

As for direct broadcasting by satellite, RTE was one of the 15 countries which participated in the pan-European tv programme experiment during 1982 and looks certain to be the body to manage the five channels allocated to Ireland within the proposed European satellite system, although as in Britain this may involve a partner relationship with a private enterprise consortium.[8]

Given the scale of the investment that would be required to establish a DBS service from Ireland (conservatively estimated at around £600 million), it is unlikely that a private investor could be found within Ireland in what is still seen universally as a high-risk business. RTE are somewhat reluctant to commit themselves to a satellite venture given their own straitened financial circumstances. However, the cultural *and* commercial possibilities of a DBS service with a footprint extending over the whole of

Britain, as well as Spain and Portugal, clearly excites them. As Fred O'Donovan, chairman of RTE put it:

> ... the coverage of the UK reverses our historical situation. For the first time we in Ireland will be able to cover the whole of the United Kingdom with our own transmissions. Properly handled, and given our willingness to become aggressive programmers, I see RTE becoming totally sufficient within five years.[9]

As ever in discussions of broadcasting policy in Ireland, considerations of cultural integrity and national sovereignty never lie far below the surface. Such considerations would seem to serve to check the ideological drift towards a radically deregulated policy for the media. For a broadcasting service which throughout its entire history has had to compete with the much larger and much better-resourced BBC for the attention of the majority of the national audience who receive off-air or cable-relayed British television and radio (now an estimated 70 per cent of the population of the Republic), the possibilities of DBS transmissions *to* Britain is a particularly appealing one.

3. Local Radio

In the field of radio it may not be generally known that Ireland has an illegal pirate broadcasting problem second in Europe only to Italy. Commercial stations with substantial advertising revenues[10] broadcast daily on regularised frequencies, parasitically lifting news material from the national stations and newspapers – with little government interference. There is evidence that specific politicians from Fine Gael and Fianna Fail with business interests in the media and advertising fields have connived in this systematic illegality. Indeed a government minister has personally introduced a programme on a pirate station!

In 1981 the then Fianna Fail government introduced a Local Radio Authority Bill which envisaged the setting up of an independent, advertising-financed local radio network completely free of RTE control. The bill, which closely resembled the British Broadcasting Authority Act of 1973, represented a major break from the public service traditions of broadcasting dominant to date in Ireland. As with the British local radio developments it was clear that business interests, rather than the identification of local community broadcasting needs, conditioned the proposed legislation. As in Britain, local radio was perceived by eager entrepreneurs as a 'licence to print money'.

However, with the dissolution of the 21st Dail in June 1981 the bill lapsed. Since then the Coalition government has been promising new legislation. At present an Oireachtas (parliamentary) Committee on Legislation is examining local broadcasting. While it is the case that commercial interests have continued to lobby extensively for a relaxation of the RTE legal monopoly over the air waves and for a revision of the Wireless Telegraphy Act of 1926 which could legally facilitate the already highly profitable pirate commercial stations, the state is displaying a caution in this area which contrasts sharply with the 'gold rush mentality' displayed by the Conservative administration in Britain in the debate over local radio there. The Labour Party has argued hard within the coalition for 'Community radio to be developed in an orderly manner by RTE and local community interests'. Its own policy document demands that, 'Radio Telefis Eireann ... have total control of radio and television wavelengths within the state ... Community radio to be developed at local level under the auspices of RTE'.[11] Fine Gael, as befits a historically conservative party with solid bourgeois roots, has committed itself, like Fianna Fail, to a largely commercial form of provision, although with the proviso that 'there will be no bias against non-profit making enterprises or against relatively small communities who wish to establish local radio services'.[12]

Despite the political strength of Fine Gael in the coalition, it now seems likely that the proposed bill will involve a considerable degree of public service regulation. The minister responsible, Jim Mitchell, has disclosed that the bill, which he hoped to put before the Dail before Christmas 1984, would involve the setting up of a 'Community Broadcasting Authority' to grant licences and ensure conformity to acceptable standards of broadcasting and to facilitate the involvement of community groups. It is now envisaged that RTE will have a substantial stake in the ownership of a number of these local stations and accordingly in programming decisions. The semi-independent broadcasting authority envisaged by the government will then be guided by public service principles of provision and not by those of a deregulatory *laissez-faire*.[13]

4. Broadcasting and Nationalism

While it is clear, therefore, that there is a degree of political support within the ranks of Fine Gael and Fianna Fail (two basically conservative parties, the latter with a strong populist following) for 'liberalising' measures in the media field, demands for privatisation of state services or for de-regulation of the communication sector do not find expression in the stated policies and programmes of these parties. How is this to be explained? Why is it that the rising tide of neo-liberalism, encouraged by a high level of public anxiety about increasing levels of public expenditure and the income tax burden, has not been able as yet to capture the commanding heights of government policy?

The answer which immediately suggests itself is one in terms of the political conflict and contradictions within the make-up of the current coalition government. Here we have a cabinet made up of members from Fine Gael, a traditionally conservative party (both in social and economic terms), and from the Labour Party. The latter, although by no means historically a mass party of the working class committed to a socialist programme, has nevertheless been in favour of enhancing state control of the economy by means of nationalisation policies. Indeed there *have* been major disagreements within the government between Fine Gael and Labour ministers about energy policy (and the resignation of one Labour minister, Frank Cluskey, over the degree of state ownership and control appropriate for the developing oil and natural gas industries). Similarly, there have been cabinet disputes over the development of local radio services and the degree of commercial involvement in these. However, to date these policy conflicts have not produced anything the public could easily recognise as an ideological fissure running through the fabric of the cabinet. Indeed, the very real political differences which do exist between the two parties seem to have temporarily submerged again with the recent publication of the government's economic plan for the period 1985–87.[14] Although this aims to cut public expenditure slightly, it falls well short of the monetarist rigour demanded by sections of Fine Gael. A shaky coalition government is not the best political implement for breaking the consensual mould around the high-spending 'benign state'.

On the other hand, it is not at all clear that any greater degree of conflict exists between the coalition partners over the status of the public sector than within the serried ranks of the opposition party, Fianna Fail. The 'Republican Party', as the latter still likes to call itself in respect for its founding fathers was, of course, historically responsible, as the party in power for most of the last 50 years, for building up the public enterprise sector. Indeed it is still prepared to commit itself in its published programme to increasing state capital spending, while effecting some reduction in overall public expenditure – an undertaking not without its contradictions given the rising proportion of current expenditure within state total spending! As a populist party which needs to mobilise a substantial working-class vote in order to get elected, and with a tradition of political organisation which relies heavily on a system of patronage and brokerage, it is, if anything, more yoked to a 'benign state' position than the coalition members.

It is, we would suggest, the continued centrality of nationalism as a political ideology in the Irish Republic, and its role in effecting political mobilisation of the population around parties *without a clear class base* that is the key factor in blunting the contemporary challenge of neo-liberalism with its anti-statism. A form of 'official nationalism', articulated by, and through, the state and its agencies, is effectively the ideological cement which ensures political adherence within the 'all class alliances' on which both of the major two parties depend for their survival. The corporate state in turn has historically been intimately associated with nationalism. To attack the former is potentially to erode the foundations of national sovereignty. *It seems at present impossible to define politically a concept of national sovereignty or to embrace an ideology of nationalism which is not deeply imbued with corporatist commitment.* This is the dilemma of the two conservative parties: their political basis rests on nationalism – nationalism ideologically underwrites the interventionist state. They are finding it very difficult to roll back the latter without undermining the former, and with it, their own political support.

In the rest of this article we shall examine the developing relationship between 'official nationalism' and the growth of the corporate state in Ireland in the particular area of broadcasting policy. In so far as nationalism is an *ideological* phenomenon, as we might expect, broadcasting has found itself throughout a history contemporaneous with that of the state itself circumscribed by a web of issues focused on Ireland's status as a sovereign power and on its cultural integrity.

HISTORICAL ORIGINS OF BROADCASTING IN IRELAND

There exists a curious historical intimacy between the development of broadcasting and the Irish Republic. One of the first objectives of the revolutionaries who launched the Rising of Easter 1916, after they had occupied the GPO, was to seize the Irish School of Telegraphy across O'Connell Street from the Post Office. As Maurice Gorham has documented,[15] a ship's transmitter in that building was made operational and on the Tuesday the station began transmitting (in morse, of course) communiqués over the name of Pearse, Connolly and Plunkett, *broadcasting* the news that the Irish Republic had been proclaimed in Dublin and that its forces had captured the centre of the city.

Gorham and a number of other commentators, Marshall McLuhan among them, have gone so far as to suggest that this represents the world's first radio broadcast. As Gorham argues:

> This was not broadcasting as we know it, for wireless telephony was not yet available and Morse messages were all that could be sent out. But it was news by wireless, not aimed at any known receiver but sent out broadcast, and that was a new idea in 1916.[16]

Whatever the merits of this claim, what is interesting in this story is the significance the urban intelligentsia who led the Easter Rising attached to seizing control of mass communication resources – even untried and untested ones. Since then seizure of centres of broadcasting has been a central military and political strategy of insurrectional movements. Initial claims to national sovereignty are established over the air waves.

When the Irish broadcasting service was eventually established in 1926 after a bloody civil war occasioned by the partition of the country, it was within a state with dominion status inside the British Empire, rather than in a radical republic. It was, therefore, a somewhat more prosaic affair than might have been expected. Significantly a public service form of provision, financed and controlled by the state, only commanded widespread political support when the representatives of a private conglomerate bidding during 1924 for a franchise to provide a commercial radio service were discovered to be involved in a tangle of political intrigue widely reckoned to be serving British Imperial interests. The conglomerate, the Irish Broadcasting Company, was tarred with the claim that its major representative, a Mr Andrew Belton, was the agent of 'a certain political-financial group of which Beaverbrook is either the head or of which he is largely representative'.[17]

The issue had become for the members of the newly re-established Dail Eirean (the parliament of the Irish Free State), one of national sovereignty and cultural integrity. As the Postmaster-General was to declare to the Committee set up by the Dail in 1924 to consider 'Wireless Broadcasting':

> We claim to be – some people say we are not – at any rate those of us

who are participating in the present parliament claim that this nation has set out on a separate existence. That existence not only covers its political life, but also its social and cultural life, and I take it to be part of the fight that this nation has made during the last six or seven years that this separate entity should not only be equipped but developed to the utmost until this country is properly set on its feet as an independent, self-thinking, self-supporting nation in every respect.[18]

In the Dail debate on the occasion of the presentation of the Committee's report, the Postmaster-General, to whose department responsibility for supervising the new radio service was eventually given, warned again about 'a sinister "external company" which was still trying to keep the Irish people from having their own broadcasting station'. The issue was settled in favour of a public service form of provision. It was felt a commercial operation would place effective control of the service in British hands, given the reality of the continued domination of British investment in Ireland. As J. J. Walsh (the Postmaster-General) summed it up, 'Any kind of Irish station is better than no Irish station at all.'

In October 1925 a Station Director's post was advertised. Significantly Mr J. C. W. Reith sat on the interview panel for the appointment, sanctifying, so to speak, the public service status of the new station. Indeed, despite the history of hostilities between the two countries, the BBC and the British Post Office (which controlled British technical resources for broadcasting) gave considerable help in the setting up of the new service and in its subsequent development. As Gorham argues:

> The BBC was the exemplar of a monopolistic broadcasting system, such as Ireland was to have, and it was already run as a public service, which it eventually became. It was always anxious to encourage similar systems elsewhere, in contrast to the American free for all.[19]

It would seem that for the Irish civil servants who came to run the new radio service (the first Director appointed, Seamus Clandillon, was a Health Insurance Inspector from the Civil Service with no previous broadcasting experience), the 'official' nationalist aspirations of the new state and its desire to utilise the new medium to strengthen national sovereignty and cultural identity were quite compatible with the Reithian concept of public service broadcasting – with its underlying social imperialist ideology. This accommodation reflected to some extent the decline in the fortunes of militant republicanism after the defeat of the Republican forces in the Civil War and the subsequent ossification of republicanism as a radical political force after de Valera's parliamentary return from 1926. The political accommodation with British imperialism that the Irish Free State involved was in fact reflected in the early dependence of the Irish broadcasting service on the BBC. The morning after his appointment as Director of the new service was announced, Clandillon was requested to leave for London to be trained in the art of public service broadcasting. And when the station at last opened in January 1926, its programming included a series of relayed programmes from the BBC.

The Wireless Telegraphy Act passed in 1926 became the legislative basis of broadcasting in Ireland. The act provided for 'the establishment and maintenance of *state* broadcasting stations'. In this it followed the recommendations of the advisory committee that 'broadcasting should be a state service purely – the installation and working of it to be solely in the hands of the Postal Ministry'.

On the other hand, the service, it was agreed, was to be *financially self-supporting*. Its revenue was to be drawn from licence fees, from a proportion of the duty collected on the import of receivers and, somewhat against the inclination of the civil servants responsible for the new service, from advertising. The Parliamentary Secretary reassured an anxious Dail that 'we are not expecting to get revenue to any appreciable extent from advertising'. The measure meant, he insisted, that 'we simply keep in existence the right to let certain time for advertising purposes'.[20] Indeed in the subsequent 17 months after the introduction of an advertising scheme, the total income raised by the operation was only £165! By April 1928 receipts from advertising for the previous year had dropped to £28 and the civil service was again pressing to ban advertisements, of which Clandillon was particularly dismissive: 'From a programme point of view they are a nuisance, and are regarded by listeners as an impertinence.'[21]

The poor take-up of advertising time was not unrelated, it has to be said, to the fact that it had been decided, following the semi-protectionist policy of the time, to restrict advertising to Saorstat (Free State-owned) enterprises and to those that did not compete with the former. Both at this time and later on in the 1930s with the advent of international commercial broadcasting in English (initiated by Radio Luxembourg in 1933), the Irish authorities were determined to stop their station being used as a vehicle for beaming commercial advertising into Britain.

As the Minister responsible explained in May 1935, this might involve a reduction in potential income but, he continued, 'there are obvious objections on the grounds of national policy to the broadcasting of non-Saorstat advertisements from state stations'.[22] He met no criticism from the Dail to this basic government policy against international commercial broadcasting.

Despite the fact that successive governments were under pressure from commercial interests to allow such advertising and were constantly receiving proposals from private operators to build commercial stations or to lease blocks of broadcast time for advertising aimed at the British consumer, there was no lifting of this prohibition right up to the time television was being introduced in 1961. A public service ideal, underwritten ideologically by a form of 'official' nationalism commanding wide popular support, became deeply entrenched in the Irish broadcasting tradition.

BROADCASTING AND THE CORPORATE STATE

Since the nineteenth century Ireland has been characterised by a particularly uneven process of capitalist industrialisation. Both the pace and extent of industrial development in the country were conditioned by its political and economic domination by Britain and by its geographical peripherality and dependency as regards the British economy. The north-east of the island was the only region of Ireland which experienced a pattern of industrial growth in any way comparable to the British experience. The partition of Ireland after 1921 bequeathed an underdeveloped and dependent economy with a weak industrial base to the new Irish 'Free State'.[23]

It is in this context of the structural weakness of native Irish capital, compounded by a sharp fall in agricultural prices after 1921 which shook confidence in the agriculture sector, that the Irish state was forced to act and develop a more interventionist economic policy. This it did despite its preference for a balanced budget and general fiscal rectitude. For during the next four decades, including the years immediately after 1958 when the Irish state committed itself to a considerable extension of its interventionist activities, the ideal objective of a balanced budget was not abandoned. A Keynesian economic logic of reflationary expansion was a long time gaining political adherents in Ireland. On the other hand, the post-1970s' intellectual and political crisis of 'Keynesianism' has not undermined the political support for maintaining and increasing state regulation of the economy to the same degree as in Britain.

The economic strategy of the Irish state during the 1920s and 1930s rested on two major areas of intervention: first, establishing a degree of tariff protection for native Irish industry – a policy considerably hardened in effect after 1932 and the election of de Valera's Fianna Fail government committed to a policy of economic self-sufficiency. This isolationist stance was not eventually abandoned until after 1958 when Lemass and the Fianna Fail government broke with their former protectionism and strove to reintegrate Ireland into the rapidly expanding global capitalist economy.

The second area of intervention was the increasing role of the state in the ownership and development of key areas of the industrial economy, usually infrastructural in character. For example, one of the first projects undertaken by the new state was the Shannon Scheme for the provision of electricity from water power, begun in 1925. This and the setting up subsequently of a state-owned Electricity Supply Board involved probably the largest capital investment undertaken in Ireland up to the present day. It also entailed the political assumption that the state must of necessity intervene in the industrial sphere to ensure the infrastructural conditions for economic development – *in order to further secure Ireland's sovereign status*. Significantly when the legislation to implement the Shannon Scheme was put before the Dail, it was passed without an opposing vote despite the implications of the measure in encouraging demands for further nationalisation in other sectors.

Right up to the contemporary period political debates between Fianna Fail and Fine Gael on the subject of what has become known as the 'semi-state sector' have been remarkably bi-partisan. As Sean Lemass, the architect of the state expansionist policy of the 1960s, declared in 1961 while Taoiseach (Prime Minister):

> Even the most conservative among us understands why we cannot rely on private enterprise alone; and state enterprise in fields of activity

where private enterprise has failed or shown itself to be disinterested has not only been accepted but is expected .... Nobody thinks of us as doctrinaire socialists.[24]

Throughout the second half of the 1920s, and in particular after 1932, and the return of de Valera to governmental power on the basis of a Fianna Fail programme for economic self-sufficiency, state intervention in the economy grew. State controlled organisations were established to run insurance, transport, sugar and steel production, industrial and agricultural credit, tourism and many other areas of economic activity. This interventionism developed in response to the twin pressures of the structural weakness of Irish native capital and a nationalism which, if now largely conservative in leaning, looked to the new state both as a guarantor of economic prosperity and as a guardian of Ireland's cultural identity. (See Table 1.)

TABLE 1
TOTAL PUBLIC SECTOR EXPENDITURE AS A PERCENTAGE
OF NATIONAL PRODUCT, 1926–77

1926	1930	1934	1939	1946	1951	1962
22.6	21.3	28.9	28.0	23.7	39.2	35.8

1962	1971	1973	1974	1975	1976	1977
33.4	43.5	44.8	49.1	54.0	55.2	51.2

Source: National Income and Expenditure issues.

It was in this context of the growing corporate character of Irish society that the broadcasting service developed. In 1927 a subsidiary one-kilowatt broadcasting station was opened in Cork, although not until the introduction of a high power station at Athlone in 1933 was a fully national service with universal reception achieved. Licence figures by 1932 were still less than 30,000. The ratio of licences to the population in the Irish Free State was only nine per 1,000 in 1929, as compared with 60 per 1,000 in the UK. The punitive duty of 33⅓ per cent on the import of receivers and the poor reception in many rural areas militated against a rapid increase in the radio audience. Nevertheless, by March 1933, largely as the result of the improved reception rendered possible by the introduction of the high power transmitter, it had risen to 33,083. By 1937 it had topped the 100,000 mark.

In 1928 the radio service 're-occupied' the GPO now reconstructed after its damage by British artillery in the 1916 Easter rising, moving into new and expanded studio and administrative accommodation. The personnel of the service survived the change of government in 1932, and Fianna Fail confirmed its commitment to developing the service and strengthening its public service function. The new minister responsible for the service expressed his personal view that he 'would prefer to see no broadcasting at all in this country rather than have a wireless service which would go outside the country [he was referring to the new broadcast coverage potential of the high power transmitter] and not be in every sense creditable to the country'.[25] Even in the aftermath of a bitter civil war which deeply conditioned political relations between Cumann na nGaedheal (later Fine Gael) and Fianna Fail, a high degree of consensus seems to have existed between the two parties as to the appropriate form of broadcasting for Ireland. Each party laid claim to the mantle of Irish nationalism and viewed broadcasting as an 'instrument of public policy' concerned with the aim of buttressing national sovereignty and defending the cultural integrity of Ireland. Neither party accepted the view that the public service ideal of broadcasting necessitated the formal independence of the broadcasting service *from* the state, as Reith did, although both accepted the principle of an impartial and permanent civil service *within* which broadcasting should be located.

The fundamental conflict between the Reithian concept of broadcasting as 'an instrument of public good', formally independent of government, and the belief among governing circles in Ireland, expressed most concisely by Sean Lemass while Taoiseach in 1966, that broadcasting was 'an instrument of public policy',[26] had not become apparent to broadcasters at this time, although from the time that the television service was established in 1961, this tension between professional broadcasters concerned with serving a wider 'public interest' and the more immediate political concerns of the government in power had become considerably more marked.

Another source of tension between broadcasters and successive governments from 1920 to 1960 was the method of funding the broadcasting service. Government demanded a public service form of provision, yet was reluctant to provide adequate funds from the public exchequer to secure the independence of broadcasting from commercial pressure. It remained in favour of increasing advertising revenue to make up annual deficits. Indeed the government from 1933 *removed* a major source of broadcast income by incorporating into its general revenue the import duty raised on receivers previously paid over in part to fund the service. The message from Sean MacEntee, Minister for Finance in the Fianna Fail government returned the previous year, was that broadcasting would become self-supporting. On the other hand, the government placed considerable obstacles in the way of the service in its attempts to increase its revenue from advertising. The wireless service faced a dilemma:

> If the advertising and other revenues failed to pay for the service, the service was a drain on the economy. If the service broke even, the advertising, the licence fees, etcetera, were an intolerable imposition on the freedom of the people or of the air waves.[27]

This contradictory stance of government towards its broadcasting service – unwilling to fund it adequately out of public revenue, but expressing extreme distaste towards advertising on the air waves – was to persist right into the age of television. It reflects the more general situation in which a corporate economy was developing in this period of governmental fiscal rectitude *without* any ideological alignment to 'Keynesian' demand management policies.

Significantly the major expansion of broadcasting resources occurred as a result of an ill-fated government scheme to establish a short-wave service capable of broadcasting to America and Europe. The broadcasting estimate put before the Dail in April 1946 forecast that total expenditure for the year would exceed revenue by £119,000. A massive increase in government subvention was projected to fund the introduction of a high-power short-wave station planned to open in April 1947. The short-wave station had been one of de Valera's pet projects since the early 1940s. During the Second World War Ireland was, of course, neutral. However, international communication from Ireland by radio was routed through London; and the British Post Office – and its censors – had control over what went through. Given the tensions that existed between de Valera and Churchill over Ireland's continued neutrality, the former found Ireland's dependence on British facilities for broadcasting to the US particularly invidious. However, in a wartime situation of acute shortages in telecommunication equipment, it did not prove possible to launch the service, and the Irish government remained dependent on Britain for its radio and telephone links with the outside world.

In response to this perceived communication dependency on Britain, the Fianna Fail government launched once again in 1946 an ambitious scheme for short-wave broadcasting. As ever, political and ideological considerations overrode the economic and technical arguments against such a service. In fact the station never got fully established as a regular service – due mainly to difficulties in securing a satisfactory wavelength. However, in the Dail those same deputies who in previous years had fought tooth and nail to restrict government expenditure on radio voted through a massive increase in capital spending in 1947 to meet the costs of the soon-to-be-redundant short-wave service.

Not even a change of government in 1948 (the coalition governments of John Costelloe) could shake the resolve of the Irish state to proceed with a project which by 1949 was looking even more unfeasible.

The lessons of this episode were not lost on broadcasters. As Gorham comments on the failure of the short wave experiment:

> The legacy that it left to Radio Eireann, on the other hand, more than doubled the station's resources. As a direct result of the shortwave project Radio Eireann gained – and never lost – a proper news service, a Symphony Orchestra, a Light Orchestra, staff script writers, outside broadcast officers, and among other things, a professional repertory company. The Irish broadcasting service had never had it so good.[28]

THE TELEVISION AGE IN IRELAND

The Irish state's traditional reluctance to provide adequate finance for broadcasting, coupled with its perpetual desire to control it, was witnessed again in the deliberations leading up to the establishment of a television service. The Television Commission set up by the government in March 1958 to investigate the possibility of launching a television station took as its cardinal principle, 'That no charge shall fall on the Exchequer, either on capital or current account, and that effective control of television programmes must be exercisable by an Irish public authority to be established as a television authority.'[29]

The government had initially announced in November 1957 that Irish television would be a largely *commercial* concern. However, by 1959 it seemed to have had a complete change of mind and announced that the new television service would be controlled and operated by an Irish *public* authority. The initial capital expenditure would be forwarded to the proposed semi-state body on a loan basis, thereby solving the problem of raising the venture capital without losing political control – and with no ultimate charge on the Exchequer envisaged.

This *volte-face* is partly explained by the general changes in government policy during this period, following the introduction of a five-year Programme for Economic Development introduced in 1958. After a period of economic stagnation throughout the 1950s and a severe deflationary crisis in 1956 and 1957, the state had begun to review the policy of protectionism and economic isolation followed since the 1930s. Between 1953 and 1958, when the rest of capitalist Europe was enjoying an unprecedented boom, industrial employment actually fell in Ireland from 228,403 to 210,324 persons. National income rose only 0.5 per cent per annum during this period. Emigration accelerated.

The government pinned its hopes for economic recovery on a programme for stimulating growth in industrial output, geared now towards external markets. In order to create favourable conditions for export-led growth, the state invested heavily in basic infrastructure (transport and communications) and directly encouraged foreign investment with a generous range of grants, loans and other investment incentives. Capital expenditure by the state rose by an impressive 239 per cent in real terms from 1953 to 1975. (See Table 2.) By 1977, 680 new industrial projects had been set up by state-aided overseas companies, representing a dramatic level of capital penetration by multinational corporations. State intervention in a situation of rapid expansion of world trade and growth of multinational capital seeking new areas for profitable investment had spectacular pay-offs. In the 1960s GNP grew in real terms at more than twice the rate of the 1950s. Investment, always a weak point of the Irish economy, increased from the low figure of 15 per cent of GNP in the 1950s, to as much as 24 per cent by the end of the 1960s. Ireland now fully integrated into the world economic system (it signed the General Agreement on Tariff and Trade in 1960 and a year later joined the

TABLE 2
STATE EXPENDITURE (IN £ MILLION)

Year	GNP	State Current Expenditure	State Capital Expenditure	Total State Expenditure
1958	600.9	145.4	37.4	182.8
1962	738.8	196.2	58.8	255.0
1966	1073.9	303.6	83.1	386.7
1970	1648.5	546.1	157.7	703.8
1974	2968.5	1091.1	411.9	1503.1
1978	6403.4	2667.6	943.1	3610.7

Source: National Income and Expenditure issues.

EEC), began to enjoy some of the fruits of the long post-war economic boom.

It was in this climate of economic optimism – the 'Irish Economic Miracle' – that the television service was launched. Ireland, thrust with the help of state intervention and multinational capital into a belated industrial revolution, was meeting the future with a new self-assurance. The 'lift off' to an irreversible dynamic of 'modernisation' seemed to have been achieved. A basically rural and conservative society was being propelled into the modernity of consumer capitalism. 'Television' like 'youth' (and Ireland had the youngest and fastest-growing population in Europe) became a metaphor for the vast social changes sweeping the country. Mass communications were indeed playing an important role in shifting traditional attitudes and facilitating the appearance of new consumption norms much more closely integrated with the capitalist market economy. Television was both conditioned by, and in turn sustained, these social and economic changes.

The television service was launched on the last day of 1961. From the outset it was decided to match as far as possible the transmission services of the British stations. As Desmond Fisher reports:

> This was not a case merely of over-ambitiousness or national pride. Approval for the television service, as 35 years earlier for the radio service, had been given by the Oireachtas out of a sense of protecting Irish culture and attitudes from the effects of British broadcasting output. Translated into broadcasting terms, this was seen to require that the Irish services were in a position to catch and hold the attention of Irish audiences.[30]

The legal and administrative basis for the new service had been established a year earlier in a new Broadcasting Act which empowered the setting up of a Broadcasting Authority, Radio Eireann (later Radio Telefis Eireann), to run the new service and take over the responsibility of radio from the Minister of Posts and Telegraphs. The new authority was now formally free of civil service and governmental control. On paper at least, it enjoyed a degree of independence which made the Reithian-inspired ideal of broadcasting as a public service, serving a 'public interest' distinguishable from, if compatible with, the immediate concerns of government, attainable for the first time.

In reality, as with the BBC, the government continued to control the purse-strings. As a state-sponsored body, RTE found itself in a position, with other such corporate bodies, where it was dependent on the whims of the state's Department of Finance for every area of its funding. Government controlled, and *continues to control*, the following areas:

- capital funding of the service, usually in the form of a repayable grant from the central exchequer;
- the level of licence fees and the collection of them. Since 1975 the Minister of P & T refers requests for fee rises from RTE to the National Prices Commission. In the last few years these have been pegged at a level below the rate of inflation. RTE reckon they lose

£6 million a year through the inefficient system of fee collection run by the P & T;
- the quantity of advertising permitted on the air (at present seven-and-a-half minutes per hour maximum for television);
- the cost of advertising on RTE.

As such, RTE has found itself constrained within the wider political objectives and economic constraints of the Irish state. In the 1960s in a period of expanding government expenditures and growth in the size and significance of the state-sponsored sector, the attention of broadcasters was focused on the *political constraints* placed on the new service by a government reluctant to grant broadcasting the autonomy it demanded. However, since 1974 (the recession of that year hit the export-orientated Irish economy particularly badly), as the state has slid into an ongoing fiscal crisis and economic growth has slowed down dramatically (GNP grew at less than one per cent per annum between 1982 and 1984), there has been a shift of attention to the economic terrain.

The early years of development of the television service were, however, untroubled by the distant dark clouds of a coming recession. The 1960s saw a steady increase in broadcasting hours, in the percentage of home-produced programmes and in the development of technical expertise in the many facets of modern television. The public service credentials of the service seemed well established, despite its dependence on advertising revenues to balance its books – credentials underwritten as ever by national and cultural aims with wide political currency. For, as the new broadcasting authority had promised in its first annual report, television would

> provide a programme which as far as possible would have a distinctively Irish quality, would reflect traditional Irish values and would recognize Radio Eireann's responsibility as a public service concerned with cultural and educational matters as well as with the provision of news and entertainment.[31]

By the early 1960s Ireland had a large and growing public enterprise sector, partly funded by, but administratively autonomous of, government. It was largely concentrated in the communications (including transport), natural resources management and finance sectors. By and large these public enterprise bodies were founded directly by the state and were not the result of a process of nationalisation of firms previously in private hands. As a result the growth of the public sector was not the outcome of a political and ideological struggle as in the case of the post-war nationalisations in Britain. The increased role of the state in the economy in Ireland, 'to supplement private initiative in industry and commerce', was presented by successive governments as a pragmatic affair addressed to remedy specific defects in the operation of the free market as experienced in Ireland – particularly the traditional chronic shortage of venture capital. In so far as governing parties did seek to legitimise the increased role of the state, it was by reference to a nationalist ideology of economic sovereignty – an ideological position which commanded bipartisan support. In the absence of a mass party of the working class committed to a programme of socialist social reform, no substantial ideological cleavages along class lines developed between the two major parties. Indeed nationalist ideology, after de Valera's accession to power in 1932, with its recurring themes of gaelic communality and endangered national sovereignty served to obliterate class identities and modes of political organisation in the south of Ireland. Nationalism, especially as orchestrated by the populist Fianna Fail party, whose politics often appear co-extensive with the practices of the state, not least because of their prolonged period in government over the last 50 years, has an 'isolation effect'.[32] It fragments the working class as a politically organised force and binds it, via clientelist links, to a populist party (like Fianna Fail) refined in the arts of political brokerage.

Precisely because of this pivotal role of nationalist ideology in political mobilisation in Ireland and its specific historical function in legitimising the growth of the corporate state, the contemporary crisis in the public finances, profound though it is (see Table 3), has not led to a situation where a major political party has led a general neo-liberal offensive on the interventionist state. In contemporary Ireland there would appear to be few votes in monetarism – even with a populist face – and the major parties know it.

TABLE 3
PUBLIC SECTOR BORROWING AND THE IRISH ECONOMY, 1953–82
(AVERAGE ANNUAL AMOUNTS DURING PERIOD IN FIRST COLUMN)

Period	National income (£ million)	Balance of payments deficit (£ million)	Public authority borrowing (£ million)	Cost of servicing debt (£ million)	Balance of payments as percentage of national income	Servicing debt as percentage of national income
1953–57	451.2	10.6	34.1	18.3	2.35	4.06
1958–62	557.9	4.5	34.2	25.1	0.81	4.50
1963–67	808.1	19.2	57.3	41.1	2.38	5.09
1968–72	1,341.5	54.0	108.8	83.3	4.03	6.21
1973–77	3,109.6	150.7	527.5	312.1	4.85	10.04
1978–82	7,068.9	870.2	1,829.2	1,035.7	12.31	14.65

Source: National Income and Expenditure, various years, 1960–81; Central Bank of Ireland, *Annual Report, 1983.*

Television as a public service developed, therefore, in a period of economic growth in Ireland presided over by the state. Indeed that growth *could* only be sustained by massive subventions by government to foreign capital (a strategy not without its ideological contradictions).[33] During the 1960s public expenditure grew substantially faster than GNP, its proportion of GNP rising from 33 per cent in 1960 to 58 per cent in 1975. The high level of state spending was only possible through deficit financing, involving in turn high levels of borrowing. Between 1961 and 1974, for instance, deficits on the government's combined current and capital account rose from £29.7 million to £178.4 million. As a result of a corresponding growth in the money supply, inflation rose dramatically from the mid-1960s onwards. Since then Ireland has had the highest rate of inflation of any EEC country (peaking at over 21 per cent in 1982, now down to around ten per cent in the depths of the recession).

BROADCASTING AND POLITICAL CONTROL

However, in the 1960s neither the limits to economic growth, nor the contradictory nature of state intervention in the economy, were fully realised by economists in Ireland – never mind politicians and the public at large. For broadcasters the sensitive aspect of their relation to the state largely resided in the issue of editorial autonomy.

Following a clash in 1966 between the then Minister for Agriculture, a certain Charles Haughey, and the RTE newsroom, the government moved to tighten its political control over broadcasting. Sean Lemass as Taoiseach reminded the Dail and Irish broadcasters that:

> Radio Telefis Eireann was set up by legislation (the 1960 Act) as an instrument of public policy, and as such is responsible to the Government. The Government has overall responsibility for its conduct, and especially the obligation to ensure that programmes do not offend against the public interest or conflict with national policy as defined in legislation. To this extent the Government reject the view that Radio Telefis Eireann should be, either generally or in regard to its current affairs and news programmes, completely independent of Government supervision .... It has the duty, while maintaining impartiality between political parties ... to sustain public respect for the institutions of Government and, where appropriate, to assist public understanding of the policies enacted by the Oireachtas. The Government will take such action ... as may be necessary to ensure that Radio Telefis Eireann does not deviate from the due performance of this duty.[34]

RTE might protest that 'the preservation of the status quo is not necessarily always in the public interest', but in the next few years the Authority was effectively brought to heel by the government.

From 1968, 'external political circumstances', to wit the deepening political crisis in the North of Ireland, which as the civil unrest grew there soon threatened to spill over into the South, became the occasion for the imposition of direct government censorship over news and current affairs coverage. This in turn led to a climate within RTE where self-censorship became the order of the day. It is beyond the scope of this article to analyse in any detail the political background of the use by successive governments of Section 31 of the Broadcasting Act to empower the issuing of ministerial directives prohibiting the broadcasting of 'any matter that could be calculated to promote the aims and activities of any organization which engages in, encourages or advocates the attaining of any political objective by violent means'.[35] But suffice it to say that the very vagueness of the directives, annually renewed by the Dail, which did not actually specify in any way the prohibited classes of matter relating to reportage of the Northern conflict nor, until 1976, actually name the paramilitary groups prohibited from appearing on television or radio, led to a developing climate of self-censorship on the part of anxious RTE journalists. It also led to an increasing level of hierarchical editorial control *within* the progressively bureaucratised broadcasting organisation itself.

The vagueness of the ministerial directions, however, did not stop the government in 1972 dismissing the entire nine-man Broadcasting Authority and appointing a new hand-picked one, after the Authority had backed RTE's right to broadcast one of their reporter's interviews with a Provisional IRA spokesman.

There can be little doubt that the 'Troubles' in the North have once again placed the 'unresolved national question' on the political agenda in the Republic – despite the evident unease of the constitutional nationalist parties about the whole issue. Indeed it is precisely the deep ambivalence of those parties to political developments in a part of the island to which the Republic's constitution still lays territorial claim that has conditioned increased government scrutiny of those areas of the media it *can* control. Indeed in the contemporary period where recession, rising unemployment (now at 17 per cent of the workforce) and cuts in welfare expenditure (including food subsidies) are undermining the legitimacy of government and in which militant republicanism, in the shape of Sinn Fein, is gaining in political strength in both North and South, the current coalition government seems to be even more paranoid than its predecessors towards media treatment of the Northern conflict.

The dilemmas of constitutional nationalism *vis-à-vis* the issue of Irish sovereignty and national identity were never more apparent in the field of media relations than in the events leading up to the introduction of the second television channel in 1978. Following pressure from groups of television viewers in areas receiving only the RTE 'single channel', namely, those not able to receive BBC and ITV transmissions and envious of those in the 'multi-channel area', the then Fianna Fail government asked the Broadcasting Review Committee to investigate the possibility of relaying British services to Irish viewers. RTE, scandalised at the possibility of the state sanctioning an increased level of penetration of a foreign broadcasting service, proposed in its submission to the Review Committee that a second national television channel be set up instead.

The Review Committee in its interim report on the matter strongly supported the RTE proposal for a second channel, concluding in a pragmatic manner that it would be uneconomical for the national service to distribute UK channels either by microwave re-broadcast or by cabling the single-channel area.

However, a change of government in March 1973 saw the installation of a new minister in the coalition government, Conor Cruise O'Brien, committed to 'pluralism' in politics and to the idea that the whole of Ireland should be 'an open broadcasting area'. In October Cruise O'Brien, noted as a bitter opponent of militant republicanism in all its guises and as a champion of 'law and order', announced that the government had authorised the provision of transmitter and microwave link network with the capacity *either* to re-broadcast one television channel relayed from Northern Ireland *or* for use to launch a second RTE channel.

The government continued to push the idea that the second television network planned should be used to broadcast BBC 1 (Northern Ireland service) rather than a second RTE channel. It did so increasingly from 1974 in the face of mounting political opposition orchestrated by the traditionally more nationalist Fianna Fail party. RTE added its weight to the strong lobby against the 'open broadcasting area' plan, publishing a position paper in June 1975, 'The Second Channel: Statement of Television Development in Ireland and the Question of National Choice'. In the document it outlined what the programming of the second national channel would look like.

In July 1975 the government bowed to public pressure and announced that a survey would be conducted to establish the views of the wider public on the matter. The resulting survey, published in October of that year, indicated a clear preference by viewers both in the multi-channel area *and* in the single-channel area for an additional RTE channel over BBC 1. The 'vote' – for the survey had become part of a bitter political campaign – was in fact decisive in deciding the fate of the issue, the overall percentages being 62 per cent for RTE2 (as it was to become) as opposed to 35 per cent for BBC 1. As Fisher comments, 'the decisive argument was that with the RTE2 choice control of the service would lie in Irish hands';[36] an argument not without a degree of irony given the fact that when the new channel actually opened in 1978, its programme content consisted largely of British and other imported material. Indeed such a programming recipe formed part of RTE's plans from the outset, given its budgetary constraints.

Once again then, as in the ill-fated short wave radio episode, arguments about endangered national sovereignty and cultural identity justified the expansion of broadcasting resources, where a purely economic rationale would have surely failed. Indeed, the second channel was delayed for over a year as a result of difficulties in financing it out of the public capital programme for 1977. The new investment was proceeded with despite the deepening fiscal crisis of the Irish state. Such is the potency of cultural nationalism.

If the launching of television in Ireland in 1961 occurred at a time of economic confidence, so the introduction of the second RTE channel coincided with the end of the long post-war boom. As economic growth has slowed down, public expenditures have continued to rise, plunging the Irish state into a fiscal crisis only temporarily relieved by foreign borrowing. (See Table 3.) With real GDP virtually flat, the unemployment rate had increased to over 16 per cent by early 1984. Despite a series of deflationary budgets aimed at controlling the public finances and endless political rhetoric about the necessity for fiscal constraint, the Exchequer borrowing requirement is predicted to remain at around 13 per cent of GNP, with total government expenditure still consuming almost one-half of national income in 1984.

As with the other state-sponsored bodies, RTE has been starved of investment. Since 1978 it has been expected to run two channels on a budget not substantially larger than it received from the government for running *one*. After substantial falls in domestic demand in the last few years (as real disposable incomes have shrunk), advertising revenues are static if not falling. Licence fees have not risen for two years.

In addition to the threat to its audience share posed by the now four British channels, the rise in the home video market has made further inroads into RTE's audience. Not unnaturally it views the possible development of pay-as-you-view and narrowcasting cable services with considerable trepidation. Commercial cable and satellite channels would undoubtedly make further inroads into RTE's share of a static advertising market. In addition, if developed on the US model, cable would lead to an atomisation of the national audience which, RTE believes, would make the defence of the public service broadcast ideal politically hard to sustain.[37] In turn, RTE argues, standards of broadcasting would almost certainly fall.

CONCLUSION

The development of Irish television may then be prematurely foreclosed by the current fiscal crisis of the state. As with the other national broadcasting services in Europe, RTE faces the challenge of the new media technologies, already weakened by inadequate government funding. As Muiris MacConghail, currently controller of programmes at RTE, comments, 'from a benign and well-meaning monopoly in a largely supportive atmosphere to a somewhat hostile environment is increasingly the order of the day'.[38]

Yet as we have argued, RTE and the political supporters of the public service ideal of broadcasting have retained a pivotal role in the definition of the new media services. Deregulatory policies founded on neo-liberal economic thinking have not made the same headway against public service traditions in Ireland as in some other western countries. In so far as the fundamental rationale for a national broadcasting service remains intimately bound up with issues of national sovereignty and cultural identity, the public service model continues to attract widespread political support in contemporary Ireland.

NOTES

1. ITAP Report of the Enquiry into Cable Expansion and Broadcasting Policy (London: HMSO, 1982), para. 8:5.
2. As Timothy Hollins comments in *Beyond Broadcasting: Into the Cable Age* (London: BFI, 1984), p. 29: 'Throughout the recession-ridden western world there is a widespread belief that cable and information technology could be important economic rejuvenators. Publicly this is described as a long-term objective; privately it is hoped cable might also act as a short-term stimulant, creating new industries, new jobs and new export opportunities.'
3. In Britain, the BBC has been credited with being 'a pre-Morrison case of "Morrisonite" nationalisation'. See T. Burns, *The BBC: Public Institution and Private World* (London: Macmillan, 1977).
4. Broadcasting Review Committee, Final Report 1974 (Dublin: Stationery Office, 1974).
5. See, for example, N. Garnham, 'Public service versus the Market', *Screen*, Vol. 24, No. 1 (Jan.–Feb. 1983).
6. Jim Mitchell, Minister for Communications, written answer to the Dail, 15 May 1984.

(Also details membership of Cable Committee.)
7. The Department of Posts and Telegraphs has already tendered for a digital microwave radio network to help link the new telephone exchanges being installed throughout the country. This £20 million investment is capable of expansion to handle other data systems, although no developments in the area of interactive services are envisaged in the next ten years.
8. A consortium Westsat involving RTE, Telecom Eireann, Allied Irish Investment Bank and Guinness Peat has been formed to bid for the government DBS franchise.
9. Interview in *Success* magazine, Dublin, May 1984.
10. The general manager of Radio Nova, the largest of the pirates, recently reported that he expects the station's turnover to reach IR£1 million this year.
11. *Sunday Tribune*, Dublin, 23 July 1984.
12. Ibid.
13. The minister has also announced that he intends to introduce legislation to make it illegal to place advertisements with illegal radio stations.
14. *Building on Reality 1985–1987* (Dublin: Stationery Office, 1984).
15. M. Gorham, *Forty Years of Irish Broadcasting* (Dublin: Talbot Press, 1967).
16. Ibid., p.2.
17. Darrel Figgis T.D., quoted in Gorham, op. cit., p.11.
18. Ibid., p.12.
19. Ibid., p.19.
20. Ibid., p.64.
21. Ibid., p.55.
22. Ibid., p.91.
23. J. Meehan, *The Irish Economy since 1922* (Liverpool: Liverpool University Press, 1970).
24. S. Lemass, 'The Organization Behind the Economic Programme', *Administration* (Dublin), Vol.9, No.3 (1961).
25. Gorham, op. cit., p.38.
26. For a discussion of this distinction see M. OhAnachain, 'The Broadcasting Dilemma', *Administration* (Dublin), Vol.28, No.1, pp.33–67.
27. Ibid., p.39.
28. Gorham, op. cit., p.161.
29. Warrant of Appointment to Mr Justice George Murnaghan, chairman of the television commission, from Sean Ormonde, Minister for Posts and Telegraphs, March 1958.
30. D. Fisher, 'The Formative Years', *Irish Broadcasting Review*, 1983.
31. Quoted in D. Fisher, *Broadcasting in Ireland* (London: Routledge & Kegan Paul, 1978), p.31.
32. For an account of this process see D. O'Connell, 'Sociological Theory and Irish Political Research', in M. Kelly (ed.), *Power, Conflict and Inequality* (Dublin: Turoe Press, 1982).
33. See J. Wickham, 'The Politics of Dependent Capitalism', in A. Morgan (ed.), *Ireland: Divided Nation, Divided Class* (London: Ink Links, 1980).
34. Dail Debates 1045, 12 Oct. 1966.
35. Section 31 Order of 1971 made by the Minister of Posts and Telegraphs, Gerard Collins, on 1 October 1971. These orders have been renewed annually by means of statutory instrument and since 1976 the political groups with whom interviews or reports of interviews are prohibited have been named in the orders. The order for 1983 made under Section 31 of the Broadcasting Act, named, for instance, the IRA, Sinn Fein, the Ulster Defense Association, the Irish National Liberation Army (INLA) and 'any organization which in Northern Ireland is a proscribed organization for the purposes of section 21 of the Act of the British Parliament entitled the Northern Ireland (Emergency Provisions Act 1978)'.
36. D. Fisher, op. cit. (1978), p.40.
37. D. Fisher, 'Challenge and Change', *Irish Broadcasting Review*, 1982.
38. Interview with Deidre Purcell, *Sunday Tribune* (Dublin), 12 Aug. 1984.

France and the 'New Media'

Raymond Kuhn

Broadcasting has been a topic of fierce political controversy in France since at least the Second World War. This is still the case today, with different aspects of the Socialist government's policy on the broadcasting media under attack from various quarters including among others the Gaullist–Giscardian opposition, the Communist Party, large sections of the predominantly right-wing press and assorted pressure groups ranging from local radio operators to viewers' associations. Familiar territory is often replonghed, notably the question of government control of news output. But this reassuring sense of continuity is somewhat misleading, for the debate on broadcasting has not remained static. While many issues (control, financing and programming, for example) are scarcely original, the technological and political environments in which the current debate is taking place have altered dramatically over the past few years.

The first, and more important, environmental change is the advent of new communications technology, particularly fibre optic cable and direct broadcast satellites. This new technology allows broadcasting to break away from constraints previously imposed by the shortage of air wave space for transmission. If their potential is realised, cable and satellite will provide more television channels for French viewers, increase the choice of outlets and lead to some new types of programming such as local productions. Inevitably their development will have consequences for the established broadcasting organisations, programme output and viewing habits, even if the extent of their impact is not yet known. What is clear, however, is that the 'new media' have already altered perceptions about broadcasting, calling into question apparently entrenched *idées reçues*. In the realm of policy formulation, cable and satellite have already made their presence felt.

The second environmental change follows the accession to power in 1981, for the first time in the history of the Fifth Republic, of a Socialist President and government, pledged to reorganise broadcasting on a variety of fronts. The 1982 statute on 'audiovisual communication', both a reaction to the past and a preparation for the future, enshrined some of the major guidelines of Socialist thinking on the broadcasting media.[1] In particular, essential elements of the traditional post-war system of a highly centralised, government-controlled state monopoly were rejected. Whether all the changes envisaged have been successfully implemented is debatable, but taken together they served to produce a picture of a broadcasting system in transition. To a large extent the new legislation signalled the end of the old broadcasting regime.

The aim of this chapter is to examine the contemporary debate on broadcasting in the light of these technological and political changes. In particular, we shall concentrate on initiatives by the Socialist government to create new sources of television programming, the so-called 'new media'. These are, first, the establishment of a new television channel, *Canal plus*; second, the introduction of cable television networks; and, finally, the commitment to direct broadcasting by satellite. None of these three initiatives figured in François Mitterrand's 1981 election manifesto.[2] They were barely matters of public political debate until quite recently. Yet it is on them that the contemporary debate on broadcasting now largely focuses.

Three main conclusions emerge from this study. First, the government's commitment to the 'new media' technologies is based primarily on its view of France's industrial and economic (not broadcasting) needs. Second, their introduction, while under the overall control of the state, opens up broadcasting to groups and interests in French society previously excluded in the traditional state monopoly system. Finally, the creation of new programming outlets has called into question the public service ethos which has provided the normative framework for French broadcasting since the war. To appreciate fully the current debate on the 'new media', however, it is first of all necessary to retrace the essential features of its predecessor – the 'old media' debate.

THE 'OLD MEDIA' DEBATE

What were the terms of the debate on broadcasting before the advent of the 'new media' and the Socialist government? During the post-war period there was a considerable degree of agreement among the major political forces that broadcasting be organised as a state monopoly with, in principle, public service norms and obligations. With little disagreement on the structure and ethos of the broadcasting system, political conflict largely centred on the problem of government control over news output: how the information services of the state broadcasting media should function to ensure balance and impartiality in political coverage.

The commitment to the state monopoly was not effectively challenged until the late 1970s. Before that, various factors combined to ensure its maintenance. The technical constraints on air wave space established a powerful, though not by itself overwhelming, case. In addition, the strong tradition of statism and Jacobin centralism could naturally be applied to broadcasting. This was certainly true in the case of the left, who feared the incursion of private interests taking over a primary instrument of cultural and ideological dissemination. This view, however, was by no means confined to the Socialists and Communists. State control of broadcasting was seen by many, including the Gaullists, as an important nation-building device in the traditionally divided and fragmented French society. Other groups had their own vested interests in the preservation of the monopoly, notably the press which feared competition for advertising revenue if it were abolished.

The Second World War had a profound influence on the French political elite's attitudes towards broadcasting. The state monopoly framework bequeathed by the collaborationist Vichy regime was continued by successive post-war governments of both the Fourth and Fifth Republics. At the same time widespread admiration of the role played by the BBC during the war resulted in a series of rhetorical commitments to establish a BBC-type public service broadcasting organisation in France. However, in terms of independence from the government and impartiality in news output, the rejection of an essential element of this foreign transplant by the French body politic was total, for the war had also revealed to politicians, notably de Gaulle, the potential of broadcasting as a political weapon which could be used for partisan purposes. No government prior to 1981 was prepared to cast aside voluntarily the state monopoly over broadcasting which in practice could be commandeered to serve its own particular interests.[3]

As a result, the various reorganisations of broadcasting undertaken by right-wing governments during the Fifth Republic, including one major statute in each presidency, all reaffirmed the monopoly status of the state services. Sporadic attempts by commercial lobbies to establish some form of private television petered out very quickly in the face of opposition from the left and, more importantly, from the dominant parliamentary force in the governing coalition, the Gaullists. De Gaulle personally was intensely hostile to proposals for commercial television. Pompidou may have been privately sympathetic, but if so he refused to support the case in public. Even Giscard d'Estaing, leader of the party thought to be most in favour of breaking the monopoly, did not pursue this option when he became President in 1974, because (he has since argued) of his dependence on the Gaullists in Parliament on whom he could not rely to pass the necessary legislation.[4] The 1974 Giscardian reform, while dismantling the ORTF (Office de Radiodiffusion-Télévision Française) and encouraging competition between the separate television companies, preserved the privileged status of state broadcasting.[5] When this was later threatened by pirate radio stations, following the example set by *Radio Verte*, additional legislation was introduced in 1978 to buttress the tottering monopoly.

With those forces supporting the monopoly in the ascendancy, the political debate centred on how the state services should be managed. One issue in this debate was financing. Here controversy focused on whether (and later, to what extent) television should be allowed to benefit from advertising revenue. In 1968, after an acrimonious debate in the National Assembly, commercial advertising was introduced to supplement income from the traditional source, the licence fee. This innovation represented not only a welcome boost to the ORTF's finances, but was also a concession to those groups which had advocated the creation of a commercial channel.

After 1968 the state sector came to depend increasingly on advertising. Moreover, while an overall ceiling of 25 per cent of total revenue was more or less maintained following the 1974 reorganisation, the two main national television channels, TF1 and *Antenne 2*, both relied on advertising for more than half of their respective incomes. Hesitantly, reluctantly in some quarters, but with a growing sense of inevitability, the left came to recognise this dependence, abandoning the abolitionist pledge made in the original 1972 Common Programme. The political debate on how to finance *state* broadcasting virtually ended at this point. Since 1981 advertising has even been allowed on the third channel, *France Régions 3*, which was previously exempt because of the powerful lobbying of the regional press barons.

Another issue was the centralist nature of the broadcasting system and its output. Demands for the decentralisation of decision-making in all spheres of activity, a feature of the 1968 protest, spilled over into the debate on broadcasting. Some acknowledgement of regional diversity in television production and programming was now required. The Gaullist approach was minimal to say the least: the regional evening news, closely controlled by Gaullist sympathisers, and a few token regional programmes of the *White Heather Club* variety. Giscard d'Estaing did little better, in spite of converting the ORTF's channel 3 into a separate regional radio and television company in 1974. While since 1981 the Socialists have boosted the regional element in state broadcasting as part of their general commitment to the decentralisation of power away from Paris, it remains to be seen whether the regional television companies created by the 1982 broadcasting reform will be a success in either programme quality or audience ratings.

In radio, however, the move away from centralism seems more marked with the introduction of public stations at the departmental level and the legalisation of private local radio, the former pirates of the Giscard presidency.[6] Current estimates of private local stations put the total at around 1,000. Their existence has opened up radio to a wide variety of forces in French society, many of which were previously ignored or marginalised by the centralised state monopoly broadcasting services. Not surprisingly, they are proving very popular with French listeners, successfully challenging the previous dominance of the national radio company, *Radio France*, and the so-called peripheral stations such as *Europe 1* and *Radio Luxembourg*.

By far the most controversial issue in the political debate on broadcasting concentrated on government control of news output. Prior to 1965, opposition spokesmen, such as François Mitterrand, were kept off the screen or suffered from malicious editing. The Ministry of Information fixed the agenda of radio and television news programmes by means of judicious appointments backed up by direct censorship if necessary. As a result, during de Gaulle's presidency state television could be accurately described as 'the government in the dining room'. The strike by ORTF staff in 1968 reflected the professional broadcasters' discontent with this system of government control which was totally at odds with the public service norms regarding balance and impartiality enshrined in the 1964 ORTF statute.

Control of political output remained a constant issue throughout the 1970s. The liberalisation of the ORTF's news services by Chaban-Delmas in 1969, a genuine though partial response to the demands of the 1968 strikers, was reversed when Pompidou dismissed him from the premiership in 1972. From then until his death in 1974, it was Pompidou's view of the ORTF as 'the voice of France' which set the tone for the relationship between the government and state broadcasting.

Although Giscard d'Estaing rejected this view and guaranteed the broadcasters professional independence from political interference, he was unable or unwilling to keep his electoral promises.[7] As the Giscard presidency ran into problems on the political and economic fronts, the temptation to use broadcasting for partisan purposes proved too strong to resist. A system of presidential controls was set up, based on key appointments in the news departments of the state companies. 'Give them freedom and independence, but do not give them yet' was the contemporary Giscardian version of St Augustine's famous plea.

The political obsession with government control of news output on the state broadcasting media has not ceased to be an issue since the Socialists came to power, despite the creation of a High Authority for Audiovisual Communication which has taken over many of the regulatory functions previously performed by the government, including the right to make top appointments in radio and television. Opposition politicians, now of the right, are vehemently critical of alleged media bias in favour of the Socialists. Viewers' associations, usually of a committed Gaullist or Giscardian hue, monitor news programming in a constant search for grievances. Those appointed to key posts in state broadcasting are scrutinised for their political sympathies and frequently condemned as unacceptably partisan choices. The controversy surrounding the appointment of Hervé Bourges as director-general of TF1 and, more recently, of Jean-Claude Héberlé as director-general of *Antenne 2* illustrates the tenacity of certain long-standing traditions and, in the eyes of some, the failure of the High Authority to resist intervention from the Elysée. Whether the allegations of the right are accurate or not, however, it is difficult to be moved by the protestations in the light of their own miserable record. In a political system where the main protagonists still regard control of state broadcasting as a natural spoil of election victory and in which political rhetoric, if not necessarily behaviour, is more polarised than in some other leading western European states, it would take a brave man – or a fool – to predict that this particular concern will ever drop completely from the political agenda. The issue of government control of television has become part of the ritual of post-war French politics: the protagonists play out their parts as though from a script, voicing their lines with no real conviction to a largely unconcerned audience.

Yet while appearing to stand still, the debate on broadcasting has moved on. It is no longer just a question of how the established state system should be run. The creation of new media outlets has recast the terms of the broadcasting debate. Old questions are now being asked of the 'new media' – and some new questions as well. But before looking at some of the principal issues in the 'new media' debate, it will be useful to sketch out the changes, anticipated or already realised, in the French broadcasting system of the 1980s, concentrating on the more important of the media – television.

THE 'NEW MEDIA'

1. Canal Plus

In November 1984 a new television channel, the first in nearly 12 years, was launched in France. The newcomer, entitled *Canal plus*, differs from the other three traditional channels in several important respects.

First, unlike RF1, *Antenne 2* and FR3, it is not owned by the French state. Rather, the dominant shareholder is the advertising agency, Havas, while other shareholders include a banking consortium, the privately-run water authority, a property company, two insurance companies and a regional press grouping. The head of Havas, André Rousselet, is also chairman of *Canal plus*.

Second, as we have seen, the other channels are financed from a mixture of licence and advertising revenue. Their programme output is made available to the viewer on payment of the annual licence, income from which is distributed among the three companies by the government. *Canal plus*, on the other hand, is funded from monthly subscriptions – 120 francs (about £10) per month – which viewers pay on top of their licence fee. To prevent non-subscribers from free-loading, the programmes are transmitted in scrambled form which the subscriber unscrambles at home with the aid of a special 'black box' provided by the company. An additional source of finance comes from sponsorship of programmes by commercial companies (although there are no advertising breaks). *Canal plus* is France's first pay-tv channel.

Finally, the three state-owned channels are subject to public service guidelines in their programming, as laid down in their operating conditions (*cahiers des charges*). These include the Reithian prescription to educate and inform as well as entertain. By the terms of Article 5 of the 1982 statute the state services are required to provide balanced and impartial news coverage, to give media access to various social groups, to help spread French culture and to encourage creative and original production and programming.

In sharp contrast *Canal plus* is bound by very few public service obligations.[8] For example, it is not specifically obliged to have news programmes, cultural programmes or programmes for children. There is no minimum quota of French-produced programming. As a result, the fourth channel is much freer than its rivals to transmit what it likes: its schedules are dominated by feature films, serials, games, sport, chat shows and short news flashes. It can concentrate on popular entertainment television aimed at the mass middlebrow audience, an essential marketing strategy if the channel is to attract and retain sufficient subscribers to make the venture a commercial success.

2. Cable Television

Although *Canal plus* represents an important new element in the French broadcasting system, a more significant change will take place when the Socialist government's plan for cable, announced at the end of 1982, comes to fruition. As it now stands, the plan is to cable one-and-a-half million households by the end of 1987 and to have half the nation cabled by the mid-1990s. If and when this takes place, France will enter the era of multi-channel television.

At the moment cable represents a dream and a promise for some; a nightmare and a threat for others. It is not yet a reality, except in a very few towns. However, despite delays, doubts and a variety of problems to be overcome, the governmental blueprint for cable is now in place and the allocation of roles among the different interested parties decided.[9] The state, through the Ministry of Posts and Telecommunications, is responsible for the installation and maintenance of the technical infrastructure, which will use the more advanced fibre optic cable in preference to the tried and tested, but much more limited, copper coaxial version. The PTT is to retain its monopoly over telecommunications services. It is also the state which is providing the bulk of the finance for the implementation of the ambitious cable plan.

Responsibility for running the programming side of cable is placed in the hands of local quangos called *sociétés locales d'exploitation commerciale* (SLEC). These will include a mixture of local authority representatives and private interests and will be headed by a local politician. The local authorities may fix their own level of participation, allowing the private interests a greater or lesser stake in the quango, but in any case they will retain a blocking right over policy decisions. There will also be a government commissioner on each body to ensure that the network respects the operating conditions imposed by the state.

These conditions were made public in the spring of 1984. As far as programming is concerned, each cable network will have to carry the output of the three traditional state channels. There is a quota of 30 per cent on imported programmes. At least 15 per cent of programming must be of local origin. One-third of network revenue must be given to finance new programming. The networks will help subsidise the cinema and television production industries. Film transmissions will be subject to the same regulations as govern the three state channels (for example, on the minimum delay between general release and television screening), except in the case of pay channels where the regulations will be the less strict ones applied to *Canal plus*. A maximum of 80 per cent of network revenue may come from advertising. Revenue will also come, of course, from subscriptions by viewers – about 120 francs a month.

3. Satellite Broadcasting

The third, and final, element in this picture of a changing broadcasting system is the decision to maintain the commitment to direct broadcasting by satellite. The history of French interest in broadcasting by satellite goes back to the late 1970s, when an agreement was reached between the French and West German governments to cooperate in this area of new communications technology. Initially two DBS satellites were to be launched, one for West Germany (*TV-Sat*) and the other for French use (*TDF-1*).

As with cable, the French DBS project has had problems to overcome. One was whether DBS was technically necessary if France was adopting cable in any case. It was argued by some technocrats inside the PTT ministry that the less expensive and technically complicated telecommunications satellites could be used to transmit programmes to central reception stations (headends) which could then be processed, amplified and transmitted to subscribers via the cable networks. The other advantage of this solution was that a control on output could be exercised at the headend by the relevant authorities, acting as a regulatory intermediary between satellite transmission and viewer reception. Naturally, such arguments were opposed by the state transmission company, TDF, which regarded DBS as its own prestige project.

Another problem was the policy stance adopted by France's media-conscious neighbour – Luxembourg. France feared that Luxembourg would launch its own DBS in competition with the French satellite, thereby compromising the latter's commercial viability. Through its important shareholding in the official Luxembourg broadcasting agency, the Compagnie Luxembourgeoise de Télévision (CLT), the French government applied pressure on the Luxembourg authorities to abandon their own project. As a *quid pro quo*, Luxembourg would be given one or two channels on *TDF-1*.

While agreement on this was being reached with the CLT, the Luxembourg government pulled the rug out from under the French by setting up a new body, the SLS, to supervise the launching of a different satellite with the backing of American private interests in the shape of the Coronet company. The French government, however, has decided to proceed with its own four-channel direct broadcast satellite in any case, allocating two channels for use by the CLT and two for use by France. Meanwhile, the conflict with the Luxembourg government was partly resolved when it agreed not to show any French-speaking output on its satellite. None the less, the success of the French DBS cannot be taken for granted, given the huge costs involved and the fluid situation in European satellite broadcasting generally.

THE 'NEW MEDIA' DEBATE

At first sight one apparently surprising aspect of the introduction of the 'new media' in France has been the lack of political debate about the desirability of their development. Arguments may rage about how they should be used and financed, who should control them and what programmes they should show. But few would appear to question whether they should exist at all. There would seem to be a new consensus across the political elite that the thrust of the government's plans, if not necessarily the mechanics, is the correct strategy for France.

Why should this be so? Largely it is because the expansion of the broadcasting media has been justified with reference to the country's *industrial* needs. The commercial importance attached by the government to the development of new technology has resulted in decisions which affect broadcasting being taken, at least initially, within an industrial policy framework. The new media technologies are part of a strategic assessment by the government that the field of communications can provide a much needed boost to both the manufacturing and service sectors of the economy at a time when more traditional industries, such as steel and textiles, are suffering from international recession and Third World competition. Emulating the commitment by the Giscardian regime, which accepted the analysis of the Nora report on the desirability of France's pursuing an integrated telecommunications policy, the Mitterrand government has determined that France will not miss out on the new 'information technology' by directing state investment into the relevant sectors of the economy.[10] Since the parties of the opposition do not apparently dispute the Socialist government's analysis, there is a considerable degree of agreement about the need for the new broadcasting 'hardware'.

The rationale behind the development of cable and satellite is clearly industrial.[11] To stimulate employment and investment in those industries manufacturing fibre-optic cable, satellites and related components; to win exports for France in what is regarded as a key area of economic activity; to ensure that France is not left behind by the much-heralded communications revolution in the way it was largely bypassed by the industrial revolution of the late eighteenth century; to provide the business and service sectors with an interactive communications system including telebanking, teleconferences and all the other two-way services promised (or threatened) by the new technology: it is with all these considerations uppermost in mind that policies are being adopted which will have profound effects on French broadcasting. Cable and satellite are important elements in an economic and industrial gamble as the French government pursues the elusive goal of 'modernisation' under its new technocratic Prime Minister, Laurent Fabius.

Even in the case of *Canal plus*, while no new technology has been required for transmission of the new service which uses the old network of the former channel 1 of the ORTF, for the reception of its programmes each subscriber has to acquire the unscrambling device made in France by Radiotechnique. In addition, many households have to purchase a new VHF aerial at a cost of approximately 550 francs. Finally, out of the 14 million households equipped with television, about six million are technically unsuited for the reception of the fourth channel's programmes. If they wish to subscribe to *Canal plus*, their owners will have to purchase a new set, which the government hopes will be French produced. The launching of *Canal plus*, therefore, conforms to a long-standing governmental objective, which predates the Mitterrand presidency, to protect and encourage the domestic television manufacturing industry.[12]

The new fourth channel is also part and parcel of an attempt by the French government to minimise the penetration of video cassette recorders into France. This entailed the decision in 1982 to impose *de facto* import controls on the importation of video recorders from Japan by channelling them through one small customs post at Poitiers. The annual tax payable on ownership of videos fits this same strategy of dampening down demand for a foreign import until, it is hoped, a domestic or European video recorder manufacturing industry can catch up on the Japanese lead. *Canal plus* is part of the same plan, since it aims to fulfil the function served by video recorders in other countries. By showing feature films and repeating them over a short time period, by transmitting for 20 hours a day during the week and 24 hours a day at weekends and by concentrating on entertainment television, *Canal plus* is intended to soak up the demand for video and keep French viewers watching a French medium, if not necessarily a French product.

Placing the development of the 'new media' within an industrial policy framework meant that much of the ensuing debate, especially in the early stages, focused on technical questions relating to the 'hardware' of the communications infrastructure. A relevant example was the dispute between the PTT ministry, in particular its telecommunications wing, the *Direction Générale des Télécommunications*, and the state transmission company, TDF, regarding the policy to be pursued on satellite broadcasting, with the former preferring the lower-powered telecommunications version while the latter advocated the more complicated DBS.[13] (Another example was the conflict between those municipalities which preferred to use copper coaxial cable in opposition to the PTT's preference for fibre optics.) This aspect of the new media debate was largely fought out between technicians: it was an archetypally technocratic rather than quintessentially political battle, even if the final decision was usually imposed by the government. Of course, industrial considerations have affected French broadcasting policy in the past when, for instance, the ORTF was obliged in the 1960s to adopt the SECAM colour transmission process and thereby act as a national shop window for a strongly government-backed domestic product. However, the extent to which the new media debate has concentrated on 'hardware' questions is much greater than previously. In the contemporary debate the medium has often seemed more important than the message.

This is evident when one considers the programming side of the 'new media'. In the case of satellite transmission, for example, having finally committed itself to going ahead with the DBS project, the government was still unclear as to how it would fill the two available channels. A similar sequence is visible with cable: first, embrace the technology and then consider the options as far as programming is concerned. To help fill the schedules of a multi-channel cable service the government appointed a team headed by the Socialist Deputy, Bernard Schreiner, to carry out the task of finding 2,000 hours of suitable programming. Archives were raided and old stocks dusted down to ensure that when cable arrived there would be programmes to show the expectant viewer.[14]

In the case of *Canal plus* there is little that is innovative in its programming, which is similar to much of the output of the traditional state channels. It does little to encourage independent productions. It is not an educational or 'cultural' channel. Nor is it an access channel. It does not cater for specialised tastes or minority groups – with the possible exception of insomniacs. In terms of programme content *Canal plus* is much less progressive than Channel 4 in Britain.

While the programme content of the new media has not been the prime consideration in their development by the government, concerns about programming *have* featured in the debate about broadcasting. The message has not been totally ignored. The government has been keen to ensure that taken as a whole the 'new media' benefit the domestic television production industry, whether this means the state sector in the shape of the *Société Française de Production* or private production companies. The programming quotas imposed on the nascent cable networks can be seen in this light. Partly this is to maintain employment in these sectors of the French economy. However, it also forms part of the government's expressed concern, personified by the Minister of Culture, Jack Lang, to protect French culture from the predatory ravages of foreign, and especially American, television imports.

The launch of *Canal plus* was itself delayed because of a dispute over programming. Discussions between the new channel and representatives of the French film industry were prolonged and acrimonious, with *Canal plus* eventually being obliged to restrict its annual feature film output and to keep certain times entirely free of films. A minimum quota of French films was imposed in the channel's operating conditions, as was the provision that one-quarter of its resources be used to subsidise the film industry. It remains a moot point, however, whether in spite of these constraints the arrival of *Canal plus* will be beneficial or detrimental to domestic film production and distribution.

The series of discussions between *Canal plus* and the film industry was not alone in demonstrating that the development of the 'new media' raised important economic, social and political issues which went far beyond the initial technical questions. The debate about the new media could never be principally a technocratic one. Nor has it been. Moreover, while the initial impetus may have been industrial, the implications of the new media for broadcasting have ensured that a whole host of interested parties have made their own contribution to the debate, which has been widened to cover the whole nature of the French broadcasting system.

The *political* debate on the 'new media' (and the 'old') is still continuing. But it is already clear that the established post-war framework of a public service state monopoly is no longer a tenet of faith of the French political elite. A reformation of thinking has taken place, involving a re-examination of long-standing beliefs and, in some cases, dramatic 'road to Damascus' conversions.

The state monopoly in broadcasting has been abandoned by the 1982 reform, with the result that other actors are now becoming involved in the running of the broadcast media to an extent unprecedented in the post-war period. The government's desire to liberalise the system has led to the participation of non-state actors, including press groups, voluntary associations and commercial interests, while its wish to decentralise has resulted in an increased role for sub-state agencies such as local authorities. Whether one considers local radio, *Canal plus* or cable television, the state has relaxed its previously iron grip on the French broadcasting system. In the cable field alone dozens of local authorities have sought the necessary agreement with the PTT. The most notable is Paris, not just due to its size and status, but also because its mayor, Jacques Chirac, is one of the leading opposition figures to the Socialist government.[15] However, cable has attracted the active interest of a host of small communes as well as large cities such as Lille and Lyons.

Clearly one should not exaggerate the extent of the state's withdrawal from its previous monopoly position. The state remains the dominant actor by far in French broadcasting, owning and managing, directly or indirectly, most of television and much of radio. Through its control of the legislative process, its financial powers and its continuing role in key appointments, the

Socialist government plays a pre-eminent part in shaping the structure of the broadcasting media and regulating their content, despite the position carved out for itself by the High Authority and the latter's frequent public opposition to government policy.

In the case of *Canal plus*, the nearest the French have ever come to a commercial channel, the state has a majority controlling interest in Havas. Moreover, on a personal level the links between Rousselet and Mitterrand are very close. Rousselet was Mitterrand's *chef de cabinet* during the Fourth Republic, managed the financial side of his first two presidential election campaigns and was his *directeur de cabinet* during the first year of his presidential term. Through Havas and Rousselet, the state remains the dominant influence in the ownership and control of *Canal plus*. As regards cable, there was never any chance of the Mitterrand government emulating the Thatcher approach of relying on private investment to install and operate the networks.

None the less, the role of the state in broadcasting matters is now a subject of heated political debate. The political parties of the right, currently favourites to win the 1986 parliamentary elections, have reneged on their previous commitment to the state monopoly. While the expansion of media outlets has provided the occasion for this change of heart on the part of the current opposition, political and ideological factors must also be emphasised in explaining this volte-face in their views on broadcasting policy.

At one level, the fact that the right are now out of government for the first time in the history of the Fifth Republic means that the state monopoly can no longer be employed to serve their partisan interests. In fact, the right argue that the state broadcasting media are controlled and manipulated by the Socialists for *their* own ends. If the public service objectives of pluralism and balance in news output are to be attained, the right claim, then the whole system has to be opened up even more to non-state actors.

Underpinning this political attack on the state monopoly in broadcasting is a more general ideological shift by the right away from statism and towards neo-liberal economic policy initiatives. France has not escaped unaffected from the perceptible change in the ideological climate of Western Europe. The challenge to the central role of the state in economic policy and social welfare provision mounted by Thatcher in Britain has been taken up by various elements within the French right, most notably within the ranks of the Gaullists. The victory of Mitterrand and the Socialist Party in the 1981 elections may have conveyed the impression that France was immune to the changing *Zeitgeist* in much of the West away from statism. But if so, the impression was misleading. In any case with the failure of the Socialist economic experiment of 1981–82 and the subsequent electoral rebuffs of the 1983 municipal and 1984 European elections, the electoral tide is now running in favour of the right. Applied to the debate on broadcasting, the ideological shift is evidenced by both the Gaullists and Giscardians favouring an increased role for private interests and a concomitantly reduced state sector.

In May 1984 Jacques Chirac, the Gaullist Party leader, announced his party's current policy.[16] TF1 would remain a state channel. FR3, the regional channel, would be opened up to interested parties from the private sector, although representatives of the state and of local councils would also be involved. No single actor would have a majority shareholding. *Antenne 2* would be wholly privatised, with 15–20 per cent of the capital being sold to small investors. The peripheral radios such as *Sud Radio* and *Radio Monte Carlo* in which the state has important and frequently majority shareholdings would also be sold off. Local television and cable services in private hands would be encouraged. (Chirac has been keen to give the private sector a large stake in the cable plans for Paris.) There would be no advertising ceiling on private local radio. Some of state radio would be hived off to leave only a basic state service. The High Authority would have its powers reduced to technical supervision and there would be only minimal regulations on programme output. Finally, with the exception of the basic phone service, the PTT's monopoly of telecommunication services would be abandoned. The contrast between these views and Gaullist policy in the 1960s is stark. There is no longer any emphasis on broadcasting as an instrument for the dissemination of French culture; little concern about programming standards; no elitist moralising à la Malraux. Instead, a vision of the future is presented with the viewer as consumer choosing among the different broadcast products offered by mainly commercial broadcasting outlets.

Former President Giscard d'Estaing has also been outspoken in his criticisms of the state's role in broadcasting. Already in September 1982, just over a year after his presidential election defeat, Giscard stated that he was now in favour of an end of the state's broadcasting monopoly. More recently, he has argued that there should be only one state television channel, that the peripheral radios be privatised and that much of *Radio France* should also be hived off.[17] A technical agency, with far less power than the present High Authority, would ensure orderly frequency allocation and management, while a monopolies commission would prevent the establishment of private broadcasting monopolies. Private television would be governed by technical regulations and minimal operating conditions.

These policy views of the right in favour of a slimmed-down state broadcasting sector have been echoed elsewhere within France. Various pressure groups are actively campaigning for greater liberalisation of the broadcasting system, particularly television. Private over-the-air television experiments have been conducted, especially in the Paris region, although these are illegal under the provisions of the 1982 statute unless authorised by the state.

Top broadcasting figures have made their own contribution to the debate. For example, in February 1984 Pierre Desgraupes, then director-general of *Antenne 2*, saw privatisation as the key to the future success of this state television company.

> If *Antenne 2* were privatised, it would finally be free to manage its programme schedules as it wished. What freedom of manoeuvre do we enjoy now, obliged to conform to unbelievable obligations laid down in our operating conditions which were the product of pressure from various interested parties ...? All of that has become intolerable.[18]

One can scarcely imagine such a view being put forward publicly by a director-general of the ORTF in the 1960s. Yet while Desgraupes' views aroused controversy and some protest, they certainly did not create a scandal.

Groups opposed to privatisation have not been silent. The Communist Party, for example, has repeated its own opposition to the incursion of commercial interests into the broadcasting sector, a move which it regards as incompatible with its concept of broadcasting as a public service. The trade union Force Ouvrière condemned the government's policy on cable as leading to the establishment of a private system of control over cable programme content. Many television producers fear that a smaller state sector would inevitably lead to cheaper programmes and more imports, with programming decisions being made with reference to purely commercial criteria.

However, with the development of the 'new media', simple defence of the state monopoly or a call for a return to a single broadcasting organisation like the ORTF are no longer credible options. With the changes in the technological environment, not only have the terms of the debate altered, but the ideological centre ground has shifted away from an unqualified statist approach towards a mixed system, albeit with a strong state presence. It is this centre ground which the Socialist government has sought to occupy.

The dispute about the optimal size of the state sector in broadcasting forms part of a much wider debate on how the public can best be served by the 'old' and 'new media' in conjunction. Not only is the concept of the state monopoly now regarded as anachronistic by a wide variety of political and social groups ranging across the ideological spectrum. The ethos of the public service is itself being questioned and subjected to a variety of interpretations. While the concept of a public service broadcasting system may still be considered as desirable by many, there is no agreement on the defining characteristics of such a service in practice.

Given the chequered history of public service broadcasting in France since the war, this situation is scarcely surprising. During the 1960s the ORTF enjoyed some successes: frequent high quality programmes, complementary scheduling across its two television channels, popular and informative current affairs programmes (especially when concentrating on foreign issues).[19] On the other hand, government control of news output and an at times heavy-handed, patronising approach to programming detracted from the reputation of the ORTF both inside and outside France, with the organisation and its output often being compared unfavourably with its cross-channel rival, the BBC.

During the 1970s the image of public service broadcasting in France worsened. The introduction of competition between the ORTF channels at the start of the decade, reinforced by the break-up of the ORTF into its constituent parts in 1974, led many to complain about a decline in programme quality as the channels were encouraged to vie with one another in pursuit of the mass audience. There was a marked decline in programme production, especially television fiction and dramas, with a corresponding emphasis on feature films, imports and chat shows.[20] The ORTF (and its successors) also encountered severe financial problems as the increase in income from the licence fee slowed down with the saturation of the market, while at the same time administrative and production costs escalated. The extension of programming hours with the launch of a third television channel in 1973 and growing use of underutilised daytime and evening slots placed further burdens on the public service, now increasingly criticised and condemned for its shortcomings. A profound sense of malaise reigned in state radio and television by the end of the 1970s, demonstrating that the problems of public service broadcasting do not date from the development of the 'new media' technologies. The advent of the latter has certainly contributed a new element to the situation; but it has not caused the present difficulties of the established channels.

Attempts by the Socialists to remedy the defects in public service broadcasting as represented by the established state companies have come up against a variety of difficulties. First, the government has not always had the courage of its professed convictions. For example, having established the High Authority to act as a buffer between the government and the broadcasting companies, the Socialist regime has on occasion sought to restrict the Authority's influence or bypass it entirely, unwilling to give its own brainchild full adult status.

Second, the problems of the state sector have proved more intractable than was anticipated. The scale of administrative costs, the overmanning in some areas coupled with serious undermanning in others, the difficulties of the state production company, the further expansion of programming hours, the introduction of new services such as the greater emphasis on regional output: these have strained the resources of the state television companies, which have not always been willing or able to adapt to changing demands.

Finally, the development of the 'new media', promising more programme outlets and the likely fragmentation of the mass audience, has helped undermine the rationale of the public service in its traditional guise. For example, the objective of balanced scheduling imposed on any one programming outlet is more difficult to defend when the viewer may exercise greater than ever choice between outlets, thereby controlling and regulating his (her) own programme intake.

The development of 'new media' outlets has proved less of an ideological problem for the right than for the left. As the scarcity which helped underpin the state monopoly gives way to relative abundance, the Gaullists and Giscardians now argue that the public is best served by a pluralistic system containing a large non-state element. The paternalistic concern with providing a balanced programme diet for the audience and the Reithian desire to raise tastes are no longer seen by the right as essential goals. In a system where the viewer can choose between different products, the need for detailed public service regulations is no longer self-evident. In this analysis the public is best served by an increase in the number of outlets, which will lead to more diversity of content and freedom of choice, resulting in greater consumer satisfaction.

The Socialists have been unwilling to accept this argument. They have waited too long to capture the commanding heights of French broadcasting simply to abandon a large part of the territory to private interests sympathetic to the right. The 'free play of the market' holds little attraction for them. Yet given the perceived need to develop 'new media' technologies for industrial and economic reasons, the changing external environment in which satellite threatens to transgress previously secure national boundaries and the financial and programming failures of the traditional state channels, the Socialists have been obliged to revise their own concept of the public service, attempting to salvage the best of the 'old' while at the same time accepting the desirability, and indeed inevitability, of some of the 'new'.[21] Some of the cardinal principles of the former public service ethos have been jettisoned, including, for example, the obligation to provide balanced scheduling which has not been imposed on *Canal plus*. Controlled liberalisation is the Socialist government's public service response to the many, and often conflicting, constraints it faces in formulating and implementing a coherent policy on the broadcasting media.

And what of the public whom the policies are supposed to serve? Which broadcasting system best provides a public service: the traditional, but now outmoded, state monopoly; the present controlled liberalisation with a large state element; or a possible future system dominated by privately owned and largely de-regulated broadcasting outlets? Any answer to this question must of necessity be subjective. Variations in tastes, standards and evaluation of programme quality, as well as differences in political and ideological beliefs, make any response highly value-laden.

Any assessment also depends on how the 'public' is defined. The subscriber to cable and *Canal plus* may find that television satisfies more of his/her wants than in the past. On the other hand, those viewers unable or reluctant to pay the additional costs involved in receiving the 'new media', and who therefore continue to rely on the traditional state channels, may find that their own programming diet is less satisfactory than previously as the 'best' programmes are creamed off for the pay-channels. In short, the development of the 'new media' is not just an *industrial* gamble. It is a *broadcasting* one as well in which the stakes are high, many goals mutually exclusive, and the outcome impossible to predict with certainty.

NOTES

1. Law no. 82–652 on audiovisual communication, 29 July 1982, published in *Journal Officiel, Lois et décrets*, 30 July 1982. See R. Kuhn, 'Broadcasting and Politics in France', *Parliamentary Affairs*, Vol. 36, No. 1 (1983).
2. D. MacShane, *François Mitterrand: A Political Odyssey* (London: Quartet, 1982), pp. 259–72.
3. R. Thomas, *Broadcasting and Democracy in France* (London: Bradford University Press, 1976), especially pp. 101–25.
4. *Télé-7-jours*, no. 1163, 11–17 Sept. 1982.
5. R. Kuhn, 'Government and Broadcasting in France: The Resumption of Normal Service', *West European Politics*, Vol. 3, No. 2 (May 1980), provides a critical account of the workings of the 1974 statute.
6. On private local radio see F. Cazenave, *Les Radios Libres* (Paris: PUF, 1980).
7. On broadcasting in the Giscard presidency see R. Kuhn, 'The Presidency and the Media

1974–82', in V. Wright (ed.), *Continuity and Change in France* (London: Allen & Unwin, 1984), pp. 178–201.
8. The operating conditions of *Canal plus* were published in *Le Monde*, 17 Feb. 1984. See also *Presse Actualité*, no. 184 (June 1984), pp. 19–34.
9. *Intermedia*, Vol. 12, No. 3 (May 1984).
10. S. Nora and A. Minc, *Informatisation de la Société* (Paris: Documentation Française, 1978).
11. Diana Green writes: 'It is important to emphasise that the government's *first* concern in launching the cable plan was industrial; the implications for broadcasting were a second-order consideration....' See D. Green, 'Cable TV in France: A Non-Market Approach to Industrial Development', *National Westminster Bank Quarterly Review* (August 1984), p. 16.
12. R. Levačić, 'Do Mercantilist Industrial Policies Work? A Comparison of British and French TV manufacturing', *National Westminster Bank Quarterly Review*, May 1984.
13. *Le Monde*, 8 and 14 March 1984.
14. *Le Monde*, 2 Feb. 1984.
15. *Le Point*, no. 607, 7 May 1984.
16. *Le Monde*, 16 May 1984.
17. *Le Monde*, 11–12 Dec. 1983 and 9 May 1984.
18. *Le Monde*, 22 Feb. 1984.
19. J.-N. Jeanneney and M. Sauvage, *Télévision, Nouvelle Mémoire* (Paris: Seuil, 1982).
20. M. Souchon, *Petit Ecran, Grand Public* (Paris: Documentation Française, 1980).
21. For an account of the changes affecting the broadcasting system introduced by the Socialists since 1981, see R. Kuhn, 'France: The End of the Government Monopoly', in R. Kuhn (ed.), *The Politics of Broadcasting* (London: Croom Helm, 1985).

Political and Market Forces in Italian Broadcasting

Donald Sassoon

Italy is the only European country with a multi-channel radio and television system much of which is not subjected to any form of state regulation. Any private person or company can set up a transmitting station, produce their own programmes or purchase them and broadcast them. The only restriction is that the broadcast must be local. The law, however, does not specify the dimensions of local broadcasting. Furthermore, a network of local companies can decide to broadcast locally at the same time the same programme with the use of previously distributed videotapes.

According to figures made available in September 1983 there are in Italy between 700 and 800 private television stations with over 5,000 transmitters and between 6,000 and 8,000 radio stations.[1] Many of these simply occupy an air wave and broadcast a signal while they try to develop proper programming, while others can only broadcast programmes around a few square miles. Only 50 per cent of television stations are able to broadcast regular programmes.

In the last few years something approaching an embryonic network system has emerged. Four 'national' companies linking together 125 stations are poised to become the keystone of Italy's private broadcasting system. They are: *Retequattro* (24 stations), *Italia Uno* (31), *Euro TV* (32) and the most successful of them all, *Canale Cinque* (38). By 1984 70 per cent of the population were able to receive these four networks. If we add to these the other local television stations and the three state channels run by the Radiotelevisione Italiana (RAI) we obtain the following result: something approaching 32 million Italians are able to tune into between seven and 11 television channels for something approaching 13 hours a day. In many large cities the choice increases to 18 to 20 channels. In some it is possible, thanks to special equipment, to receive foreign broadcasts from Switzerland, France, Monaco, Austria and Yugoslavia. This has enabled Italy to have the highest density of radio and television stations in the world: there is one radio station for every 16,000 inhabitants against one in 25,000 in the USA, and one television station for every 93,000 inhabitants against one in 274,000 in the USA.[2]

An unregulated system of broadcasting means that the only rules which are applicable are those established by existing *general* legislation such as those regulating pornography. There are no *special* restrictions concerning the broadcasting of sexually explicit material, no rules concerning unfair treatment of minorities or individuals, no obligation to report facts in a fair and unbiased manner, no restriction on the kind of programmes to be shown during the day when children may be watching and no requirements to broadcast a certain amount of cultural or educational material. A private television company can broadcast, if it so wishes, non-stop adult movies or cartoons or both.

State television is, of course, subjected to all these restrictions and is therefore competing from a position of inferiority. Italy's private system of broadcasting thus provides an example of what might happen to a West European country which decided to develop a system of unregulated cable television. If this system was financed by advertising, as private radio and television companies are in Italy, there would probably be very similar effects in terms of what happens to advertising revenue, the content of television output and the ethos and organisation of established 'public service' broadcasting.

In this article we shall examine all of these but before doing so it will be necessary to explain the origins of the present system.

STATE TELEVISION: ORIGINS AND DEVELOPMENTS

The RAI is a public company which is entirely owned by the Istituto per la Ricostruzione Industriale (IRI), a stateholding company which had been created in the 1930s by the fascist regime. Television broadcasting began in 1954 and was available to nearly half the population. Two years later it covered virtually the whole territory. A licensing fee provided television with its sole source of revenue until 1957 when the RAI was allowed to accept advertising. This was strictly regulated: it had to be 'bloc' advertising at the beginning or at the end of a programme.[3] This is still the case.

Soon after 1945 the RAI came under the political control of the Christian Democrat Party (DC), which had emerged from the war as the leading Italian political party. Between 1945 and 1954 the DC relied heavily on the political machine of the Roman Catholic Church in order to maintain its electoral base. In the early 1950s it began to use its control over the public sector to develop its own network of clienteles so that it would not have to be so dependent on the Church. In this period, under Amintore Fanfani, the Christian Democratic Party began to appoint its own supporters to positions of power and influence. This was also a device used to develop its own network of experts and specialists.

The RAI was obviously an important terrain for this kind of political 'colonisation'. Television was seen as a powerful instrument of propaganda which could be far more easily controlled than Italy's highly diversified press. It was also a potential cultural industry which would give jobs to technicians and intellectuals. The DC did not intend to control the content of the entire output: what really mattered was the news and current affairs section. Fiction programmes were allowed freedom from overt political control. In fact they were dependent on prevailing conceptions of decency which, until the mid-1960s, tended to be those of traditional Catholicism. These could not compete with Italy's thriving cinema industry.

In the late 1950s a private group, *Il Tempo-TV*, began to exercise pressures for the development of commercial television. The DC tried to prevent it and the Constitutional Court was asked to arbitrate. This decided that the state monopoly of broadcasting was legal and justified on a purely technical reason: the shortage of frequency bands available. The Court, however, also declared that some sort of competition was necessary and this led the RAI to begin broadcasting on a second channel (RAI-2) in 1961. By 1967, RAI-2 could be received by 86 per cent of the population.[4] RAI-2 was politically controlled just like RAI-1 but its programming policies were of a more cultural nature and the bulk of the audience continued to turn to RAI-1.

Political opponents of the DC, much of the press and the intellectuals continued to criticise the RAI: news programmes showed government ministers performing edifying tasks such as inaugurating schools, kissing children, receiving flowers, being greeted and acclaimed. Opposition leaders (in Italy's case, Communist Party leaders) were never to be seen, their policies never mentioned. Only in 1963, during the electoral campaign, did the Communist leader Palmiro Togliatti appear for the first time on the screen in a political broadcast in which he was interviewed by the press.

It is difficult to assess the political consequences of DC political control over the RAI in terms of votes. Television certainly did not enable the DC to increase its electoral base. After its victory in the 1948 elections the Christian Democratic Party tumbled to 40 per cent in 1953, moved up to 42 per cent in 1958 and then settled around the 38–39 per cent mark until 1983 when it lost heavily and went down to 33 per cent. The Italian Communist Party, on the contrary, moved from 22 per cent in 1953 to around 25–27 per cent in the 1960s. In 1976 it reached its peak (34.4 per cent) although it lost a few points in 1979 and 1983 (down to 30 per cent). At the European elections of 1984 it obtained 33.3 per cent of the votes overtaking for the first time the DC, if only by 0.3 per cent. The total of the Communist and Socialist vote in Italy has been around 40–45 per cent, which corresponds to the percentage of votes that left-wing parties obtain in most other West European countries, including those where television is not under the direct control of political parties.

In spite of widespread criticisms and the lack of any evidence of electoral gains, the DC never relented in its pursuit of control over the RAI. In 1961 it named as director general Ettore Bernabei who would remain in charge until 1974. Bernabei was a personal friend of Fanfani and had been the editor of the DC daily, *Il Popolo*. Bernabei's rule saw a further expansion of the patronage system of the DC, but the general approach had to change radically to take account of the presence of the Socialists in a new coalition system.[5]

Between 1948 and 1963 the DC had governed Italy in alliance with three minor parties of the centre: the Social Democrats, the Republicans and the Liberals. During this period, and particularly between 1958 and 1963, Italian economic development reached a very high rate of growth: the so-called 'economic miracle'. This expansion had been largely left to the private sector. When this period of growth came to an end in 1963 many of Italy's traditional problems had remained unsolved, such as the gap between the developed north and the agricultural south, and new ones had been created by the uncontrolled internal migration which had deprived the southern countryside of its labour force and overcrowded the industrial cities of the north. The DC, under the leadership of Aldo Moro and Amintore Fanfani, decided that it was necessary to ditch the anti-interventionist Liberal Party, include the Socialist Party in the coalition and initiate a programme of reforms. This was all the more necessary so as to stop the Italian Communist Party from extending its influence. The entry of the Socialist Party in the coalition government brought to the DC a partner which intended to obtain some share of control over the public sector (which, under the aegis of the new centre–left government, expanded very rapidly). The DC could no longer hope to have the exclusive monopoly over appointments in the public sector; now it had to negotiate with the Socialist Party (PSI). This was done through a quantitative increase in jobs. Thus the entry of the Socialists into the RAI in the 1960s under Bernabei was simply part of a process which was going on elsewhere in the public sector.

Bernabei increased the personnel of the RAI in an uninhibited manner, not only to accommodate the Socialists but also to make friends and extend his own power and that of his party. To counter the constant criticisms of intellectuals he developed a system of consultancies and freelance contributors well in excess of what was needed. Writers and journalists, academics and other personalities would be paid a retainer, on a yearly basis, plus a special contribution for occasional services.[6] When the student movement erupted in 1968, soon to be followed by the wave of workers' unrest in 1969 (the so-called 'hot autumn'), dissent threatened to engulf large sections of educated public opinion. The Bernabei system could no longer hope to diffuse criticisms by the simple policy of co-option.

The structural reforms promised by the centre-left government never materialised. After the social unrest of 1968–69 the DC faced a deep crisis. In 1974 it tried to re-establish control over the Catholic electorate by initiating a referendum to reverse the 1970 Divorce Act. It failed. In 1975 the Communist Party made sweeping gains in the local elections and took control, with the Socialist Party, of most major cities: Milan, Florence, Venice, Turin and, eventually, Rome and Naples. In 1976 the Communist Party further increased its electoral strength at the general elections. It was now the party of 34.4 per cent of Italians, a few percentage points behind the DC.

The DC felt it could no longer monopolise the public sector (and hence the RAI). Consequently, it offered the PSI a wider share of political power. The subsequent battle for control allowed other political forces to enter the fray and in particular the PCI. This led to the most important reform of the RAI to date.

THE REFORM OF THE RAI AND THE END OF DC MONOPOLY

The PCI was ill-equipped to enter the battle for the reform of broadcasting. Its main guiding principles were all connected to the conception of broadcasting as a 'public service' and the necessity to democratise it. Democratisation entailed the transfer of control over the RAI from the government to Parliament. This was also the only way in which the PCI could obtain some influence over the RAI because, although excluded from government, it had obviously a very strong presence in Parliament. The PCI was also committed to improve relations with the PSI, but if it had decided to fight unrelentingly against the carving-up of the RAI (the so-called *lottizzazione*) it would have had to oppose the PSI. Of course, the PCI could have also attempted to bypass the PSI and deal directly with the DC in the hope of obtaining a share more or less commensurate with its strength. But this strategy would have damaged the prestige of the PCI as the one party unsullied by corruption and would have divided it from those RAI journalists and technical staff and the broadcasting unions who saw the PCI as their main representative. Virtually paralysed in its attempts to initiate a more thoroughgoing reform, the PCI ended up by insisting on two principles: democratisation (that is, parliamentary control) and decentralisation.

The principle of democratisation was enshrined in Law 103 (1975).[7] This established that the RAI was now under parliamentary control. A parliamentary committee on broadcasting was set up. This consisted of 40 members appointed by Parliament in proportion to the strength of the parties. The task of this committee was to ensure that the state television system was managed according to the principles of political pluralism and that it fulfilled the obligations set out in its charter and those established by the law (for example, that there should be open access, educational programmes, etc.). The parliamentary committee was also required to appoint ten out of the 16 members of the *Consiglio d'Amministrazione* (the Board of Governors), the remaining six being appointed by the 'shareholders' of the RAI, that is, the IRI.

The principles behind the reform were good. The application of the principles less so. Within the parliamentary committee a majority was constituted which reflected the government. In other words the same parties which were in coalition in government joined together to appoint governors who could be relied on to support them. Furthermore the president of IRI, whose job it was to appoint six governors, was himself a government appointee and was instructed to follow the advice of the government department in charge of IRI. The PCI was given less than its fair share of the governors, but that was immaterial in view of the fact that *all* governors were political appointees and that the majority of the Board would in any case have been made up of loyal supporters of the governing majority. Thus control by the executive branch was reasserted via the devious route of establishing parliamentary control. The governors always behaved as 'politicians' and sought to defend the interests of their masters. This was, once more, seen essentially in terms of ensuring a 'correct' news coverage. The political importance of television fiction bypassed them nearly completely.

Law 103 established the 'official' reform of the RAI. Alongside it there was a parallel hidden 'reform': the formal carve-up of the two channels between the DC and the PSI. A 'secret' agreement (which leaked immediately) was reached in a locality near Rome between the representatives of the coalition parties.[8] The most significant point of this agreement was that RAI's two main television channels were given two distinct structures. RAI-TV 1 would be under DC control, whilst RAI-TV 2 was placed under Socialist control.

This has been the situation ever since. In 1984 the state of play was the following: the President and Vice-President of the RAI are members of the PSI, while the director-general is a Christian Democrat. The DC also 'has' the directors of RAI-TV 1 as well as the director of the news programmes on the first channel, whilst the Socialists control the entire second channel. Radio has suffered a similar political carve-up: Radio 1 has a Social Democrat for director, but its news are jointly run by a Socialist and a Communist. Radio 2 (including the news) is the exclusive property of the DC. Radio 3 (which is similar to its British equivalent) is mainly devoted to cultural programmes and is run by an independent close to the PCI while its news bulletins are run by a Social Democrat.[9]

The extent of politicisation in Italy is such that virtually all journalists and many RAI employees are members of political parties. In the shake-up that followed the DC–PSI agreement journalists were allowed to opt for one or the other channel. Most Socialists opted for the second channel, whilst the Christian Democrats opted for the first.[10]

The carve-up was not 'fair', not even by the rules of the *lottizzazione*: by choosing the first channel the DC obtained the channel with a mass following and thus retained the lion's share of the RAI audience.

As a sop to the decentralising demands of the PCI, a third television channel was also established. This was expected to devote a large amount of programming to broadcasts of a local and regional nature. It never stood a chance because the first and second channels were beginning to face the challenge of private television and more and more economic resources were poured into them in order to make more popular programmes and to purchase films from the USA. As a result, the audience share of the third channel has always been insignificant.

In retrospect the attempt by politicians to monopolise television can be seen to have had little effect. Mass behaviour is not affected by news programmes alone but by the entire communication system. Television too depends on a cultural industry of great diversity: press, publishing, theatre, cinema, the educational system and all other disseminators of information including those of other parts of the world. The colonisation of the RAI by the governing parties could not prevent the growing autonomy of the broadcasting media from the political elites because these (that is, the media) were becoming increasingly subordinated to the (largely American) world communication and cultural industries. Furthermore, the crucial event which would transform the contours of Italian broadcasting and enable the development of a sizeable private sector was about to empty the political carve-up of the RAI of much of its significance. This event was the decision, in 1976, of the Italian Constitutional Court that the state monopoly over broadcasting was not legal.

DEVELOPMENT OF PRIVATE BROADCASTING AND ITS CONSEQUENCES

A year after the 1975 Reform Law was passed, the Constitutional Court assembled once again to consider the question of the state monopoly over broadcasting. It decided that this was now valid only at the national level. Local private broadcasting was to be allowed. In so doing the Court probably destroyed also the emerging hopes of the cable industry because over-the-air broadcasting is much cheaper: it does not require an expensive network of cables and any additional expenditure on the part of viewers over and above the licence fee.

The way was now open for the unrestricted expansion of private radio and television stations. Of course the government could have stepped in and established some sort of regulatory framework, but the DC, having seen its power at the RAI somewhat diminished, hoped that it could reassert it, at least partially, in the developing private sector. There were no great pressures for regulation from the PCI whose position was still that television should be a 'public service'. It took a few years before the Communists accepted the idea of private broadcasting. It should also be said that the diffusion of private broadcasting companies was greeted by near-universal approval. The prestige of the RAI, never very high, had been tarnished by the spectacle of political parties fighting over the spoils. It was also assumed that competition would improve programmes all round. The press could have been expected to resist private broadcasting which would be an obvious competitor for advertising. It did not do so because most of it is under the control of large publishing conglomerates such as Mondadori and Rizzoli who were quick to enter the field of private broadcasting. The far-left groups as well as radicals and libertarians felt that this was a golden opportunity for the diffusion of community programmes with a high political content. As the initial capital required for this kind of operation was quite low, they hoped to initiate a whole network of 'alternative' broadcasting. Eventually even the PCI established its own network of radio stations (and some television stations) in the major cities, although with little success. Italian intellectuals, who have always had a snobbish attitude towards television, hoped that the new private sector would open up the possibility for more and better cultural programmes.

The hopes of all these were soon dashed. Those who benefited were some of the entrepreneurs who threw their energies into this new enterprise (but many had their fingers burnt and withdrew) and, of course, the audience whose demand for more popular television could no longer be satisfied by the RAI. As could be expected the cultural content of the private programmes was quite low. Most private radios offered an undiluted diet of pop music and some amateurish news reporting. Private television stations soon found out that they could never afford anything more than games shows, old films and a constant run (and re-run) of American products.

There is no doubt that the bulk of the audience wants to watch films. The ratings for the main types of programmes give a 75 per cent for films, but there is also a strong demand for news (74 per cent).[11] This is probably due to the low level of press readership and the habit of eating dinner during the news (that is, between eight and nine in the evening). At 8.30 p.m. the news programme is over and virtually all television channels schedule the beginning of their main programme. The search for a film starts. This is when the private television audience reaches its peak: 13 million viewers between 9.00 p.m. and 10.00 p.m.

Taking a day at random in the Rome area it is possible to classify thus the supply of television: 16 channels, including the three RAI channels, offer 196 hours of television, 23 per cent of which is produced by the companies themselves, and the rest purchased; 4.6 per cent of the total output is devoted to sports; 6.4 per cent to news; 11.4 to games and pop music; 15.4 per cent to cartoons; and 61.7 per cent to purchased films. Thirteen out of the 16 channels show films after 8.30 p.m., most of which (and of the cartoons) have been purchased abroad and dubbed in Italian. Nearly all imported films are made in the USA.[12]

Thus the Italian television system has become a huge network of terminals transmitting programmes produced in and around Los Angeles. In 1981 Italian television companies (both private and the RAI) imported 2,369 films plus 2,043 made-for-TV films and episodes of television serials. This makes a total of 4,412 units of which only 18 per cent were bought by the RAI. The total sum spent for all TV imports *and* for films to be shown in cinemas was 102 billion lire in 1981. In the same year Italy exported television material and films worth 29 billion. The deficit is therefore one of 73 billion lire (roughly £12.6 million), which indicates that the financial resources available for television and film are not invested internally but are directed towards the USA. In practice the Italian broadcasting system acts as the distribution network for products manufactured by a few multinational companies: centralisation of production and decentralisation of distribution go hand in hand.

This is, of course, not only an economic problem but also a cultural one: there is an increased Americanisation of Italian society. It will be remarked that this is not imposed on the Italian viewer by some evil outside force. Nobody compels anyone to watch *Starsky and Hutch, Dallas* and *Happy Days*. This is true, but it is not the whole story. Television viewing is now the principal, though not exclusive, focus of people's leisuretime throughout the advanced industrial world. There is no other activity to which masses of people can turn so frequently and so easily. Italians may well want to see films, but there is no evidence that they get the films they really want or might want if they had a wider choice. On the contrary, there is some evidence that the audience is getting bored. They do not switch off but they use frenetically the now widespread remote control instrument in a desperate search for 'something better on another channel'.

The dominance of American-made products is not only due to a cultural hegemony which has been established by the Hollywood film industry between the wars, but also to the fact that it is much cheaper to buy their products than to make new and original ones. Private television stations do not have the resources to invest heavily in their own production, although soon, the larger ones will. As for the RAI the fear of being left with a small share of the audience has driven it to compete with the private companies on their own ground, diverting resources towards the purchase of foreign products.

The spread of private television companies has also had a massive impact on advertising. In the first place the widespread diffusion of local television has enabled local advertising to find a space. Until then national advertisers could use the press, the RAI, the cinema, etc., to the benefit of products with a national market. Local advertising had no outlet until private local radio and television stations emerged. This in turn caused the development of new advertising agencies specialising in local advertising. To sell a 'spot', however, it is necessary to have a programme of fairly good quality. The early programmes were mainly chat-shows and badly dubbed poor quality foreign films, and so the agencies themselves began to purchase a better product which they passed on to the companies together with the advertising spot. The local companies became mere relay stations whilst the agencies continued their 'vertical growth' by purchasing equipment from electronic companies.[13]

Soon there emerged something akin to a network situation. The advertising companies became *de facto* distributors. They convinced a number of local television stations to carry the same programmes at the same time with the same advertising (which by now is both local and national). They thus provided the stations with the advertising revenues which would be returned to them to pay for the programmes, thereby establishing their control over most of the financial aspects of private broadcasting. The advertising companies/distributors then organise the production and distribution of comic books, novels, T-shirts, toys and other goods which relate to the programmes shown.[14] Thus the local television companies, far from being examples of a new dynamic entrepreneurship are but the agents of a few oligopolies which dominate the market. They are mere terminals for distribution.

Some local broadcasting stations are financed by capital already connected to advertising. Backed by powerful interests they soon emerged as the market leaders. The top three private television companies have cornered most of the advertising revenue going to the private TV sector.[15] Of these the most powerful is *Canale Cinque* whose owner, Silvio Berlusconi, has become the virtual master of the entire private system since he bought both *Italia Uno* and *Retequattro*. Berlusconi's own financial empire includes housing estates, shopping centres, and electronic companies, the right-wing Milan newspaper *Il Giornale* and Italy's leading television weekly magazine. His complex network of couriers distributes videotapes to hundreds of relay stations around the country thus creating the effect of a national network. The system he has created includes a financial company, Cofint-Finanziaria, a company for the purchasing and distribution of videotaped programmes, a production centre, a technical centre with a high and low frequency band, a television broadcasting station *Telemilano* (the original element in the network), and an advertising company. Technically speaking *Canale Cinque* is a network which broadcasts daily the entire programme schedule of *Telemilano*.[16]

In 1982 *Canale Cinque* bought the Italian option for the entire output of the major American TV company, CBS. Another company, *Retequattro*, made a similar deal with ABC. The RAI was forced to follow suit with NBC, but by June 1984 it still had not received from the Ministry of Trade the authorisation to purchase the necessary foreign currency. In 1984 the RAI was able to obtain the exclusive Italian rights for the Los Angeles Olympic coverage, but this meant that the Eurovision network (of which the RAI is a member) had to pay over the odds to defeat Berlusconi's challenge. The RAI had to agree to participate in this operation to the tune of six million dollars. Without Berlusconi, it would not have had to pay more than two-and-a-half million dollars.[17]

In 1983 Berlusconi bought *Italia Uno* thereby establishing a commanding strength. In 1984 he bought from Mondadori, Italy's largest publishers, *Retequattro*. Thus Berlusconi has acquired control over all three leading private TV stations, and consequently over 80 per cent of advertising revenue. He is likely to expand this further by also obtaining control over the remaining two minor networks, *EURO-TV* and *Rete A*. It was quite clear that Mondadori had tried to find another buyer. Its president, Mario Formentor, declared, when he accounced the sale in September 1984, that at first he had been trying to sell to another firm (the building company of Vincenzo Romagnoli) until he realised that Romagnoli was acting on behalf of Berlusconi. While the negotiations were going on, Mondadori's shares began to show a constant fall in value because of heavy sales. It has been widely suggested in the Italian press that this was a concerted action inspired by Berlusconi.

Having achieved the conquest of virtually all major national private networks, Berlusconi's next move could well be to weaken further the RAI. He has already begun to exercise considerable pressure on the government to abolish the RAI's licensing fee or to forbid it to carry advertising. He is also asking that he should be allowed to broadcast news every half-hour and has declared that 'any new law on broadcasting must not re-examine problems which have already been overtaken by the workings of the market'.[18] Clearly from now on the struggle will be directed entirely against the public sector. It is quite possible that the Berlusconi empire is not constitutional because the Supreme Court had already made its opinion known that even an oligopoly would not be legal. But this is not likely to deter Berlusconi. As a member of the secret masonic lodge P2 (his name was on a list deemed to be authentic by the parliamentary commission investigating the allegation), he has obviously enjoyed the help of influential political friends and has always acted in the knowledge that there would not be any regulation which could be an obstacle to his plans.

The entire operation which led to the establishment of a number of private networks occurred under the aegis of a *laissez-faire* ideology which had a major libertarian component. It was not only a question of establishing a free market in the broadcasting sphere, but also a demand for a pluralistic system of broadcasting which would not be confined to the state sector. Given the RAI's traditional subservience to the governing political parties, the development of private broadcasting had considerable public support. Yet no-one should be under any illusion that the development of the private sector was occurring despite the political establishment. There is little doubt that active encouragement had come, at crucial stages, from the governing parties. Only this can explain the extreme reluctance to initiate any legislation throughout the period of expansion of the new private system and the extreme ease with which thousands of television and radio transmitters have been installed throughout the national territory. Italy has a maze of regulations and a large and well-entrenched bureaucracy notorious for its delaying tactics. It is not unusual to have to wait months and even years in order to obtain permission to enlarge one's house or open a newsstand. Yet the widespread diffusion of transmitters occurred without any reaction on the part of the authorities. Clearly the dream, or perhaps the utopia, of a hundred stations broadcasting against the monopoly of state television has faded away. Power and control were at first diffused, then concentrated in a few hands and an oligopolistic situation was created. By the end of 1984 even this situation came to an end. There is now a duopoly: RAI and Berlusconi's TV empire.

ADVERTISING AND AUDIENCE SHARES

Available figures show that the remarkable growth in advertising which occurred between 1977 and 1981 benefited the private sector more than the RAI. Between 1978 and 1980 the RAI's share of advertising revenue decreased. In 1981 it increased again.[19] This is probably due to the fact that the amount of advertising broadcast in the private sector is reaching saturation point. The private companies may well have reached what is considered to be the natural limit of advertising per hour, namely, 14 per cent (eight-and-a-half minutes) whilst the RAI, which broadcast more hours, has still some way to go. But there is another explanation for the RAI's increase in revenue after 1980 and it is political.

During the battle for control between the DC and the PSI the RAI had succeeded in acquiring some form of independence. In the years 1976–79 the Italian Communist Party had supported the Christian Democrat government as part of its strategy of 'historic compromise'. This encouraged many producers and journalists to behave more independently. It was assumed that the difficult situation in which the DC was finding itself (electoral losses, necessity to co-operate with the PCI, etc.) meant that political control over the RAI could not be so tightly exercised as in the past. This was not the case. The DC and the PSI re-established control through the financial side: the real value of the licensing fee was allowed to decrease, while at the same time the amount of advertising revenue the RAI was allowed to obtain was not increased.[20] This amount, according to the RAI Reform Law (Law no. 103), must be established by the appropriate parliamentary committee, in other words, by its governing majority. Thus the RAI lost revenue on both the advertising and the licensing fronts. In 1980 many independent-minded functionaries and broadcasters were sacked and 'political protection' returned; advertising revenue and the licensing fee went up.

Clearly, the control exercised by political parties has had no tangible benefits for the RAI. The necessity to be on good terms with the governing political parties has meant that no-one can be particularly original, daring or critical; routine is much safer. There is also a growing inefficiency. In spite of its large personnel (14,000 employees, 800 executives, 1,100 journalists) there is a massive use of outside facilities and personnel on contract. For example, the RAI has paid an outside company ('Video Italia') to edit its own presentation spots: about 100 a year (length of spot: 40–50 seconds). The contract amounts to 3,500 million lire a year (roughly one-and-a-half million pounds). The RAI's director-general is not allowed to negotiate contracts for sums greater than 100,000,000 lire (£43,000), so these kinds of deal must be authorised by the majority of the 16 members of the Board of Governors (whose expertise on matters of television financing is not particularly great).[21] Clearly the chances of kickbacks are very high.

The leading private television companies have made major inroads into the RAI audience. The ratings for December 1983 made available by the ISTEL research organisation (considered fairly reliable by both the private and the public broadcasting sectors) show that *Canale Cinque* has now got the second largest share of the peak-time audience (8.30 p.m. to 11.30 p.m.):

	Percentage
RAI-1	28.9
Canale Cinque	25
Italia Uno	14
Retequattro	12
RAI-2	9.9
RAI-3	1.4
Others	8.8

This means that the three leading private networks have three million peak-time viewers more than all three RAI channels put together (the total audience is 27.380 million). This is not a 'freak' result; it is confirmed by the average ratings for the whole autumn of 1983. It also shows a trend unfavourable to the RAI, because the ratings for the spring of 1983 had seen the three RAI channels 'beating' the top three private networks by three million peak-time viewers.[22]

THE FUTURE OF ITALIAN BROADCASTING

The development of the private broadcasting system could not have taken place without the deliberate help of the governing political parties. Its appearance can be justified on many counts: the RAI monopoly was increasingly untenable; there was a widespread demand for television products that the RAI alone could never hope to satisfy; competition could have improved the public service; there was a need for more local broadcasting and so on. What is not so obvious is why the ruling coalition has never regulated this system, why it has allowed this untrammelled growth and why, nine years after the decision of the Constitutional Court, there is no evidence that the government is about to produce even the draft of a comprehensive regulatory bill.

1. The Position of the DC

The Christian Democratic Party never fought very hard to defend the monopoly of the RAI. In the first place it was clearly beginning to lose the total control it once enjoyed. The fact that it had to share power with the PSI had already been a sign that it could not assume that it could control in perpetuity a monopolistic public system. In the second place it hoped that it would be able, sooner or later, to deal directly with the emerging networks. The DC may have had to give up important sectors of its empire, but it has retained absolute control over the banking system. This has given it access to the private sector of industry which depends on the banks for much of its finances. Through the banks the DC can always negotiate with the private television companies.

The best card the DC can play with respect to the private sector is the regulatory system. It can tailor it so that it will benefit those companies which will accept to collaborate, but there is no point in playing this card before the private system has gone through an initial phase during which a few companies will have acquired a dominant role. This phase has now been reached, but various things have happened to the DC in the meantime: it has suffered a serious defeat in the 1983 general elections (a defeat which was confirmed in the European elections of 1984); it has had to give up the Prime Ministership to the Republican leader Spadolini in 1982 and to the Socialist leader Bettino Craxi in 1983, the first time since 1945 that non-DC politicians have obtained this post; it is at the mercy of a Socialist Party which has always had the option of joining the PCI in opposition, thus depriving the DC of the necessary parliamentary support. A weakened DC may not be able to impose on restless coalition partners the regulatory system it wants, but it is still strong enough to prevent any regulation whatsoever.

Finally, the DC is in reality concerned mainly with the television coverage of news and current affairs. Here the RAI still reigns supreme and, within the RAI, the DC-controlled RAI-1 has the overwhelming share of the audience for news programmes. Thus the leadership of the DC can obtain the 'right' sort of messages where it really matters. DC backbenchers have a different attitude; they need private radio and television because they can obtain from them what they cannot obtain from the RAI: publicity for their own activities at the local level. The opportunity to establish a local television image can be crucial to DC politicians during an election campaign. Italian voters must vote for a party, but can then write in the names of their favoured three or four candidates from within that party's list (the so-called preference vote). Before the development of the mass media, local candidates could keep in touch with their electorate through public meetings. Now they can no longer obtain a large audience; everyone stays at home watching television. Local notables can only enter private homes through small television stations which beam their message for a distance of 10–20 miles.[23] They will, of course, pay for it, but they can also do so by blocking in Parliament any reforms because, as far as local television stations are concerned, the best way in which they can be helped is by leaving untouched the present *laissez-faire* system.

2. *The Position of the Socialist Party*

Some of the arguments used to explain the position of the DC can be applied to the PSI as well. However, the support that the PSI has given to the private companies is also due to its general strategic perspective. Since Craxi became the Socialist leader, the party has attempted to create for itself a new image. It has proceeded to shed many of its traditional working-class connotations and to espouse a view of modernisation characteristic of many new and old centrist parties in Europe (such as the British SDP). According to this analysis it is necessary to link up with the emerging middle classes of technicians and professional people who are in the forefront of technological progress and whose aspirations have been repressed by the existence in Italy of a Christian Democratic Party which has always protected backwardness and inefficiency in order to maintain its electoral strength. Nor can the PCI be the vehicle for these new groups because – the PSI claims – it is still a traditional working-class party which will protect these entrenched interests against any rationalisation of the economy. Given this outlook, the PSI has cultivated from the very beginning the new private television sector. It welcomed the end of the RAI monopoly, declaring that a mixed market system would open up opportunities for all.

The PSI has also tried to develop the image of a party which seeks to defend and extend civil liberties and the right of the individual against the populist spirit of DC clericalism and the collectivist spirit of the PCI. The diversification of the broadcasting system was seen as a golden opportunity for expanding access and was made to fit the new libertarian image of the PSI. The fact that the reality of oligopolistic control contradicted the dream of 'let a hundred television channels bloom' never seemed to matter.

3. The Position of the Italian Communist Party

Until the 1970s the PCI had conceived of the television system purely in terms of a 'public service' which had to remain under the control of the state. It had not appreciated that television had also become an industry which would soon have to face competition from the private sector and be subjected to the requirements of the market as well as to political and professional control.

In the 1970s and 1980s the party began to understand the great importance of the mass media as a crucial sector which linked industry, culture and the new technologies. It established a special section of the Executive Committee which dealt exclusively with the media and was the only political party to present a comprehensive proposal for reform during the life of the 1979–83 Parliament. The main points of this proposed law were:[24]

(a) The Constitutional Court's principle that companies must operate only at the local level must be upheld. However, the local dimension cannot be too restricted and so it is suggested that the 20 Italian regions be the framework for roughly as many private companies.
(b) Networking would be allowed provided that effective anti-trust legislation ensures that ownership is not concentrated in a few hands.
(c) Private companies would be required to produce and transmit their own programmes for at least 30 per cent of their total weekly broadcast time.
(d) A national broadcasting authority would be created with specific tasks: to allocate frequency bands, specify when and how much of the inter-

nally produced programmes would have to be shown and supervise the application of codes of conduct. The governing body of this authority would be appointed in part by the government and in part by the parliamentary committee on broadcasting (although clearly this might launch a new *lottizzazione* struggle).
(e) A single national news programme should be broadcast by the private sector which would be in charge of its production. 'Live' news broadcasts would be provided by a publicly owned company.

Virtually every political party has agreed with at least some of these proposals. For instance, the DC accepts the principle of a single national news programme and of a statutory limit to advertising. Along with the small Republican Party it also accepts the need for anti-trust legislation which is, however, opposed by the Socialists (who seem to have become the main upholders of unrestricted capitalism).

The Communist proposals, in spite of the positive comments with which they have been received, are unlikely to become law. The chances are that there will not be any regulation of the private sector for some time to come. The present government coalition is too weak and divided and faces powerful interests. Furthermore, all existing proposals for reform do not get to the heart of the matter, which concerns both the relationship between the private and the public sector and the connection between television broadcasting and the entire information industry.

CONCLUSION

A modern mixed system can no longer assume a rigid demarcation between the public and private sectors of broadcasting; both are subjected to market forces and both must be liable to some form of state regulation. There is no reason why the two should be kept separate. The state could, through the RAI, establish some sort of framework within which a system of mass production of television products can be established and in which the private sector can play a part. So far the private sector has been an importer. A way should be found to transform it into a producer. The RAI has been successful in forging links with the film industry by acting as a producing company as well as a distributor of films both on television and in the cinemas. Well-known directors such as Olmi, Bertolucci and the Taviani brothers have produced important films through this system. It could be expanded on a more commercial basis and the private sector could be involved in it. This would allow Italian broadcasting to compete with American products, particularly if it were to take advantage of the fact that a number of European and Third World countries are increasingly concerned at American 'cultural imperialism'.

The advent of satellite broadcasting will go a long way towards destroying the national basis of television systems. In these circumstances reforms can no longer be conceived purely at the national level. The tasks facing the Italian political elite are thus considerable; it must achieve the modernisation of Italian telecommunications and promote – with other European countries – a concerted entry into the technological software market as well as into the international TV market. It must try to eliminate at least the worst aspects of *lottizzazione* (which has not given it the advantages expected) through the professional training of competent cadres and the establishment of some form of demarcation between technical and professional competence on the one hand, and political control on the other.

The main danger facing Italy at this stage is in the field of information technology. The development of unrestricted private television has dealt a blow to the possibility of the expansion of cable systems. Viewers who can receive up to 20 channels for free are unlikely to pay to get 30 more channels transmitting *Dallas*-type programmes all over again. The long-term purpose of rewiring an entire nation is not to provide programmes (these are only the means to convince consumers to pay for the installation of cables), but to provide the whole country with an interactive (two-way) system of information; consumers will no longer be the passive recipients of messages manufactured and transmitted by a few senders, but will actively intervene in a network of data which will permit shopping, learning, working and communicating by cable. The unrestricted over-the-air broadcast explosion may have cut Italy off from these crucial developments. The consequences may be that Italy will be left out of the advanced sectors of the 'information revolution'. For a country which is still paying the price for having been a 'late comer' in the industrial revolution, this is a daunting prospect.

NOTES

1. Figures made available by the RAI-Documentazione e Studi.
2. Figures in Carlo Gagliardi, 'La televisione in Italia: tendenze del sistema misto', *Sociologia e ricerca sociale*, no. 9 (1982).
3. Franco Chiarenza, *Il cavallo morente* (Milan: Bompiani, 1978), p. 91.
4. Giovanni Cesareo, *Anatomia del potere televisivo* (Milan: Franco Angeli, 1970), p. 80.
5. For an analysis of Bernabei's management see F. Pinto, *Il modello televisivo* (Milan: Feltrinelli, 1980).
6. Cesareo, op. cit., pp. 45–6.
7. A fuller description of the law can be found in Fabio Luca Cavazza, 'Italy: From Party Occupation to Party Partition', in Anthony Smith (ed.), *Television and Political Life* (London: Macmillan, 1979), pp. 105–8.
8. See Chiarenza, op. cit., p. 22 and Massimo Pini's autobiographical 'confessions', *Memorie di un lottizzatore* (Milan: Feltrinelli, 1978), especially pp. 63–72.
9. *Il Gazzettino*, 5 Feb. 1984.
10. C. Fracassi, 'Poltrona per poltrona tutto il potere lottizzato alla RAI-TV', *Paese Sera*, 6 March 1982.
11. Data in Giuseppe Vacca, *L'Informazione negli anni ottanta* (Rome: Riuniti, 1984), p. 155.
12. My calculations on the basis of data in S. Balassone and A. Guglielmi, *RAI-TV L'autarchia impossibile* (Rome: Riuniti, 1983), pp. 64–8.
13. Renato Venturini, 'Verso un sistema misto', *Studi sociali*, no. 1–2 (1983), p. 106.
14. Ibid., pp. 111–2.
15. Data in Vacca, op. cit., p. 167.
16. See Venturini, op. cit., pp. 111–2, and the *Financial Times*, 14 March 1984 for information on Berlusconi.
17. Chiara Sottocorona, 'Effetto biscione', *Panorama*, 19 March 1984.
18. Quoted in Mimmo Scarano, 'Il predatore del network', *Rinascita*, no. 35 (1984), p. 7.
19. Data in Balassone and Guglielmi, op. cit., pp. 81–5.
20. The Italian licensing fee is one of the lowest in Europe: approximately £32 for colour

television (only one-third of receivers are colour). The real value of the fee dropped 16 per cent between 1974 and 1979, but by 1981 it had returned to its 1974 level.
21. See reports in *La Repubblica*, 22 Feb. 1984.
22. See ISTEL reports in *Il Giornale*, 24 Jan. 1984.
23. Venturini, op. cit., pp. 98–9.
24. See Luca Pavolini, 'TV, la legge bloccata', *Rinascita*, no. 1 (Jan. 1983); Antonio Bernardi, 'Regolare cosi RAI e private', *Rinascita*, no. 5 (Feb. 1984) and reports in *La Repubblica*, 30 Nov. 1983.

Pluralism in the West German Media: The Press, Broadcasting and Cable

Arthur Williams

An argument often advanced by the proponents of the new communications technologies, particularly when they direct their attention away from the needs of trade, industry and the telecommunications sector and address themselves to the implications of cable and its adjuncts for the mass media, is that these promise to increase variety and afford a greater range of choice for the public. This argument is adduced in the Federal Republic of Germany, but with a change of emphasis from the general term 'variety' to the more specific 'plurality of opinion' (*Meinungsvielfalt*).

Leaving aside the stock semantic blunder ('new technologies mean new media mean new content in the media'), suppressing the suspicion that what practising politicians mean when they talk of a greater plurality of opinion is really more outlets for one shade of opinion, namely, their own, and acknowledging that a greater plurality of opinion in the mass media is a natural selling point in any western democracy, it is interesting to ask why this particular concept should be so important in West Germany. More specifically one may wonder whether there is good reason why it should be emphasised at this particular juncture – as it has been, for example, by the Federal Chancellor, Helmut Kohl, in his second declaration of government policy (4 May 1983), and by the Prime Minister of Rhineland-Palatinate, Bernhard Vogel, at the inauguration of the Ludwigshafen cable broadcasting project (1 January 1984), the most advanced of the four West German pilot projects.

This article seeks to demonstrate that in the political life of the Federal Republic, in the press and in broadcasting, the first three post-war decades produced developments which, although different in detail and in emphasis, all point to a narrowing down of the spectrum of opinion informing the public and public decision-making. Against this background, and particularly in the light of patterns that have evolved in the press and broadcasting, progress to date in the various cable projects and the attendant legislative activity will be examined to see how far cable broadcasting can be expected to fulfil its undoubted promise: to make more programmes available, give more groups access to the media, bring the press and broadcasting together in a new relationship, bridge continents via satellite and at the same time facilitate very specific local services. It will be argued that present evidence suggests that the goal of greater *Meinungsvielfalt* will not be attained in the immediate future, but rather that existing patterns are likely to be replicated and reinforced – particularly through the opening up of broadcasting to the press.

However, although this much seems clear, a note of warning must be sounded at the outset – the subject is extremely complex, the picture generally very blurred, and progress to date in both pilot projects and legislation markedly limited. Any evaluation must be made on the narrowest of bases and must be understood to be essentially speculative.

THE BACKGROUND TO THE NEW MEDIA

The Political Scene

In the contemporary political scene, the emergence of the Greens as a new group in the Bundestag in 1983 has important symbolic value. It is possible to see their success and certain aspects of the legislation promulgated in the last decade (for example, data protection, equality for women) as a focusing of attention on some of the basic rights of the constitution whose implications had been previously neglected.

During the first two decades of the Federal Republic, the experience of history (the centrally managed abuse of power of the Third Reich following the pernicious fragmentation of Weimar), the force of the constitution (decentralisation), the electoral system and the modifications to it (strengthening the barriers against small parties and effectively creating a three-party system), the ban on groups perceived as unconstitutional (SRP, KPD; later the *Berufsverbot* or *Radikalenerlaß*), the pressures of the geopolitical situation and the need of the population for economic and political stability and respectability – all of these combined to locate the seats of power and influence in a number of institutions and groups, none of which was large enough to be individually dominant, but which were few enough in number and sufficiently aware of their shared experience and common goals to allow the formulation of policies in all crucial fields to which all could subscribe (continuity through change). The apogee of this 'neo-corporatism' came during the *Große Koalition* of the two great catch-all parties, CDU/CSU and SPD, in the *konzertierte Aktion* which brought together the unions, the employers and the various branches of the economy, represented by their respective associations, in an attempt to resolve the incipient economic problems of the period; it underscored the 'centrality'[1] that had become characteristic of West German political life and the impression that the vehicle for West Germany's rise to respectability was a strong, largely conservative and technically very expert 'upper middle management' in both the economy and in politics. As a reaction to these structures, with their strong bureaucratic and academic traits, but also as a mark of their success, a generation has grown up whose lodestar is the codex of individual liberties founded in the dignity of man – the fundamental value which the whole of the West German *Basic Law* is intended to safeguard and foster. The voice of this generation, raised initially outside parliamentary forums during the student protests of the 1960s, is only now, after almost two decades of unrest (Baader-Meinhof) and experimentation (*Bürgerinitiativen*), beginning to formulate and articulate its views and values in such a way that they are heard and noted in the central arena.

The Media

The media are understood in West Germany to have an important function of formulating and articulating opinion and criticism in a manner consonant with the public interest – which can be taken to mean reflecting a fair, balanced plurality of opinion (see below). This concept is not without its problems; at the very least, it must imply an openness to a spectrum of views closer to that found in the public at large than that represented in parliamentary assemblies and within the established political parties and interest groups. Given the decentralisation of life in the Federal Republic, it is reasonable to seek evidence of this wider spectrum not at the national level alone, but also in relation to more specifically defined publics. The federal structure would make the *Land* the natural unit; as we shall see, in many instances the subregional unit is of greater significance in this context. It is at this point that cable broadcasting could prove to be the medium most appropriate to the emergent spirit of the age – the vast majority of the extra-parliamentary groups are formed in response to developments of *local* importance.

To demonstrate the potential suitability of cable, it is first of all necessary to establish the salient facts about the existing media, from which it will be readily obvious that cable encroaches much more on the realm of the press than that of broadcasting. There is a certain division of labour between the press and broadcasting which ensures that the two are in many ways complementary and coexist with little actual difficulty. The daily press is primarily local with only four or five recognised supraregional newspapers; the broadcasting corporations tend to serve areas identical with one *Land* (two out of nine serve more than one *Land*) and the second television service, *Zweites Deutsches Fernsehen (ZDF)*, is the only truly nationwide service. The press is privately owned and relies heavily on revenue from advertising, while broadcasting is carried out by public corporations which draw most of their income from licences. Advertising in the daily press is generally of local origin, whereas in broadcasting it is predominantly associated with big, national brand names.

A few statistics will bear out the stability of the media system at the beginning of the decade:[2] no new broadcasting house had been established since the early 1960s; the circulation of the daily press had increased steadily to reach 21,230,100 by the end of 1982; the use of the media had reached saturation point by 1980 (97 per cent of all households possessed a television, 98 per cent owned a radio and 78 per cent took a newspaper daily); finally, shares in the advertising market are now steady at 30 per cent for the daily press, 17.3 per cent for television and 7.4 per cent for radio. By this time also, the two media of broadcasting and the press had settled firmly into patterns which, while still showing important characteristics inherited from the Western Powers of Occupation, have an unmistakable West German stamp.

Broadcasting[3]

Differences in the broadcasting system were created by the preferences of the British and Americans for divergent structures of control, by the differing sizes of the *Länder* (making for variations in income according to size of population) and by the availability of equipment. The result, by the mid-1950s, was nine very different broadcasting houses serving 11 *Länder* with distinctive methods of control in the north and the south, between which there was also a broad left/right political division. All of them were expanding their range of radio and television programmes. The former British Zone stations, unlike the rest, did not carry advertising in their radio programmes. Before the *Länder* joined forces in 1961 to found *ZDF*, considerable cooperation had already developed between the broadcasting houses, including a joint first television channel in which they all have a proportionate share and which is transmitted, except on rare occasions, by all of them. The sharing arose because it was the only way to ensure a full programme for every broadcasting house.

This arrangement is part of the financial equalisation (*Finanzausgleich*) by which the larger corporations pass on some of their income to the smaller ones – to even out some of the inequalities that arise because the licence fee has to be standard for all areas. The broadcasting houses and the *Länder* have formulated many administrative agreements of this kind; they maintain equality, ensure individual survival and promote corporate identity. As early as 1950, the broadcasting houses formed their own working group, the *ARD* (*Arbeitsgemeinschaft der öffentlich-rechtlichen Rundfunkanstalten der Bundesrepublik Deutschland*) through which they organise, for example, international and national representation, carry out joint tasks such as research, specialist reports and training schemes, run the nationwide news service on the first television channel and negotiate such matters as the pooling of programmes; recently, through the *ARD*, they have purchased the rights to televise large numbers of American films.[4]

The pooling of programmes which, at its inception in 1970, saved DM 70 million annually, relates particularly to the entertainment programmes that frame the 20-minute session of commercials each weekday evening and to material for the third television programmes, essentially educational and cultural programmes broadcast on spare first channel time within one region or adjacent regions.

Given existing political differences, programmes passed from region to region have to be non-political in nature or carefully balanced, as in the case of the joint first television channel (DFS), and indeed also in that of the nationwide second channel (ZDF), and purged of any extreme or abrasive item. Thus the obligation to serve the whole country, and to some extent even to serve larger regions, tends to weaken the force of programmes that might be considered important in terms of the range of opinion presented to the public. Broadcasting, particularly television, is integrated and integrative – an *Integrationsrundfunk* which tends to reduce rather than to emphasise differences. The conservative effect of the system is further underpinned by *Proporz*, the 'proportional thinking' typical of all West German politics and, given the importance of the parties, also of many aspects of administration. *Proporz* transmits the balance of parliamentary opinion into the infrastructure of society.

A reduction of differences triggered by the need for different sovereign bodies to cooperate and to coordinate their activities and promoted by the normative nature of the system (*Rechtsstaat*) can also be observed at the level of media legislation. The differences created by the Allies have been greatly reduced; the various broadcasting laws, although not identical, all acknowledge the same principles highlighted and consolidated by a number of events over more than two decades, and in particular by rulings of the Federal Constitutional Court. The process of self-definition has brought the crucial nature of public accountability, the relative roles of the state, the political parties, the broadcasters and the public, and the terms under which commercial companies can be involved in broadcasting under scrutiny. The process was rounded off by the redrafting in 1980 of the law governing the North German Broadcasting Corporation (*Norddeutscher Rundfunk, NDR*) and the third Television Judgment (*Fernseh-Urteil*) of the Federal Constitutional Court in 1981.

NDR[5] inherited the characteristics of the British model of control. In this 'parliamentary' model, the parties represented in the *Landtag* appointed members to the controlling organs of the broadcasting house in proportion to their parliamentary strength. The contrast between this model and the American 'pluralistic' or 'social groups' model, in which the 'socially relevant groups' (the churches, the two sides of industry, sports associations, etc.) appoint their own members directly alongside the representatives of the political parties, was marked and became a matter of increasing public concern.

Meanwhile, the understanding of the role of the political parties was deepening: the redrafting of the Bavarian Broadcasting Law in 1973 established the 'Bavarian' model, a refinement of the 'social groups' model, which limits to one-third the proportion of broadcasting council seats held by 'political' representatives (serving members of parliaments, others in political office); and the accompanying amendment to the Bavarian Constitution lays down the fundamental importance of public accountability. The new *NDR* agreement observes these principles and adds the interesting innovation of leaving a few broadcasting council seats free for allocation to new groups – elsewhere all seats are earmarked for named groups.

The three *Länder* served by *NDR* (Hamburg, Lower Saxony and Schleswig-Holstein) also used the opportunity of the new agreement to provide for innovation and more variety in the region – they wished to see more account taken of their individual characters. New technologies would be introduced alongside existing *NDR* services and these latter would be augmented by the introduction of new regional and local programmes.

The new *NDR* treaty removed the major anomaly in the system; even so, public control is still channelled through established interest groups, while the controlling organs and the services, even the new subregional programmes, remain essentially integrative. Nevertheless, as a statement and a symbol, the redrafting of the *NDR* treaty marks the end of a process of self-definition in West German broadcasting, establishing a firm basis for a future which will be marked by competition between the public corporations and the private companies.

The three classic judgments of the Federal Constitutional Court of 1961, 1971 and 1981 are the triangulation points in this process of definition. While the 1981 judgment relates directly to the sanctioning of commercial companies, the fundamental principles of 1961 retain their monumental significance:[6] the distinction is made between broadcasting and telecommunications; the central authorities are debarred from involvement in broadcasting and the role of the *Länder* as legislators defined; broadcasting must never be the monopoly of one individual or group; all relevant groups in society must be involved in the control of broadcasting; and programmes must reflect a fair balance of opinion.

The latter has been misinterpreted in practice. In the 1961 ruling it is linked to a discussion of the difference between broadcasting and the press. Access to broadcasting is limited both by the technology and by the cost, and therefore pluralism, the implementation of constitutional freedom, has to be effected by administrative arrangements and guaranteed in law. This is the crucial issue, not the established administrative form of the public corporation or a measured proportionalism in the programme. A further vital point, often forgotten but important for the future, stresses the relatively large range available in the press – the judges never maintained that access to the press was free, they simply took account of the greater variety of supply available. This was clearly a situation which could change in respect of both broadcasting and the press; it is a matter ultimately of the judgement of relative merits at a point in time. The structures of the press as they existed in 1961 are no more sacrosanct than the public broadcasting corporations – together and relative to each other they simply represented an acceptable plurality of opinion at that time.

The 1981 judgment[7] advanced the definition of pluralism in respect of broadcasting by distinguishing between *Binnenpluralismus* (internal pluralism) and *Außenpluralismus* (external pluralism). The former is the established representation of a plurality of interests in the controlling organs of the broadcasting house, with the programme as a whole presenting a balanced package; the latter obtains when a number of quite different groups broadcast programmes within the same system to the same public and so together, although individually distinctive, generate a proper pluralism in the total programme.

The laws drafted to accommodate commercial broadcasting attempt to meet these requirements by creating new institutions in which there is a pluralistic representation of the public and which, by the control of franchises, ensure that the resulting programmes display a general balance. They attempt to combine the two forms of pluralism and even allow for a shift from one to the other as facilities improve. They still differ in other important respects (see below), but the emergence of this degree of conformity shows the normative process already at work.

The draft legislation provides for existing services to continue; there is a tendency to think of the old and the new as separate systems. However, in a cable system they will stand together roughly as *ARD* and *ZDF* do now; the key question about an acceptable variety will have to be asked of them all together. Since some of the new programmes will be produced by newspaper publishers, the contribution of the press to the general balance will also have to be considered (as, indeed, it was in 1961); and since the cable system will, for many years to come, consist of small islands, the question of balance will have to be asked of these areas individually and in the comparison of these with non-cable areas. The latter is impossible at this stage, but a discussion of the press will underline the importance of the definition of the composite, local media package.

The Press[8]

As in broadcasting, the British and Americans adopted different principles in the allocation of licences: the British authorities licensed individuals or groups representing particular political views, so that these could compete openly in public; under the American system, licences were issued to boards of editors of different persuasions who were expected to iron out their differences at the pre-publication stage in order to present balanced views to the public. Delicensing brought a massive increase in the number of newspapers, particularly in the American Zone[9] – probably determined by demographic factors (many pockets of rural communities) rather than a reaction to the American system.

The Allies attempted to establish quality newspapers in key centres, with the intention of providing models for the future. These papers still form the backbone of the West German press: the new titles, virtually all of them traditional *Heimatzeitungen* (local newspapers) or *Generalanzeiger* (popular local newspapers with no particular affiliation), came late on the scene and were generally too small to compete with the already established titles. While an expanding population with increasing personal wealth probably helped many of these papers to survive longer than might otherwise have been the case, the newspaper world was becoming ruthlessly commercial: it was the age of the *Bild-Zeitung*, the first tabloid launched by Axel Springer in 1952, and of the concentration that would swallow up many of the new titles and virtually the whole of the party press.

The new titles of the early 1950s did nothing to promote plurality of opinion: the *Heimatzeitungen* have to operate within the bounds of local opinion; the *Kaufzeitung* (sold only in kiosks or on the street) deals in sensation; neither excels in hard news, commentary and criticism. *Kaufzeitungen* survive because of their popularity; the local press has to attract as many advertisements as possible and also has to keep costs to a minimum – this explains the mesh of associations and services created to support these papers.[10] Everything is provided: news and features, technical and marketing advice, matrices and, in advertising consortia, advertisements. There is also a great deal of cooperation between individual publishers, particularly between near neighbours, which has further reduced and often eliminated differences between newspapers.

It is important to understand not simply the extent of press concentration in the Federal Republic, but also its nature and its effect on the local districts. Between 1954 and 1983, while daily circulation rose from 13.4 million to 21.2 million, the number of press units with editorially independent political sections fell from 225 to 125.[11] During the same period, administrative reforms reduced the number of local districts from 558 to 329; of these larger districts 46.8 per cent are served by one publishing unit only (local monopolies). Significantly, in the *Länder* most interested in private broadcasting the percentage of local monopolies is above the national average: Saarland 83.3, Rhineland-Palatinate 77.8, Lower Saxony 63.8 and Schleswig-Holstein 53.3. As we shall see, the same publisher often holds a monopoly position in a number of neighbouring districts, creating a subregional or regional monopoly situation.

One needs to be aware, in identifying these local monopolies, of the deceptive nature of the national picture. One has, first of all, to discount the *Kaufzeitungen*, which are dominated by the 5.4 million circulation of *Bild-Zeitung* and tend to distort the picture,[12] and to concentrate on the subscription newspapers (*Abonnementzeitungen*). Here there is no national monopoly: the five largest publishers account for only 26.1 per cent of a total circulation of 14.3 million. However, local situations vary greatly and the names associated with monopoly or near-monopoly positions are significant in the context of a discussion on cable broadcasting. In Hamburg and Berlin, the Axel Springer Verlag, through various titles, controls 86.4 per cent and 71.4 per cent of the respective daily circulations. In the Saarland, the *Saarbrücker Zeitung* (ten editions) controls the whole circulation of 192,700; in addition, it controls two editions of the *Pfälzischer Merkur* which appears in Pirmasens (Rhineland-Palatinate). Three publishing groups (of eight) dominate the scene in Rhineland-Palatinate: *Die Rheinpfalz* (Ludwigshafen), the *Rhein-Zeitung* (Koblenz) and the *Allgemeine Zeitung* (Mainz). Respectively, they control 31.6, 29.2 and 21.5 per cent of total circulation in the *Land* and each is a virtual local monopoly. They illustrate the pattern reproduced across the Federal Republic of local monopolies centred on the cities.[13] As we shall see, these groups are involved in common cable enterprises.

Also involved in the cable projects are groups from other branches of the publishing industry where the concentration phenomenon is very apparent; they are the publishers of *Publikumszeitschriften* – illustrated magazines, journals for hobbies and other specialisms. These publishers are also involved in book publishing, book clubs and all the associated activities. The names to note in this connection are: the Heinrich Bauer Verlag (32.3 per cent of the market), the Axel Springer Verlag (13 per cent), the Burda-Gruppe (11.2) and Bertelsmann/Gruner+Jahr (7.4). When all of its activities are taken into account, this last is Europe's largest publishing concern, but all of these groups are capable of offering a wide range of services using the new technologies: entertainment programmes of various kinds, educational courses, specialist data and advisory services and also news coverage. Their natural outlet is not the local cable network, but the nationwide, even international link-up provided by satellite. Some of them have interests which could embrace both levels. For example, the Verlagsgruppe Georg von Holtzbrinck (Stuttgart) is West Germany's largest publisher of paperbacks but it is also associated with several newspapers including the *Saarbrücker Zeitung*.

As in broadcasting, the final shaping of the West German press has taken place since the mid-1970s. The process of concentration has slowed down and while there are economic and demographic reasons for the changing pattern emerging here, some emphasis must be placed on changes in public awareness of the processes afoot in the press. This had grown slowly through the 1960s with the reports of the First Michel Commission (1964–67) and the Günther Kommission (1967–68). The central government then drew up plans (1974) to introduce framework legislation for the press (which although perfectly constitutional came to nothing) and amended the law against restraints on trade (*Gesetz gegen Wettbewerbsbeschränkungen*) in 1973 and 1976 to include (§§22–24) specific reference to the press: the definition of market dominance (*Marktbeherrschung*) and of the point at which mergers become notifiable (*Fusionskontrolle*) are now much more critical in the case of the press than elsewhere in the economy (amalgamations with a total annual turnover of DM 25 million are automatically reviewed, whereas normally the figure is DM 500 million). Apart from voluntary restraint by publishers, the Federal Cartel Office (*Bundeskartellamt*) has taken action several times since the mid-1970s, assessing mergers for both the effect on the readership and on the advertising market. It is aided in its work by reports from an independent advisory body, the *Monopolkommission*, instituted in 1973; apart from periodic reviews, the *Monopolkommission* can report on individual cases on request or on its own initiative. Since 1975, regular official statistics on the press have also been issued and the principal academic research into concentration regularly updated.

The change in public attitudes is indicated by a general loss of confidence in the media, particularly the daily press,[14] and by the increase in the number of 'alternative newspapers', many of which are strictly local (*Stadtteilzeitungen*). Some 3,000 titles have been noted, as has a rapid growth (since 1975), in spite of their irregular circulation.[15] Further compensation for the stagnation of *Abonnementzeitungen* has come in Sunday editions (notably in Baden-Württemberg), the regionalisation of *Kaufzeitungen* and in new, group-specific periodicals. Very few of these publications appear daily and many have been short-lived, but they point up the significance of local ties and of the interests of definable groups. Clearly, the established press is not meeting these needs adequately.[16]

Thus we have in the press, as in broadcasting and in parliamentary forums, evidence of developments which entail the reduction of variety and strongly suggest that the plurality of opinion in the Federal Republic has been undernourished and for some identifiable publics even constrained. There has been some reaction to this situation, but it has either remained outside the established channels for the articulation of opinion (for example, extra-parliamentary opposition, alternative newspapers) or, where it has gained access to them, found only a small niche (the Greens in Bonn, NDR broadcasting council seats, regional programmes).

There is a distinction to be made here between the press and broadcasting. The public broadcasting authorities have followed the principles laid down for them – at least as far as their governance is concerned: the plurality of opinion in the controlling bodies has been maintained and strengthened, their accountability to the public has been reaffirmed and they are also seeking to increase their regional services. The press has been governed by other considerations (mainly commercial) and has failed not only to maintain the range and diversity that it originally represented, but also, to a serious degree, to uphold what many would see as an acceptable plurality of opinion. The public accountability of broadcasting would appear to be the decisive factor distinguishing it from the press.

Let us now examine the new developments to see whether they promise to fulfil the expectations placed on them and analyse the function they perhaps should have, given the situation as set out here, of reinvigorating the plurality of opinion in the West German media.

NEW DEVELOPMENTS IN THE MEDIA

Four developments occasioned by technological advance are of relevance to the broadcasting system and to the relationship between the press and broadcasting: *Videotext* (teletext), *Bildschirmtext* (*Btx – Prestel* equivalent), local broadcasting projects and, lastly, the cable/satellite projects.

Videotext

Videotext was introduced in the Federal Republic in 1980 for an experimental period of two years on the basis of an agreement reached only with difficulty between the public broadcasting corporations and the *Bundesverband der deutschen Zeitungsverleger* (*BDZV* – the Federal Association of Newspaper Publishers).[17] The fact that the test phase has twice been extended is due to the reservations of the publishers about the apparent advance of the broadcasting companies into the supply of news by text. Five supraregional newspapers have been involved in the tests and while this cooperation has worked well, there are still problems to be resolved created by the incipient regionalisation of the *Videotext* services by the broadcasting authorities; they have so far been centralised with the administration in Berlin. The newspaper publishers regard the regional and particularly the local sphere as their own. However, *Videotext* has been well received and the formalisation of arrangements is imminent.[18]

Bildschirmtext

Btx was tested in two pilot projects (Berlin and Düsseldorf) between 1980 and 1983 and the Prime Ministers of the West German *Länder* have agreed to introduce the system throughout the Federal Republic.[19] The original date for this was September 1983, but was postponed for technical reasons until mid-1984. While the detailed studies which were to accompany the projects have not yet been published, the interest shown by the publishing world is well known: some 30 per cent of the groups offering *Btx* services are publishers and they account for approximately 50 per cent of those services. Much of the newspaper world has already taken the step into the electronics age, but more relevant here are the plans of the big publishers to offer comprehensive specialist services in *Btx*.[20] If *Btx* is a threat to the existing media, it would appear, like *Videotext*, to threaten the press rather than broadcasting; it could prove to be a viable substitute for a number of services that rely traditionally on the printed word – consumer advice, commercial information, tourist information, regional and local advertising. In the latter respect it could affect the local press which has no competition from broadcasting, but where any strengthening of positions as a result of *Btx* could drive smaller units out of business.

Local broadcasting

The precarious position of the local press would appear to be further threatened by a number of embryonic local broadcasting projects. However, these are of very limited scope as yet. Most of the West German broadcasting houses have steadily increased their subregional services,[21] but for specific local broadcasting projects only the *Monrepos* agreement[22] and three other isolated schemes are of relevance.

Under the *Monrepos* agreement, the public broadcasting houses serving Baden-Württemberg and the Association of South-West German Newspaper Publishers plan to establish a maximum of four local radio services (*Stadtradio Freiburg* went on the air on 1 October 1984; Ulm is to follow) and two television stations (one in Mannheim). The agreement is that these services function under the umbrella of the broadcasting corporation in whose area they are located, but that at least two local publishing houses are involved in each case. Each station is independent editorially and is financed by the contracting parties; no commercial income is envisaged during the trial period.

The other three schemes bear very similar names to some of the services organised by the public broadcasting corporations, but they belong to the press; they are the 'city video' services provided in Frankfurt by the *Frankfurter Allgemeine Zeitung* (*FAZ*), in Koblenz (*Rhein-Zeitung*) and in Bielefeld and Paderborn (C.W. Busse, publisher of several newspapers in Westphalia). These indicate something of the interest of the publishing world in video developments. It is significant that *FAZ* and the *Rhein-Zeitung* are already involved in the cable projects and that other publishing concerns are investigating the possible use of similar techniques.[23]

Cable/Satellite

The four cable projects were designed to test different combinations of factors, with the Ludwigshafen project intended to open up broadcasting to private (commercial) groups. It is in Ludwigshafen that the probable pattern of future press involvement will emerge most clearly. The Dortmund project specifically excludes commercial interests; in Berlin, the newspaper publishers have decided not to become involved, preferring to await satellite developments;[24] and the level of press involvement in Munich is low. As we shall see, there is a certain overlap between Munich and Ludwigshafen, and again between Ludwigshafen and the project which is moving ahead in Luxembourg.

West German publishers are involved in the Luxembourg project, which in practice has two distinct aspects: a television channel, *RTL-Plus*, which is at present being broadcast by conventional means from Luxembourg to the Saarland and some neighbouring areas, and plans, already well advanced, to reach further into the country via satellite. Curiously, this dual project epitomises the pattern emerging in the Federal Republic; a major publisher (Bertelsmann) has a 40 per cent share in the *RTL-Plus* project and has made no secret of the fact that it sees Luxembourg as a stepping-stone to a full-scale satellite Pay-TV service,[25] while the (smaller) West German newspapers involved are interested only in the area in which they already operate. Here again the germ of a generally valid pattern can be discerned; the local publishers harvest the advertising revenue their programmes generate and thus strengthen their position in the local advertising market – in Ludwigshafen and in all the discussions of legislation to date, the local advertising market has been reserved for those groups who normally service it (that is, the local press), while public broadcasting corporations may not compete in this market.

Progress to Date

The small degree of innovation to date can be conveyed by a few statistics. In Ludwigshafen, only four of 23 radio channels and eight of 19 television channels have been made available to the body which controls the commercial franchises, the *Anstalt für Kabelkommunikation (AKK)*;[26] the public broadcasting corporations are responsible for all of the other channels. Of the four *AKK* radio channels, one has to be an access channel (*offener Kanal*), and of the other three, only one has been allocated (*Radio Weinstraße*). Again, in television there is one access channel; two have been allocated to very heterogeneous groups (one is called the *Mischkanal* – 'mixer channel'); on two others public broadcasting corporations are attempting new styles of (non-political) programme; a sixth channel is the international satellite *Sky Channel*, leaving only two in the hands of commercial groups with a clear identity. These include local publishers.

The *AKK* has also been given control of one satellite channel (ECS 1 *Westbeam*) which it has allocated to a consortium of 21 varied partners. It is here that big names from the West German publishing world appear: Heinrich Bauer Verlag KG (Hamburg), Burda Verlag GmbH (Munich), Verlagsgruppe Georg von Holtzbrinck GmbH (Stuttgart), Otto Maier Verlag GmbH (Ravensburg) and Axel Springer AG (Hamburg).

The dimensions of events to date are further indicated by the fact that an adequate pool of applicants for franchises in Ludwigshafen was formed only when the *AKK* had extended the deadline, while the Munich project started three months late. Dortmund and Berlin are not even on the slipway. The number of households participating in the Ludwigshafen project when it commenced (1 January 1984) was a little over 1,000 with a further 5,500 expressing positive interest – the Federal Post Office had provided facilities for 40,000 households and the law establishing the project had, in fact, set 30,000 as a prerequisite for commencement. The lack of public enthusiasm for the project is palpable and explains in part why the Federal Minister of Posts and Telecommunications has negotiated for four satellite television programmes to be received into eight cable networks, with plans to increase the number of towns with facilities to receive satellite programmes to 72. The original aim was to test the technology for the satellite–cable link-up. Clearly, by linking small local audiences via satellite, a public large enough to attract major commercial interests can be created and so save the brave new world of cable broadcasting from being trapped at birth.

The Federal government's cabling plans have also run into serious financial and technical problems. Any hopes of a rapid advance in fibre optics have been dashed by the action of the *Bundeskartellamt* against the grouping of companies formed in Berlin to develop the technology,[27] and the original costings for the coaxial (copper) cabling of West Germany have been shown to be unrealistic;[28] the cost of participation in the cable projects is also considerable,[29] and the same appears to be true of *Btx*.[30] To be economically viable, every element will have to be used to the full – a factor also apparent in the choice of satellite systems where only one of five is to be a direct broadcasting satellite (DBS), while the others are multi-purpose telecommunications satellites.[31] Many of the satellite projects, of course, involve international cooperation.

BROADCASTING PROJECTS AND THE PLURALITY OF OPINION

In spite of the fact that none of the new developments can be said to be flourishing, it should be possible, if the objective is to increase *Meinungsvielfalt*, to detect some signs that greater plurality is being encouraged. Not only does this appear at this stage not to be the case, but the opposite seems the more likely outcome. In respect of the crucial areas of (particularly local and subregional) news and current affairs, more will be provided by existing groups and, as has been indicated above, these groups already occupy strong positions in the subregionally organised press; moreover, they form the links between the three projects that are actually on the air.[32]

The *RTL-Plus* regional news magazine, *Regional 7*, is the joint product of the *Saarbrücker Zeitung* and the *Rhein-Zeitung*. Each enjoys a local monopoly as a newspaper; by broadcasting to an audience in the Saarland they can only strengthen their position in the advertising market vis-à-vis *Saarländischer Rundfunk* (Saarland Broadcasting Corporation), which is heavily dependent on income from advertising, and vis-à-vis any potential newcomers in the press. An examination of the Ludwigshafen groupings reveals the small Luxembourg group as the western edge of a net which could stretch across the whole of the south of the Federal Republic. One of the major publishers involved in the *Westbeam* consortium is the Verlagsgruppe Georg von Holtzbrinck, the main shareholder in the *Saarbrücker Zeitung*; the *Rhein-Zeitung* is involved in both places. The apparent duplication both within the *Westbeam* consortium and between it and the other *AKK* franchises is startling. The Aktuelle Presse-Fernsehen GmbH & Co. KG (Berlin/Hamburg) of the *Westbeam* consortium is an association of 160 newspaper publishers, the *Geschäftsführer* (managing director/secretary) of which is Gerhard Naeher of the Axel Springer Verlag; the Axel Springer AG (Hamburg) is a member of the consortium. The Programmgesellschaft für Kabel- und Satellitenrundfunk mbH, Frankfurt (*PKS*), a group of mixed business interests, features in the *Westbeam* alongside *FAZ* and the Otto Maier Verlag, with whom it holds a joint franchise for one of the Ludwigshafen cable channels; it also has a channel in Munich. Similarly, the Allfunk GmbH, Koblenz, stands in its own right in the *Westbeam* group beside the three companies which founded it: Mainzer Verlagsanstalt und Druckerei GmbH & Co. KG (Mainz), *Rheinpfalz* Verlag und Druckerei GmbH (Ludwigshafen) and Mittelrhein Verlag (Koblenz). The names of the newspapers these publish are familiar: *Allgemeine Zeitung, Die Rheinpfalz* and *Rhein-Zeitung*. The Allfunk GmbH also provides the regional programme for the *PKS/FAZ* channel, and *Die Rheinpfalz* has a 64-per-cent controlling interest in the Erste Private Fernsehgesellschaft mbH, Ludwigshafen (*EPF*) – the other shares being held by a group from Baden-Württemberg (ten per cent), where the newspaper has further associates,[33] and by the Neue Medien GmbH (26 per cent) founded by the *BDZV*. A similar group, the Neue Mediengesellschaft Ulm GmbH, is one of the *Westbeam* groups.

It was inevitable that the publishing world would be the most vigorous investor in the new broadcasting opportunities. Not only have the newspaper publishers consistently sought since the early 1960s to break the public monopoly in broadcasting, but their investment in the new technologies has been considerable and these technologies have brought, by their very nature, the print and broadcasting media very close together. It is also fair to say that no other group had the relevant expertise and facilities available. Nor can it be considered unexpected that only newspaper publishers of a certain size would have the resources to become involved and that they would avail themselves of the opportunity to strengthen their position.

This much was predictable and while the groupings they have formed might not have been, given the reputations and investment at stake and the ability of the press to defend itself, it can be expected that these groups will not now be easily removed or their activities curtailed. Ludwigshafen can be regarded as both a potential harbinger of similar developments elsewhere and also possibly as the first step in the creation of a large-scale network in broadcasting based on a few newspapers.

In the short term, the project has given the principal newspapers in the region an additional outlet and a platform on which to promote themselves both as newspapers and as broadcasters. The few individual citizens who are connected to the cable network may see a little more from newspapers of which they would otherwise be only peripherally aware, but there is no doubt, if the project grows and is extended to other parts of the *Land*, that these newspapers, which together control 82.3 per cent of *Abonnementzeitung* circulation in Rhineland-Palatinate, would dominate commercial news services in the *Land* in both media. Given the associations they already have (with the *Saarbrücker Zeitung* through the RTL-Plus project and with Stuttgart publishing groups) and given that their experience would make them important contributors to any plans by the *BVDZ* to promote companies to exploit commercial broadcasting opportunities, the prospect is real that increasingly close links will be forged between a number of already powerful regional newspapers and a virtual news empire created covering much of the south-west of the Federal Republic. Nor would this be a completely unnatural step: the public broadcasting corporations in the area already cooperate closely and plans have been discussed from time to time to fuse them; the idea of the south-west state has a long history; finally, the politics of the newspapers concerned and of the *Land* governments match up. Indeed, such a development might be seen by many in the region as the appropriate antidote to the domination of the public broadcasting services by the north German, left-wing corporations – which is still perceived as such in spite of the modifications that have taken place since the mid-1970s.

The prospect that such a scenario might materialise ought to be a matter of serious concern to the present SPD opposition; their representation in the media, certainly in proportional terms, would be reduced and with it, potentially, also their chances of an early return to government. Yet the SPD, who have always opposed private broadcasting and, during the 1970s, gave the development of the new technologies only cautious support, seem to have accepted, in the reorientation after their fall from power, the inevitability of technological progress and swallowed their objections for fear of appearing to prejudice the chance of a possible boost to the economy.

The clearest and most consistent opposition to the new technologies is now articulated by the Greens who protest that what is needed in broadcasting is not an increase in the quantity of programmes but, rather, an improvement in quality. They stand firmly for public control and increased variety under the aegis of public broadcasting authorities. This is hardly surprising: neither the short-term nor the long-term prospects appear good for the new voices in West German politics; they will have to rely on alternative newspapers, perhaps the few open channels in the new broadcasting schemes and possibly on local projects such as the *Monrepos* experiment, although it is worth noting that the Greens in Baden-Württemberg are not satisfied that even these arrangements will prove adequate to their needs and those of society.[34] The fear is real – and, as we have seen, not unfounded – that even the Ludwigshafen project, whose structures are undoubtedly adventurous and innovative, will prove to be utterly conservative in media terms and to the right of centre politically. The enthusiasm of the CDU leadership for the new technologies and private broadcasting is clearly understandable both in terms of the party's free enterprise philosophy and in terms of their general party-political interests.

However, here we are projecting speculation well into the future when there is one shaping influence which has still to be considered: the legislation which will have to be enacted by each and every *Land* to regulate the changes in the media. Such legislation, to conform with the Constitutional Court ruling of 1961, should take account of the plurality of opinion reflected in broadcasting and the press together. Ideally, such legislation should also take account of the potential of cable and satellite both to cross borders and to create closely defined local broadcasting networks.

NEW LEGISLATION AND THE PLURALITY OF OPINION

The question of legislation to take account of units smaller than the *Land* is a very new one and addresses a problem the general awareness of which is low: the (re)definition of the forum (or public) in which the concept of pluralism or plurality of opinion is to be safeguarded. It is here that the greatest difficulties lie for the legislator and where we must look for indications of future perspectives. By contrast, cross-border broadcasting, whether international or between *Länder*, is relatively clear-cut.

The role of the Federal Minister of Posts and Telecommunications has not been changed by the recent surge of activity; he still needs the cooperation of the Länder in matters relating to the broadcasting of programmes – all of the projected tests will be carried out on this basis. Broadcasting across borders, in practice, will be a serious problem only where it occurs by a direct method, where it involves groups not based in the Federal Republic and where it is of a political nature incompatible with the internal situation; anything that cannot be received directly relies on a cable system and can be controlled at the point of entry to that system (for example, *Sky Channel*); any West German group is subject to the law whether it broadcasts from inside or from outside the country (the *RTL-Plus* group could be scrutinised by the *Bundeskartellamt*) and the basic freedom of information is not limited to internal sources. A case which was not covered by one of these considerations would be extremely difficult to contend with; only international conventions could help. Within the Federal Republic, given the force of the constitution and of established traditions, it is inconceivable that one *Land* would permit broadcasts to a public in another without a formal agreement; in fact, this would rarely be necessary because the projected legislation generally allows for such an eventuality, provided that the *Land* broadcasting law is not infringed.

There is no obligation on the *Länder* to formulate identical legislation; indeed their cultural sovereignty presupposes individual identities. In the case of the new broadcasting legislation, while the drafts respect all the basic principles (veracity of reporting, right of reply and so on), and while they tend to combine the two forms of pluralism defined by the Constitutional Court (1981) and even seek ways to effect a transfer from one to the other, there has not been even a preliminary agreement between the Prime Ministers about the points we have highlighted here. Thus, with the *Länder* proceeding at different speeds, there is a fragmented appearance about the documents that are available. Relating to the projects, these are: two bills still awaiting enactment (Bavaria, Berlin) and two acts (North Rhine-Westphalia, Rhineland-Palatinate); relating to future full-scale systems, there are two drafts intended as a basis for discussion between the Prime Ministers (Baden-Württemberg, Lower Saxony), bills in the Saarland and Schleswig-Holstein, and one act on the statute books (Lower Saxony).[35]

The Bavarian bill, which will assimilate the Munich project and extend it to the rest of the *Land*, is interesting because it is the only document that places a clear emphasis on the development of local and 'supra-local' companies (*örtliche* and *überörtliche Kabelgesellschaften*, §§22–24) whose task will be to ensure that local programmes find a place within the regional services. The bill states that the local press will be involved in these companies, but makes no further stipulations. The Saarland bill mentions neither the local situation nor the press, but it does cover the possibility of different programmes emanating from closely related groups (§40.3) by stating that associated companies as defined by §15 of the 1965 *Aktiengesetz* (law governing the operation of joint-stock companies) will be regarded as one unit.

This latter formulation was used in the Baden-Württemberg draft (§17.2) and is found in the Schleswig-Holstein bill (§5.4). A comparison of this bill with the Lower Saxony law is helpful – the two *Länder* are neighbours; between 1976 and 1980 both tried to break away from *NDR* and establish their own broadcasting services; they have a roughly comparable press situation.

Neither Schleswig-Holstein (§5.4.2) nor Lower Saxony (§12) proposes to encourage local broadcasting wholesale. Rather, the emphasis is on full regional programmes; any local dispersion of these may not exceed one quarter of the total time. At this point, with §23, Lower Saxony goes a step further and imposes an additional restriction: any periodical publication with more than 20 per cent of the total local circulation may not provide more than 50 per cent of the material for the relevant local programme. Since the law (§5.2) also contains the ban on multiple involvement by associated companies, any local programmes, although of very limited scope, will not be allowed to become the extended arm of one locally dominant press group. Thus, there are in the documents to hand a few positive indications of an awareness of the need to take account of the local or subregional district, to limit the possibility of multiple involvement by closely related groups and to reduce the potential for duplication between the press and broadcasting. This amounts to a step in the direction of preventing the extension of monopoly positions in the press into broadcasting.

However, nowhere are all of these factors present together. Apart from the inconclusive discussions between the Prime Ministers of the *Länder* there may be good reason for this: for example, the significance of the 20-per-cent circulation clause, which seems the most progressive element, would vary greatly according to the extent of the programmes or services to which it was applied. One can envisage circumstances under which it might encourage pluralism: sufficient programme time to make even a portion of a programme an attractive proposition and an area large enough for several groups (newspapers and others) to be interested in creating news programmes. Under other circumstances it might make local news services virtually impossible: in a small community with a monopoly newspaper and very few facilities for the development of alternative sources.

The fact is that the legislators are trying to anticipate developments which are, as we have seen, at present in an early and confusing stage. They are seeking to promote change in the broadcasting system and at the same time to prevent abuse of the opportunities this affords. It is possible that these two goals are incompatible in the short term – particularly while any negative trends are unproven. On present evidence, the legislation in train offers little more hope of positively promoting an increase in *Meinungsvielfalt* than do the developments in Ludwigshafen. The confidence of Helmut Kohl and Bernhard Vogel would appear to be unfounded.

However, we stand at the beginning of a process of change and no matter how fast or slow its progress, all the experience of the past 35 years would suggest that eventually the normative pressure of the system will make its impact. The *Länder* have failed to draft a model for the future to which they could all subscribe; indeed there is no evidence to show that they have even discussed one. The less they have in common now, the longer and the more painful will be the process of establishing and implementing norms.

The ingredients for this process are already present: on the one hand, actual developments which seem to endanger the plurality of opinion and, on the other, first indications in legislation of an awareness of where this danger arises. There are three ways at least – and they may be complementary – in which the two sides of the equation can be brought together: through a special commission of enquiry; through action taken by the *Monopolkommission* and the *Bundeskartellamt*; or through a ruling of the Federal Constitutional Court.

There is nothing at present to suggest that positive action will be initiated in the near future to expedite the process of establishing and implementing generally accepted norms; the scene seems to be set for a re-enactment at a new level of many of the manoeuvres performed during the shaping of the press and broadcasting systems. It seems likely that the process will be a long one and probable that when a clear pattern finally emerges, the main emphasis will be on the protection of the plurality of opinion and not on positively increasing it. There seems little hope in the short term that cable broadcasting will do anything to enliven the political scene – except if it becomes itself the centre of political controversy through the efforts of the Greens and their allies to draw attention to the negative implications of developments to date. In the long term it appears essential if *Meinungsvielfalt* is to be strengthened in a radical way in the Federal Republic, that the activities of the publishing world be subjected to closer public scrutiny and be made more accountable to the public – both in relation to its new role in cable and satellite broadcasting and, since the two media are no longer separate, also in relation to its established role as a producer of daily and weekly newspapers and magazines.

NOTES

Since the completion of this article, a number of events of relevance have occurred and a number of articles have been published which contain useful supplementary information and analyses.

- The Lower Saxony Law has been challenged in the Federal Constitutional Court. The ruling is not yet available.
- The bills in Bavaria (15 Nov. 1984), the Saarland (27 Nov. 1984) and Schleswig-Holstein (28 Nov. 1984) have become law.
- The two satellite channels have begun to broadcast: *3 Sat* (ZDF, ORF, SRG) on 1 Dec. 1984 and *Sat 1* (the commercial *Westbeam*) on 1 Jan. 1985.

- Constitutional questions raised by the new legislation are discussed by Rolf Groß: 'Verfassungsrechtlich bedeutsame Schwerpunkte der Mediengesetzgebung', *MP* 9/1984, pp. 681–96.
- The extent of the variety offered in Ludwigshafen is analysed by Udo Michael Krüger: 'Kabelpilotprojekt Ludwigshafen – durch Vielfalt zur Einfalt?', *MP* 10/1984, pp. 749–55.
- The economic dimension of press involvement in broadcasting is the subject of 'Zur wirtschaftlichen Lage ausgewählter privater Rundfunkveranstalter aus dem Pressebereich', *MP* 9/1984, pp. 669–80; 'Zeitungssterben vorprogrammiert. Anmerkungen zu einer Untersuchung von Eberhard Witte und Joachim Senn', *MP* 10/1984, pp. 758–61; and of part of the main report of the *Monopolkommission* for 1982/83 (*Ökonomische Kriterien für die Rechtsanwendung*, Baden-Baden, Nomos, 1984) which is reproduced in *Rundfunk und Fernsehen* Vol. 32, No. 3 (1984), pp. 363–78: 'Monopolkommission: Wettbewerbsprobleme bei der Verbreitung der Neuen Medien'.
- *Die Zeit*, 31 Dec. 1984, pp. 9–11 has a *Dossier* which reviews developments in cable and satellite to the end of 1984.

1. The term is Gordon Smith's. The following are relevant to this section: William E. Paterson and Gordon Smith (eds.), *The West German Model: Perspectives on a Stable State* (London: Frank Cass, 1981) (first published as a Special Issue of *West European Politics*, Vol. 4, No. 2, May 1981); Herbert Döring and Gordon Smith (eds.), *Party Government and Political Culture in Western Germany* (London: Macmillan, 1982); Arthur Williams, 'West German Social Policy Since 1969: A Discussion of Perspectives', *Quinquereme*, Vol. 6, No. 2 (July 1983), pp. 167–87.
2. Statistics are drawn from a number of sources; some of the calculations are my own. *Media Perspektiven* (*MP*) is the most dependable and consistently up-to-date source. The standard references are Helmut H. Diederichs, 'Daten zur Konzentration der Tagespresse und der Publikumszeitschriften in der Bundesrepublik Deutschland', most recently *MP* (7/1983), pp. 482–99, and Walter J. Schütz, 'Deutsche Tagespresse' and 'Die redaktionelle und verlegerische Struktur der deutschen Tagespresse', most recently *MP* (3/1983), pp. 181–203 and 216–28. See also note 31 below.
3. See also Arthur Williams, *Broadcasting and Democracy in West Germany* (Bradford: Bradford University Press, 1976).
4. Haug von Kuenheim, 'Für mehr als eine Handvoll Dollar', *Die Zeit* (23 March 1984), p. 74; *MP* (2/1984), pp. 157f.
5. See also Arthur Williams, 'West German Broadcasting in the Eighties – Plus ça change ...?', *ASGP Journal*, No. 7 (Spring 1984), pp. 3–35.
6. Text in: Wolfgang Lehr and Klaus Berg (eds.), *Rundfunk und Presse in Deutschland. Rechtsgrundlagen der Massenmedien* (Mainz: v. Hase & Koehler, 1971), pp. 221–56; here p. 254f.
7. Discussed in: Arthur Williams, 'West Germany: The Search for the Way Forward', in Raymond Kuhn (ed.), *The Politics of Broadcasting* (London: Croom Helm, 1985).
8. See also John Sandford, *The Mass Media of the German-Speaking Countries* (London: Oswald Wolff, 1976), pp. 1–60.
9. Harold Hurwitz, 'Die Pressepolitik der Alliierten', in Harry Pross (ed.), *Deutsche Presse seit 1945* (Munich: Scherz, 1965), pp. 27–55; here p. 50f.
10. Günter Böddeker, *20 Millionen täglich: Wer oder was beherrscht die deutsche Presse?* (Oldenburg: Gerhard Stalling, 1967), explores this process, particularly pp. 175–99.
11. The number of editions with distinguishable local sections fell from 1,500 to 1,255 and the number of publishers editing their own newspapers from 624 to 385.
12. For example, the Axel Springer Verlag controls 30.2 per cent of total daily circulation, but there is a great difference between its involvement in *Kaufzeitungen* (82.9 per cent) and *Abonnementzeitungen* (4.9 per cent).
13. Walter J. Schütz, 'Deutsche Tagespresse 1981', *MP* (9/1981), p. 665 categorises 67 West German cities.
14. Marie-Luise Kiefer, 'Massenkommunikation 1964 bis 1980. Trendanalyse zur Mediennutzung und Medienbewertung', *MP* (4/1981), pp. 261–86.
15. Werner Herminghaus, 'Stadtteilzeitungen – Keine Alternative, aber ein Ansatz zu einem neuen Lokaljournalismus', *MP* (8/1980), pp. 558–60; Wolfgang Beywl, 'Lokale Alternativ-

presse – Eine erste Bestandsaufnahme', *MP* (3/1981), pp. 184–90.
16. Ulrich Pätzold and Horst Röper, 'Neue Ansätze einer Pressekonzentrationsforschung', *MP* (2/1984), pp. 98–106 (see also note 23 below) demonstrate this process and argue a strong case for a revision of the research methods used by Schütz.
17. Text in *ARD Jahrbuch 80*, Hamburg, Hans-Bredow-Institut, 1980, pp. 327–9 and *MP* (5/1980), pp. 337–41.
18. Hansjörg Bessler, 'Videotext-Nutzung im Feldversuch ARD/ZDF', *MP* (1/1983), pp. 39–46; Alexander Kulpok, 'Vier Jahre Videotext-Feldversuch ARD/ZDF. Eine Bilanz', *MP* (3/1984), pp. 202–10.
19. Text in *MP* (2/1983), pp. 130–33 and (3/1983), p. 229f.
20. Gruner and Jahr set up a department in 1982 aiming to supply medium-size companies with information about market research, marketing and advertising. See also: Brigitte Kammerer-Jöbges, 'Die Bildschirm-Aktivitäten der Presse', *MP* (4/1984), pp. 264–72.
21. Examples are: *Kurpfalzradio* in Heidelberg, *Citywelle* in Munich, *Frankenchronik* in Nuremberg, *Nordhessen-Journal* in Kassel, *Radio Stuttgart* and many third radio and television programmes.
22. Text in *MP* (5/1983), pp. 356–7.
23. Ulrich Pätzold and Horst Röper, 'Vom Zeitungsverband zum Medienverbund', *MP* (4/1984), p. 245f. give an interesting 'fictitious' example of the advantages gained from this.
24. Marie-Luise Kiefer, 'Kabelprojekt Berlin ohne Berliner Zeitungsverleger', *MP* (4/1984), pp. 259–63.
25. *FAZ* (9 March 1984), pp. 4 and 17; *Frankfurter Rundschau* (9 March 1984), pp. 4, 5 and 9; *MP* (3/1984), pp. 259–63: 'Ein altes Unternehmen auf neuen Wegen: Anmerkungen zur Bilanzpressekonferenz der Bertelsmann AG am 7 März 1984'.
26. The structures in Ludwigshafen and elsewhere are discussed in the chapter in Kuhn, op. cit.
27. Joachim Nawrocki, 'Abschied vom Kartell', *Die Zeit* (25 May 1984), p. 13.
28. Wolfgang Hoffmann, 'Die Fehler des Ministeriums', *Die Zeit* (29 June 1984), p. 21.
29. Heidi Dürr, 'Ein sehr unscharfes Bild', *Die Zeit* (11 Nov. 1983), p. 29; Elke Halefeldt, 'Regionaler Einstieg ins bundesweite Fernsehen? Privater Rundfunkveranstalter in der Bundesrepublik', *MP* (1/1984), pp. 33 and 35f.; *Frankfurter Rundschau* (30 March 1984), p. 11.
30. *MP* (3/1983), p. 230.
31. Heinz Blüthmann, Rainer Frenkel, 'Kabel frei!', *Die Zeit* (30 Dec. 1983), p. 10; Rolf Groß, 'Zum Stand der Diskussion über den Satellitenrundfunk', *MP* (1/1984), pp. 45–50.
32. Various sources, in particular: *FAZ* (2 Jan. 1984), pp. 1 and 4; (30 March 1984), p. 5; *Frankfurter Rundschau* (13 Dec. 1983), p. 10; (14 Dec. 1983), p. 12; (27 March 1984), p. 11; (30 March 1984), p. 4; *MP* (1/1984), p. 34f.; (3/1984), pp. 228–31; *Die Zeit* (30 Dec. 1983), p. 9f.; (13 Jan. 1984), p. 50.
33. It has financial links with the Verlagsgruppe *Stuttgarter Zeitung* and with the Gruppe Württembergischer Verleger; the three constitute the Federal Republic's second largest group in *Abonnementzeitungen* (7.2 per cent). The Baden-Württemberg branch accounts for 37.2 per cent of *Land* circulation. There are further business links with newspapers in Hessen.
34. Die Grünen Baden-Württemberg, *Programm zur Landtagswahl 1984*, pp. 44–7.
35. Texts in *MP*: Baden-Württemberg (3/1982), pp. 202–13; Bavaria (8/1982), pp. 531–3; (2/1984), pp. 140–48; (4a/1984), pp. 305–13; Berlin (4a/1984), pp. 314–24; Lower Saxony (11/1982), pp. 723–32; (6/1984), pp. 486–96; North Rhine-Westphalia (6/1982), pp. 409–17; Saarland (4a/1984), pp. 325–41; Schleswig-Holstein (41/1984), pp. 342–53.

Broadcasting and Politics in the Netherlands: From Pillar to Post

Kees Brants

Writing about broadcasting and politics in the Netherlands is like contributing to yesterday's paper. Time after time the student of politics and mass communications is confronted with developments which make seemingly established structures and well-founded assumptions look out of date. Cable, satellite, telematics are all media which have not yet found a place among the more traditional means of communication. A picture of the Dutch media is, therefore, a 'still' in a moving process. At the same time, writing about this topic is like rewriting history. The same old issues seem to be at stake and quite often the same old arguments are used by the same actors; only the names have changed.

The discussion on the relation between broadcasting and political institutions (once again re-emphasised with the appearance of the new media) centres on the question of control. In the Netherlands and other countries where television started as a non-commercial communication system, there were three related reasons why the state and/or political parties emphasised relative control over this new electronic medium. First, the scarcity of channels made it necessary for governments to be involved in their allocation and regulation. Second, television was seen as a powerful means of educating the masses, the political socialisation of whom should stay within the margins of a supposed consensus on norms and values dominant in Dutch society. Third, and related to this, powerful television was seen as dangerous if placed in the wrong hands. Already before the Second World War, the Dutch Labour Party was considerably worried about cultural norms and values vanishing because of the impact of mass media such as radio.

Several types of study have dealt with the questions: who controls the media and with what effects on media content? Two approaches are of particular interest here, and although they differ from a normative point of view, both apply to the study of broadcasting and politics in the Netherlands. In the first analysis, media institutions are studied in relation to the socio-political environment. In particular, as Curran *et al.* have summarised, 'Questions concerning the interaction between media professionals and their "sources" in political and state institutions appear to be crucial for understanding the production process in the media'.[1] The pluralist version of this approach sees this interaction as a mutual dependency, a role relationship in which the politicians are as much dependent on the media to make their view public, as are the media on the politicians as a source of information and a deliverer of communication goods.[2]

This approach could provide some insight into the Dutch broadcasting situation which for so long has been dependent on the intricate political culture known as 'pillarisation': a party system based on religious and ideological cleavages. Within this political culture the media operated more or less as the mouthpieces for the separate political elites. This situation has changed considerably over the last 20 years and so has the interaction between media professionals and political institutions. The first part of this article deals with this changing relationship within the political culture of the Netherlands.

The second part concentrates on changes within the media, in particular those affecting the broadcasting system: first, the change in programme styles (from partisan ideology to market orientation) and, second, the introduction of the new media. Another theoretical approach could be of help here: the study of the political economy of media institutions, which stresses the economic situation of the media as a dependent variable for content; media ideology as a reflection of the economic base. In this view, capitalist organisation of the media, which in public broadcasting means the necessity of attracting large audiences, has led to entertainment-orientated programme policies involving no risk and which in the end tend to legitimise the existing order. Although overemphasising the economic base can lead to a blind spot as far as the relative autonomy of the ideological level is concerned, this approach has shown the importance of the study of ownership and control.[3]

Government and the major political parties in the Netherlands have traditionally had a large say over a number of issues concerning control, like the appointments of the media elite, media finance, content (to a certain degree) and hard- and software.[4] With the emergence of the new media, control is gradually shifting from public to private, institutionalised interests. The scarcity argument no longer seems valid, with cable and satellites offering an abundance of channels. The electronic media are more often seen as a powerful means of leisure than a threat to public consciousness while, according to some, public service broadcasting is not necessarily best guaranteed by public ownership.[5] This shift, which has affected not only the structures of broadcasting but also the terms of debate on political communication in the Netherlands, will be dealt with in the second part of this article.

I. BROADCASTING AND POLITICS: THE DECLINE OF 'PILLARISATION'

Dutch society has long been renowned for its 'pillarised' structure: social movements, educational and communication systems, voluntary associations and political parties were organised along the lines of religious and ideological cleavages. The Netherlands has long been one of the most typical examples of segmented pluralism: 'It is pluralist in its recognition of diversity of religious, socio-economic, and political affiliations; it is "segmented" in its institutionalization of most other forms of association along the lines of politico-religious cleavages.'[6]

The media in the Netherlands are often judged as the showpiece of pillarisation, with its typical mixture of traditional, mostly religious ties and progressive, open pluriformity. The latter characteristic however, appeared only after the broadcasting system was opened up for newcomers at the end of the 1960s. Until that time, political communication formed a closed system, of which religious and ideological cleavages formed the borderlines.

Already before the war, but more especially after it, the Netherlands was characterised by four large social blocs: the Roman-Catholic and the Protestant pillars (at the time encompassing more than 50 per cent of the population), the Socialist movement (about 25–35 per cent) and the Liberal sphere (only ten per cent to 15 per cent). Between the different blocs people lived more or less separated from each other. Communication took place only via the respective elites, who told their followers what, and particularly what not, to think and believe. Within the boundaries of one's own religious or ideological group, one could be looked after from the cradle to the grave.

Within each of the Catholic and Protestant pillars a closely-knit conglomerate of clerical, social and political organisations joined large groups of people from different socio-economic backgrounds through a common religious belief. A picture of society as it was supposed to be, as seen through the pillar's own 'glasses', was painted by each elite and generally endorsed by the followers. Within the Catholic pillar, for example, political life revolved around the Catholic People's Party (KVP), while employers, employees and intellectuals all had their own Catholic organisations. There were separate Catholic newspapers and weeklies, schools and universities, clubs and youth associations. From the Catholic football club to the pigeon-owners' association, everywhere an adviser kept the flock together and on the right path.

Pillarisation is often explained as an emancipation movement only,[7] but it should also be seen as a deliberate attempt to keep workers free from Socialist (and to a lesser degree, liberal and humanist) influence by appealing to their religious feelings and as an attempt to canalise and neutralise growing class awareness.[8] Sometimes a 'correction', a stiff warning was therefore needed, for not all followers were as docile as expected. When Socialism knocked successfully at the door of the Catholic worker after the war, the Bishops ordained in a Decree in 1954 that Catholics could no longer be members of a Socialist trade union, read Socialist papers, listen to the Socialist broadcasting company VARA or visit Socialist meetings – all on pain of excommunication. They advised against cooperating with the Labour Party (PvdA), although not daring to go as far as forbidding Catholics to vote for it. Some see this Decree as a final spasm of the Catholic pillar, but for the time being it was a successful attempt to keep political communication within the Catholic pillar closed.

Opposite these Catholic and Protestant pillars was the Socialist movement, aiming for a completely different social order. Although without a church as an integrating organisation, it did have an ideology. The Socialists did not organise across classes, but were concerned only with workers. Class cooperation versus class struggle was one of the fundamental cleavages between the religious and the Socialist pillars. Forced by the way Catholics and Protestants organised themselves and the resulting isolation, an organisational structure came about within the Socialist movement which was quite similar to the Catholic and Protestant pillars. Here too, social life was steeped in organisations with an ideological foundation.

From a socio-economic point of view the Liberal sphere is the mirror-image of the Socialist movement. It is not a pillar in the proper sense of the word, since it does not strictly organise people and institutions along ideological or religious lines. There is, of course, no (or no one single) church in the Liberal sphere, but there are employers, intellectuals and in general members of the higher middle classes and their organisations. Contrary to the other pillars the Liberals were not as isolated or self-contained. Some of the Liberal organisations – not least their media – even stressed their cross-national and inter-class attitude which, contrary to their pillarised counter-parts, was said to reveal an openness to other opinions.

With diversity at the mass level, accommodation and conflict resolution in the political system were possible only because the leaders of the different pillars agreed to certain rules of the game, of which business-like politics, tolerance and secrecy were the main components. Lijphart has called fragmented but stable democracies like the Netherlands 'consociational democracies', where the elites have the ability to accommodate the divergent interests and demands of the different subcultures.[9] The rules of the game of policy-making are a necessary part of the political culture in consociational democracies, since there is a shared commitment to maintain the system. As Wigbold has put it, 'Holland's much praised tolerance was based less on respect for others' convictions than on a gentleman's agreement to respect others' territories'.[10] In order to avoid awkward questions from the rank and file, the diversity at mass level necessitated a policy of secrecy, a consciously created 'information gap' about what was going on. Until the mid-1960s, the post-war period was characterised by a high degree of harmony in both the political and economic spheres.

The media – themselves confusingly often called 'pillars' as well – fitted quite nicely into this cleavaged structure. The press included a large number of neutral papers, but the majority (measured by circulation) was clearly connected to the major pillars, with the Catholic and Socialist pillars most strongly represented. The same picture generally applied to radio. The connection with other pillar organisations was even stronger here, because already in the 1930s the government – afraid of the intrusive nature of this new and powerful medium – had ruled that only broadcasting organisations with strong ties to the different pillars should be allowed on the air. As a result, a Socialist corporation (VARA), a Catholic (KRO) and two Protestant corporations (NCRV and VPRO) were established. The only neutral corporation, AVRO, had strong links with the Liberal sphere, which is not surprising considering its commercial (Philips) background.

Television was slow to come to the Netherlands. Five years after its introduction in 1951 there were still only 25,000 sets. Ten years later there were more than two million, but in the meantime the tenuous balance in broadcasting had been badly disturbed. The broadcasting corporations mainly saw a possibility of strengthening ideological values through the new medium, because radio had not proved so powerful after all, but several commercial interests saw other opportunities.

To begin with, television in the Netherlands had started under heavy pressure from Philips. The Socialist prime minister at the time was afraid of the degradation of culture and also feared that the new, powerful medium might lead to indiscriminate spending by the working classes – sentiments that could be heard in the religious parties as well. But the economic importance of Holland's largest industry proved too great. With British commercial television as an example, a number of banks, industries and national dailies initiated a set-up for commercial television. The official broadcasting corporations, fearing heavy competition from commercial television, used all their power within the pillars to put pressure on their counterparts in Parliament. Although there was some sympathy for commercial television within the government, the main political parties (with the exception of the Liberal–Conservative VVD)[11] put a stop to these plans for the time being. But when pirate ships started to broadcast from the North Sea and even commercial television was beamed from an oil rig outside territorial waters, the government not only sent in the Navy, it felt it had to do more.

With the popularity of the pirate stations growing, their support within government grew as well, but still the established broadcasting corporations and the parties affiliated to them held on. In 1965, the confessional-Liberal government failed to reach a decision and resigned on the broadcasting issue. Three commercial groups had again applied for time on the air and they found support in government from the Liberal ministers and some of their Roman Catholic colleagues. The minister of Culture, however, refused their bid, in his turn supported by the religious parties and the PvdA.[12]

Despite some dissenting voices within the government, generally speaking the broadcasting organisations formed the mouthpieces of the party elites within the pillars. The electorate formed a stable group the political parties could count on at election time. The media had a strongly integrating function within the pillars. They orientated themselves towards the elite and therefore communicated the 'right message' from leaders to rank and file. They were the 'spreaders of the word', so to speak. The media showed and confirmed the correctness of the pillar's ideology; political communication formed an almost closed system.

Depillarisation

This neat arrangement came to an end in the middle of the 1960s. Depillarisation and a decline of religious feeling shook the foundations of both political and media systems. Rapid industrialisation, technological developments, a rising level of education and a growth of the tertiary sector with its expanding new middle class (typical of all post-war western societies) strongly affected the precarious balance along the religious dividing lines in Dutch society.

In the wake of these structural changes in society (and at the same time amplifying them) religion lost its unifying and integrating function: the pillars lost their flock. The organisations, associations and political parties became less segmented and more pluralistic, while interactions between members of the pillars increased rapidly.

The Catholic pillar was hardest hit (but certainly not it alone). Its electorate went adrift and so too did the members of the Catholic organisations such as the trade union NKV. The Second Vatican Council in fact both represents a time exposure and a catalytic agent of this development: the old power structures came under fire and a new radicalisation set the pace for new developments. The closeness of a strict church gave way to an openness in which differences of opinion, even different beliefs were nurtured. Hesitantly, politics and social life were affected.

The resulting amalgamations between organisations from the different pillars were not always smooth operations. A federation of Catholic, Socialist and Protestant trade unions ended, after long and difficult negotiations, with only the first two united, ten years after the bishops had lifted the ban on Catholic membership of the Social Democratic union (the Decree was removed in 1964). Where workers did not succeed, employers did. The Catholic and the Protestant employers' associations not only merged but also cooperated with the much larger Liberal organisation. The political parties did not merge until 1980. The Dutch reformed (ARP), the Protestant (CHU) and the Catholic party (KVP) formed a new Christian Democratic party (CDA), after having lost much of their support: from 76 seats (out of a total of 150) in the Second Chamber in 1963 to only 48 in 1981.

Depillarisation and the decline of religious feeling have especially affected the political parties at electoral and membership level. It is no longer considered in the nature of things to vote for the party of one's own pillar. In addition, there has arisen an anti-system movement on the one hand, while on the other, the concept of democracy has been given new content. After years of docility by the rank and file there was an ever stronger call for participation at the base of society. The anti-system movement found expression in two anti-poles: the anarchistic Provo-movement and the more 'Poujadist' Farmers' Party. The first, although an Amsterdam phenomenon, inspired many political innovations. Provo bit the generous hand of the consumer society which fed it; it pointed an accusing finger at authoritarian opinions and at the rigid political system and was both an anti-Vietnam movement and a green party *avant la lettre*. Although the Farmers' Party was less provocative and did not seek clear political innovations, it was inspired by the same government interference and increasing bureaucracy against which Provo, in a certain sense, was protesting.[13]

The appearance of new parliamentary and extra-parliamentary groups, all with different and increasing demands, brought pressure to bear on the nature of the political culture. The pacification and accommodation so familiar in the business-like cooperation between the pillars at elite level had to make way for an ideological confrontation between groups with a relatively strongly politicised following. Openness and contestation became the new creeds, not the best basis for negotiations. Cabinet formations – which had never proceeded without a hitch, but in an atmosphere of secrecy had not taken longer than two months – took 163 days in 1972–73 and in 1977 even 207 days.

Television, in spreading the word, triggered many developments, but at the same time it was part of the changes. The uncertainty of the party elites regarding a changed political culture was shown by the medium, to which the old party politicians were not yet used. They did not need to be, because until then the medium had been a platform. But with the loss of steady support they had to aim their propaganda at a new phenomenon, the floating voter; preaching at their own parish was *passé*. Between 1948 and 1967 support for the religious parties dropped from 56 per cent of the total vote to 48 per cent (by 1981 it had dropped to 35 per cent). At the same time, the rank and file, locked up for so long in the closeness of pillar and sphere, caught a glimpse of an other world. Until the mid-1960s there was only one channel on Dutch television. Every organisation had its own evening to broadcast documentaries, current affairs programmes, shows, church services – everything with its own Catholic, Protestant and Socialist flavour. With people watching every night, television broke the isolation of the pillars and opened the window to show how the other half lived. With only one channel, people were 'forced' to look at other ideologies and religions and were surprised to find that they were human too.

While the parties had to search for floating voters, the media had to aim for new consumers. Traditional supporters, who followed the creed of their religious or ideological background when they subscribed to a broadcasting corporation (or its programme magazine which had a direct binding function), could no longer be counted on.[14] The end of the 1960s and the beginning of the 1970s mark the change from pillarisation to market segmentation in the media; the diversity is no longer based on beliefs but merely on commercial considerations.

After one centre-right cabinet had fallen on the broadcasting issue the year before, a centre-left cabinet initiated a Broadcasting Act in 1966–67 which changed the existing system. The problem of commercials was solved by the establishment of a separate Advertising Foundation (STER), which broadcasts blocks of advertisements outside the actual programmes. Commercial broadcasting companies were still not allowed. The system was opened up, however, to newcomers (with 15,000 members one could become a candidate with limited broadcasting time). With regard to the allocation of broadcasting time, based on the number of members or subscribers to the programme magazine, the Act distinguished between A-, B-, and C-companies according to the number of members. A Dutch broadcasting foundation (NOS) was founded next to the existing corporations with a much more independent position than previous bodies of cooperation. The NOS provides not just coordination and technical facilities, but also so-called 'meeting-point programmes' and programmes explicitly suited to a collective approach (news, national festivities, sports).

Although the Broadcasting Act explicitly states that corporations must provide a 'complete' programme which contains a 'reasonable ratio of culture, information, education and amusement', opening up the system meant more 'neutrals', next to the already existing AVRO, and more programmes aimed at the general public. First came TROS which originated from the short-lived tv-experiment from an oil-rig station, and later

Veronica, the official offspring of the radio pirate of the same name. Pop-programming, introduced in the Netherlands by *Veronica*, was quickly followed by the other radio stations. For television, American serials, shows and quizzes turned out to be more successful than specifically pillar-orientated programmes of pillarised corporations. Apparently, for the public the content of programmes rather than their source now counted most. In the race for the viewer and high ratings the five original broadcasting corporations soon followed suit. The success of TROS-programming even led to the invention of a new word for mediocre, commercial programming: *verTROSsing*. Both opponents and supporters used it as a term of abuse and magic formula respectively. Paradoxically, the unbinding of religious ties also led to a modest re-pillarisation, when right-wing Protestants started a fundamentalist evangelical broadcasting corporation (EO), which at the moment has B-status.

While entertainment and drama took the lead part in Dutch television, market orientation also had its effects on news and current affairs programmes. Originally current affairs programmes were the visiting cards of the broadcasting company. Through their partisan stand they visualised and affirmed the company's ideology: VARA interviewed a PvdA-minister, the KRO a Catholic union man and the NCRV chose someone from the Protestant elite. These programmes were shown at prime time – propagating political beliefs was a prime function – but they attracted a limited number of viewers. Due to the market orientation the programmes were first moved to the late hours. Then TROS introduced the news show: a mixture of short, political and light items, in which personal drama, factual news and off-beat elements took the fore. Gradually the other companies followed in the wake of the TROS success. Objectivity, human interest and the personalisation of political reality – the elements of professionalisation – took over from the partisan stand customary in broadcasting until then. Political communication had already changed with the change in the electoral market place. Programming for specific target groups was no longer the common feature, the general public having become the target. Stopping at the borders of one's own pillar would mean losing track of reality and voters.

Control

Central to the discussion on the relation between broadcasting and politics during this period is the theme of control. Until the mid-1960s, control of appointments, often via interlocking directorships in high places, was quite usual within the different Dutch pillars. The main political parties, trade unions and social and welfare organisations had 'quality seats' on the boards of their affiliated broadcasting companies. The chairman was quite often a former parliamentarian or a future minister. Since that time, however, the strong hold of political parties over the broadcasting organisations has slackened with depillarisation and secularisation.

Yet in spite of this tendency (which is stronger with the press), to a large extent the broadcasting corporations still operate as platforms for the respective parties in pillars and movements. Broadcasting, although in turmoil, is one of the places where pillarisation still holds on to a certain extent. The present and previous chairmen of the AVRO, for instance, have both been junior ministers for the VVD. But the formal relations of the 1950s and early 1960s have mostly been turned into informal ties between parties and organisations. For example, while the PvdA has no more official links with the VARA, at election time the Labour leaders can be sure of prime time coverage. And as a KRO publication put it: 'A broadcasting corporation which calls itself Catholic must have very strong reasons for publicly criticising a political party which calls itself Catholic.'[15]

In general, however, while formal ties with political parties have slackened, the government's hold has intensified somewhat. The chairman and one quarter of the NOS-board are appointed by the Minister of Culture, while a government commissioner supervises the proper functioning of the companies and can take repressive disciplinary measures. As to media-finance, the government determines the broadcasting licence fee, while the NOS-budget is also subject to ministerial approval. The commercialisation tendency has not changed this formal control.

With the exception of the government commissioner, control of appointments and finance do not necessarily mean control over the form and content of programming. In some ways one could say that this control is also to be found in the same 1967 Act, which charges the broadcasting corporations with providing a total programme which 'contains a reasonable ratio of culture, information, education and amusement'. Fear of mediocrity, a playing down of mass (popular) culture and emphasis on the educational side of television was the main theme in every government or party note. As we have seen, however, the cultural diversity which resulted from religious and secular cleavages has turned into a diversity based on commercial considerations. The market behaviour on the part of some media (an overdose of American series and serials, news shows and in general a tendency to let viewing figures decide programme policy) has forced the others to adopt a similar policy.

In order to control the equal diversity and strengthen the informative, educational and cultural side of broadcasting, the government has had to take action. Classical constitutional rights prohibit state interference in the private sphere: *laissez faire, laissez aller*. The rise of social constitutional rights, particularly in the welfare state, has, however, turned private matters into a social concern. Government feels the responsibility to emphasise the supply-side of mass communications, not – as in the Law of Rents, for example – the demand-side, the consumer. Mass communications' cultural goods have become a matter of concern for respective governments, especially with the advent of the new media. It is to this discussion – state relations with broadcasting in the new media age – that we now turn.

II. THE STATE, COMMERCIAL INTERESTS AND THE NEW MEDIA

There were two reasons why the traditional broadcasting system for which the Netherlands has been famous came under fire. First, as outlined above, the concealed form of commercialisation and the overflow of entertainment, at the expense of culture, information and education, changed the original, more pedagogical function the traditional political parties had in mind for television. Second, another technological innovation – cable television – threatened to run wild, with cable offering endless new opportunities to commercial interests.

To these pressures government reacted in two stages. In 1975 a centre-left government tried to bring things to a halt with a *Media Memorandum* and a separate Cable Note aimed at serving and saving the *status quo* in the broadcasting system. At the beginning of the 1980s technological developments overtook the then centre-right government on all sides. Cable was no longer a lone feature, but was joined by satellites, video and telematics. The Policy Note of 1983 and subsequent measures were an attempt to keep pace with developments and take decisions at the same time, with unmistakable effects on the whole media system.

The *1975 Media Memorandum* of the centre-left Den Uyl government was part of a general culture policy in which the distribution of income, knowledge and power had a central position. Particularly the last two points were supposed to find expression in the policy's starting points – democracy, freedom of expression, diversity and participation. These were basic principles in line with the division of power and access the Den Uyl government envisaged and principles which the Minister of Culture and Welfare (CRM) saw endangered by the workings of the market mechanism.

Part of the Memorandum was devoted to measures supporting the difficult financial situation of the Dutch press, but what interests us here are the suggestions concerning broadcasting. In the first place the Memorandum proposed that less broadcasting time be allocated to the NOS and that it be relieved of its task of producing 'meeting point programmes'; second, that the possibility of repressive ministerial control on broadcasts be struck from the Broadcasting Act; third, that membership of a corporation remain decisive for the allocation of time on the air, but that two so-called 'couplings' be dropped (the first coupling determined that only he who paid the licence fee in a family could be a real member of a broadcasting company in the sense of determining allocation of broadcasting time. Because of the second coupling, subscription to a programme magazine also counted as membership of the company concerned. Quite a number of people subscribed to a magazine, not because they liked the company's programme or adhered to the ideology, but because the magazine itself was attractive or cheap); fourth, that regional broadcasting be financed by the regions, produced by the NOS or representative cultural institutions (not including the press) and eschew advertising; and finally, that cable broadcasting, as far as its exploitation is concerned, be considered as a form of regional broadcasting, thereby also excluding advertising and commercial participation. In a separate Cable Memorandum the state-owned PTT was given the power to determine technical regulations. At the same time, for reasons of standardisation, preference was given to one system with a limited number of channels.

At a hearing by a special parliamentary committee which preceded the parliamentary debate, some 25 different interest groups (press and publishers' organisations, broadcasting companies, unions and hardware industries) appeared, while most organisations also produced an extensive written reaction. The publishers and printing organisations even went so far as to publish their own paperback, entitled: 'The media say NO to Van Doorn's Memorandum', with a rather unsavoury picture of the minister on the cover. They also sought support in parliament; the broadcasting organisations contacted the party of their own pillar, while the publishers were more inclined towards the right-wing VVD. Commercial interest groups on the whole were very unhappy about the proposals, even when in the years to come (as it turned out) most were never implemented. Commerce still did not have a foot in the door with cable and regional broadcasting, while the proponents of the old system felt their situation to be at least not wholly undermined.

By the end of the 1970s and the beginning of the 1980s, however, neither new technological developments nor commercial influences could be kept out any longer. We shall limit ourselves here to the national broadcasting system itself and the rise of cable broadcasting, but in the field of telematics, video, the press and notably satellite, both developments and expectations formed an extra impulse for the government (by then centre-right) to take steps. The Dutch channel on the European Communication Satellite (ECS), for example, has been allocated to the private company Euro-tv, while the Russian satellite Gorizont was being relayed by a number of Dutch cable companies. The lack of clear regulations and the possibility of linking satellite with cable prompted new measures.

As we have seen, the national broadcasting system underwent fundamental changes in the 1960s during which a closed communication system was opened up, both for newcomers and in the sense that, as a result of secularisation, the originally steady membership dissolved in favour of more neutral and entertainment-orientated corporations. In 1967 there was only one neutral corporation, whereas by 1977 TROS, *Veronica* and AVRO had 51 per cent of all broadcasting membership and in 1984 this had already risen to 55 per cent. This market segmentation led to fierce competition with the traditional corporations following in the more commercial footsteps of the neutral TROS and VOO (*Veronica*). Programming became a sort of marketing strategy in which viewers' polls helped the companies in deciding when to broadcast what: serials and shows at prime time, news shows and controversial programmes (if any) in the late hours. For the viewers themselves, programmes were no longer traceable to an original religious, ideological or neutral background. But since the amount of viewing time depended on the number of members or subscribers to the programme magazine, the viewers were constantly reminded which corporation they were watching and which telephone number to call for membership. The minister placed restrictions on this, but the corporations found an answer in superimposing their name at regular intervals during films and serials.

The broadcasters use all means available in order to reach the consumers. The programme magazine is promoted as a family magazine, with articles, interviews and background far beyond the scope of programme information as originally intended. New subscribers are offered all kinds of presents and goods: from books to trips abroad offered at reduced prices. The programmes themselves are more and more merchandised, with T-shirts of the A-team, Sesame-Street puzzles and Muppets-puppets. The popular serial figure, they hope, can be traced back to the original broadcasting corporation and so the buyer can follow the track back home: Hans and Gretl in consumer land.

The openness and diversity for which the Dutch broadcasting system had previously been famous, had now turned on itself. The circle of commercialism, in an essentially non-commercial system, had closed, with the growing neutral organisations smiling in the middle. How far would government have to go (how far indeed was it prepared to go) to protect the originally public service system, especially now that commercial threats entered the country via satellite and cable? Sky Channel and plans in Luxembourg for a commercial satellite programme aimed at a Dutch-speaking audience, particularly threatened the existing, in principle, non-commercial broadcasting organisations. The Labour Party and Christian Democrats (still) put up a fight against commercialism, but the conservative VVD – in power with the Christian Democrats – was in favour of opening up the system, as it had been already in the 1960s.

The developments around cable broadcasting, in fact, are closely related to the existing broadcasting system. Already at the beginning of the 1960s, cable started with communal aerials as a means of improving the quality of reception and getting rid of a skyline crowded by antennas. With the change of the Telegraph and Telephone Law in 1969, the PTT lost its monopoly on the installation and operation of cable systems, but retained the right to stipulate technical requirements. Although the centre-left government tried to prescribe only cables with a limited number of channels in the 1975 Memorandum, this was rejected by Parliament which wished to avoid forestalling technological developments and to allow for systems with more possibilities.

The present cable networks have a capacity of 12 to 30 channels and in some places a limited two-way system. The most advanced system, however – the Deltacable star network with more than 100 channels – has been installed in only a few places. Opportunities are all there. After Belgium, the Netherlands is the most densely cabled country in Europe: 80 per cent of all households are connected, growing to an expected 85 per cent in the middle of the 1980s. With the growth of cable networks and the enormous software options, the PTT, broadcasting organisations, network-owners and commercial interests all claimed sole right to the new medium. So far the cable channels are used for broadcasting the two Dutch channels, two Belgian stations, three German, some British programmes and, if available, regional broadcasting stations.

The network-owners can decide what programmes they want on their channel, but only up to a certain point, because the Minister of Culture can determine whether satellite signals can be distributed through the cable, whether pay-tv will be tolerated and whether regional and local programmes will be permitted. At the moment there are five local stations, which broadcast a few hours per day, and some 50 more are waiting for ministerial approval.

At the beginning of the 1980s, radio and tv-pirates who 'broke into' the communal aerials triggered official and judicial rulings. While the official local cable tv-stations so far allowed and the regional radio stations were not permitted to use commercials, the illegal stations did. The tv-stations showed mainly feature films and pornography, while the radio stations limited themselves to pop music, with a reasonable number of exceptions ranging from squatters' to feminist stations. In 1981 the High Court ruled that copyright must be paid for feature films and that cable firms are liable, since they are able to 'close' their network when official programming has ended. Since then, most tv-pirates have disappeared. The thousands of radio pirates, however, continue to broadcast on the FM channel.

1983 Policy Note

The pirates speeded up government thinking and generally provoked reactions from interested parties. Already in 1979 the government had decided on setting out a 'coherent media policy'. Publishers, software firms and newly formed conglomerates in which supermarket chains, publishers and software industry cooperated, were pressing to get in. Satellites were going up, foreign programmes could no longer be stopped at the border and the traditional broadcasting corporations were getting nervous.

In 1983 the government published its Media Policy Note. So heavy was the pressure by different actors trying to steer and influence the direction and content of the Note, that numerous concepts were considered and successively leaked out. The leaking of the 1975 Memorandum, in order to test its political viability, must have served as an example. The civil servants at the Ministry, who were supposed to write the Note, were so torn between rival opinions that in the end they had to be supervised by a psychological bureau! But this was without success, because it was the minister himself who eventually wrote the compromise to suit all parties, or at least those in government. Several senior civil servants resigned when the Note was published, stripped of its fringes and reduced from nearly 200 (one of the leaked versions) to 16 pages.

There was pressure within government as well. With five colleagues and a junior minister looking over his shoulder and signing the Note as well, the Minister of Culture had to leave out more than he could incorporate. Himself a Christian Democrat, four of the others who signed were Liberals, including the Minister of Economic Affairs who is supposed to have had a large say in the final product.

In the Policy Note the Minister aims at a fair division of the media space, with the old media for the old broadcasters and opening up the new media for the new interests. The existing national system should be protected by allowing the broadcasting companies extra time on the air. The requirements for broadcasting corporations to represent 'genuine streams' in society (the minister has updated the definition of pillarisation), counteracting the tendency of *vertrossing*, was strengthened. So was the requirement to present a general programme (mentioned already in the 1967 Broadcasting Act) with culture, information, education and entertainment in reasonable proportions. The need for broadcasting to avoid commercial activities was reaffirmed.

At the same time the Note opened up the way for pay television, from which the existing broadcasting companies should be excluded. Pay-tv is supposed to be self-financing via subscription with no advertising permitted. In September 1984 the minister gave permission to eight applicants and programming is expected to start at the beginning of 1985. Subscription for each channel (firm) will be around 30 to 40 guilders ($10) per month. The largest applicant, ATN (a subsidiary of Holland's biggest publishing house VNU) has claimed, however, that pay-tv in the Netherlands is only viable for two pay-tv distributors. Two other successful applicants, Filmnet and (Swedish) Esselte (the latter also has permission for use of the Belgian channel on the European Communication Satellite) have already started talks on a merger, supported by a banking consortium.

According to that same principle of fair division, the European Communication Satellite is to be opened up for both commercial operators and the broadcasting corporations. Cabled satellite programmes, the Note ruled, should not contain advertising especially aimed at the Netherlands. In the course of 1984, however, some cable networks had started relaying London-based *Sky Channel*, which is completely financed through advertising and has more viewers in the Netherlands than in Great Britain. As long as advertising is not exclusively aimed at the Netherlands, the minister will not take steps, but as a protection for the broadcasting organisations and the commercial viability of pay-tv he has issued the extra ruling that foreign satellite programmes may not be subtitled.

As to the financial aspects of the future policy, the Note is rather vague. As the saying goes in Dutch: the sun goes up for nothing. This becomes painfully clear where the minister gives broadcasting companies extra time with one hand, but refuses extra money, for example, by raising the licence fee. The public will have to spend extra money on pay-tv, since that goes through individual subscription. But that is not the only new financial drain. Local and regional broadcasting – until now financed through national sources – will have to be paid for through local and regional means. Advertising is not allowed here, but by way of compensation the press may start graphic advertising on local television in connection with two other new features: cable newspaper and cable text.

A simple calculation of the extra money required for cable subscription, pay-tv, regional and local programming (not to mention such new gadgets as video and telematics) shows that the new media might well cost households up to 1,000 guilders ($300) per year extra. To add to the costs borne by the public (but cutting those of the broadcasting companies), the High Court has ruled that relaying national programmes via cable is a new 'publication' for which copyright should be paid. This also goes for foreign programmes. In the end the consumer will have to pay. The existing broadcasting companies now fear that all these extra fees and costs will mean a loss of members/

subscribers and therefore broadcasting time. Should they lose the copyright on the extensive publication of the programmes – a main reason for buying the programme magazines and subscribing to individual corporations – this might well be, they fear, the final blow for the traditional 'pillars of Hilversum'.

CONCLUSION

There certainly seem to be more issues at stake in the 1980s than there were in 1975. The number of leaked versions of the 1983 Policy Note already showed that more pressure was being brought to bear than eight years before.

In the first place, until the last Note, all rulings on the media were firmly based on some sort of idea about culture and education, while market preferences were kept at a distance. The protection of Dutch cultural achievements and diversity are still thought important, but there seems to be a noticeable shift in favour of industrial policy considerations. The Note, although only 16 pages long, is quite outspoken about this:

> The Cabinet is ... not merely tenaciously holding on to existing interests, however correct it may be to defend them, but also ... wishes to explore possibilities of media policy opened up by new technology. In the Cabinet's opinion, commercialism is not a phenomenon deserving of disapproval. For culture is not always an alternative to money when it comes to keeping society going. And at the same time, in its widest sense, culture means the development of human activity, not stagnation.[16]

The CDA apparently did not agree with this interpretation of culture, for after the Note had passed relatively unscathed through Parliament, the minister's own party, the CDA, tried to find support for the idea of a separate Third Channel for art and culture, which would give the traditional corporations ample ammunition in their fight against pay-tv and satellites. But in order to get this idea through they had a lot of bargaining to do. When their coalition partner (VVD) turned the idea down, the CDA reached an agreement with the opposition party, PvdA. In its turn, the Christian Democrats would have to support a PvdA motion allowing the broadcasting organisations access to pay-tv. At the beginning of 1984 both motions received a majority, but after consultation with the minister, the CDA decided to stick to a Third Channel only if the licence fee would not rise more than marginally. In the middle of that same year PvdA and VVD opposed the ministerial ban on subtitling foreign satellite programmes, but the government ignored this parliamentary majority.

The different coalitions for and against the motions (and the powerful position of the government) once again demonstrates that on the broadcasting issue cleavages can run deep along quite different lines from major economic and political stances. On economic points the CDA and VVD seem to have a happy marriage, but on social points CDA leans more towards the PvdA, while the latter finds support from the VVD on ethical issues. Broadcasting politics seems to balance precariously on all lines. In 1965, be it hesitatingly, Christian Democrats opposed VVD-supported plans for introducing advertising in broadcasting. In fact, this has been an issue over the years with both Christian Democrats and Socialists showing anti-commercial sentiments. The Socialists saw it as a tool for manipulating the market by capitalists and the Christian Democrats regarded it as anti-religious. Even now, with 15 years of advertising on Dutch television, Sunday is still free of commercials. And for a few years the Christian Democrats had the seven o'clock commercials banned, as they argued that these would have a bad influence on children. The two parties presenting the 1983 Policy Note again had rather opposing views on, and different relations with, the media. At the press conference, at which the minister presented the Note, he explained in so many words that the final result was a compromise between the Liberal aim of reducing government influence and the Christian Democrat plea not to stir up trouble in the existing broadcasting system.

In the second place, the media themselves had direct lines to the parties in and outside government. While pillarisation might be outdated, the original broadcasting corporations still have informal contacts with political parties: VARA with PvdA, KRO and NCRV with CDA. The more commercially orientated TROS, *Veronica* and AVRO enjoy contacts with the VVD. And since they were part of the changes proposed in the Note, they often made use of their own means of communication to make their objections public. When, in one of the leaked versions of the Note, a sharp control of the 'complete programme' formula was announced, TROS and *Veronica*, with their emphasis on entertainment programming thought this was meant for them. In their programmes (even with special jingles) they immediately started a campaign against the minister and his plans.

In the third place, there was the electronics industry and the publishers who had been knocking on the door for years and who could hardly be kept waiting any longer with all their new electronic equipment. At least, they thought so and the VVD agreed with them. They reminded the government that at its start in office it had especially emphasised innovative industries and here was a good opportunity to turn rhetoric into action.

Compared to earlier drafts of the Note, the final document is somewhat less restrictive in tone and in practice offers relatively more to business interests. One half of the Cabinet was eager to reduce public control which restricted, as the VVD put it, any initiatives smelling of commercialism. Part of the Policy Note satisfied this half: the new media will be industry's playground. The other half of the Cabinet feared that 'helping' (*sic*) private initiative might mean the end of the existing broadcasting system. They too can find paragraphs in the Note to satisfy their views: the old channels are still for the old media and, as a compromise, public and private systems may both share the European Communication Satellite. In general, this is the starting point of the Policy Note: preserve the old, nourish the new.

In the fourth place, there is the issue of political control. A special chapter in the Note is dedicated to 'Government keeping its distance'. The measures mentioned here mean a reduction of control at governmental level. There is a tendency towards decentralisation which in reality will mean that local and regional councils still make final decisions. Yet government control is not on its way out. In the case of the NOS, for instance, the government until now appointed directly or indirectly a majority of the Board. In the Note the minister proposed to give the corporations a majority, but he will still appoint the chairman and 'some' members. Apart from this, the minister will install a Commissariat for the Media with extensive jurisdiction over the content and form of both national, regional and local media. The importance of this Commissariat, to which the government will appoint five members, is as yet unclear, but it will also control the limited commercial activities of the – in principle, still non-commercial – broadcasting organisations.

The changes in the media market, in the fifth place, are expected to have a noticeable effect on political communication in the Netherlands. The growing number of channels, the internationalisation of supply and content, and the decentralisation of media use will make it more difficult for political parties to reach and mobilise the public. Abundance does not necessarily mean more choice. The growing competition for the viewer and the latter's growing necessity to make a choice from the abundance have so far resulted in an increasing uniformity of the programme format and a decrease of political diversity.

This brings us, finally, to the one actor that is highly involved in broadcasting politics but rarely mentioned in the Note: the public. As usual with new media, its role is a passive one. It is expected to consume and, in the end, pay. 'Viewers equal consumers' would seem to be the hallmark of the new media age in the Netherlands.

NOTES

1. J. Curran et al., 'The Study of the Media: Theoretical Approaches', in M. Gurevitch et al., *Culture, Society and the Media* (London: Methuen, 1982), p. 20.
2. J. Blumler and M. Gurevitch, 'Politicians and the Press: An Essay in Role Relationships', in D. Nimmo and K. Sanders (eds.), *Handbook of Political Communication* (London: Sage, 1982).
3. Cf. for a first contribution G. Murdock and P. Golding, 'For a Political Economy of Mass Communications', in R. Miliband and J. Saville (eds.), *The Socialist Register* (London: Merlin Press, 1974). See also J. Curran and J. Seaton, *Power Without Responsibility* (London; Fontana, 1980) and G. Murdock, 'Large Corporations and the Communication Industries', in M. Gurevitch et al. (eds.), op. cit., pp. 118–51.
4. K. Brants and W. Kok, *Political Communication and Agenda-Building*, paper presented at the IPSA conference, Edinburgh, 1976.
5. This view is to be found particularly in conservative circles. For an interesting discussion on the ideological notion of public control see J. M. Piemme, 'Monopoly and/or Public Service: The Belgian Instance', *Media, Culture and Society*, Vol. 5, No. 3/4, pp. 297–303.
6. V. R. Lorwin, 'Segmented Pluralism: Ideological Cleavages and Political Cohesion in the Smaller European Democracies', *Comparative Politics*, Vol. 3, No. 2 (1971), p. 141.
7. The Labour movement, aiming to further their class interests, the Catholics, in search of equal treatment in a dominantly Protestant-Liberal nation, and the orthodox-Calvinist 'simple folk' (as they were called), protesting against the dominance of the Liberal bourgeoisie and unorthodox Protestantism, all see themselves as emancipation movements.
8. According to Stuurman, pillarisation is one of the forms in which the working class, farmers

and middle classes are divided up into fractions, some of which are 'organised' under the specific fractions of the ruling class. In his dissertation, Stuurman gives several examples of this 'organisation', which is sometimes overt but often part of a process of ideological integration. S. Stuurman, *Verzuiling, kapitalisme en patriarchaat* (Nijmegen: SUN, 1984).
9. A Lijphart, 'Consociational Democracy', *World Politics*, Vol. 21, No. 2 (1969), pp. 207–25, and also *The Politics of Accommodation: Pluralism and Democracy in the Netherlands* (Berkeley, CA: University of California Press, 1968). The sketch of the Netherlands as a closed system of subcultures is, to a certain degree, ideal typical. Certainly, pillarisation covered the country as a woollen blanket, but the closeness was not so strict as not to let exceptions and 'escapes' take place. Otherwise the abrupt and fundamental changes which took place in the 1960s cannot be very well explained.
10. H. Wigbold, 'Holland: the shaky pillars of Hilversum', in A. Smith (ed.), *Television and Political Life* (London: Macmillan, 1979), p. 196.
11. The VVD (People's Party for Freedom and Democracy), at present the third party in the country, is a traditional liberal party with progressive stands on ethical issues (abortion, freedom of expression), but with strong conservative overtones, particularly on socio-economic issues. The VVD is comparable to large parts of the British Conservative Party and in this text will be called Liberal, Conservative and Liberal-Conservative synonymously.
12. P. Gros, *Grijsboek televisie* (Amsterdam: De Bezige Bij, 1966), and H. Schaafsma, *Geschiedenis van de omroep* (Amsterdam: Wetenschappelijke Uitgeverij, 1970).
13. Ph. van Praag and K. Brants, *Depillarisation and Factionalism: The Case of the Dutch Labour Party*, paper presented at the ECPR conference (Florence, 1980), p. 8.
14. For more information on the rules governing membership of broadcasting corporations and the allocation of transmission time between the different companies, see H. Wigbold, op. cit., p. 220.
15. *Visies op kommunikatie. Denken uit de KRO bij zijn vijftigjarig bestaan* (Bilthoven, 1975), p. 85 (Author's translation).
16. 'Tweede Kamer der Staten Generaal, zitting 1982–1983', 18035 nr.1, *Medianota* (Den Haag, 1983), p. 7 (Author's translation).

Broadcasting in Spain: A History of Heavy-handed State Control

Esteban López-Escobar and Angel Faus-Belau

The long period during which virtually all public aspects of Spanish life were dominated by the Franco regime was marked among other things by close governmental control of broadcasting for political, ideological and cultural ends. The death of Franco in 1975 raised expectations in many quarters both inside and outside the country that an era of change was about to begin in Spanish politics. Applied to broadcasting, these hopes were translated into a desire that the establishment of democracy would open up radio and television to new political, social and cultural elements, as the broadcast media escaped from the previously stifling grip of Francoism.

The subject matter of this article is the relationship between government and broadcasting in post-civil-war-Spain, spanning the period of the Franco dictatorship, the transition to democracy and the election of the present Socialist government in 1982 with its mandate for reform.[1] The main theme of this study is the overriding continuity of this relationship, in spite of changes of regime, governmental elites and broadcasting legislation from the Francoist period to the present day. A liberalisation of broadcasting, whether in terms of the establishment of private competition for state television or in terms of a more impartial and balanced news output, has not taken place.

BROADCASTING IN THE FRANCO ERA

As far as radio is concerned, during the authoritarian regime of General Franco there was a mixed system of ownership, including both the state and private interests. This was at a time when in many other Western European countries the state exercised monopoly control over radio. This mixed system of ownership still exists today although, as we shall see, there is a tendency towards the strengthening of the state sector. To understand this historical development of Spanish radio, however, one has to go back to the circumstances surrounding its introduction in the 1920s.

By the promulgation of the *Reglamento* of 14 July 1924, all radio stations which were then operating in Spain on an experimental basis had to cease broadcasting and request the relevant authorisation to transmit.[2] The first licence was granted to Jose Maria Guillen Garcia who along with a group of Catalonian businessmen had created EAJ-1 *Radio Barcelona*. The most notable characteristic regarding the origins of radio in Spain was that private interests were the motivating force behind all radio stations prior to the Civil War.

The most important step in the early development of Spanish broadcasting was the creation of *Unión Radio*. Without belittling the contributions of other radio stations, it can be argued that the history of Spanish radio has been to a large extent the history of *Unión Radio* and of its successor, *Cadena SER (Sociedad Española de Radiodifusión)*. This is so not only because SER is the largest private radio network in Spain (and indeed in Europe when measured by the number of stations),[3] but also because it has been the most innovative and forward-looking in its use of the medium over the 60 years of its existence.

The outbreak of the Civil War, at which time there were 68 radio stations operating in Spain, marked the end of the initial development of Spanish radio.[4] On 19 January 1937 *Radio Nacional de España* was established in Salamanca by the newly emerging Francoist wartime coalition to broadcast its political propaganda. This event marked the beginning of state-controlled radio. The new station held a monopoly over radio news during the post-war period, since all other stations were compelled to link up to it twice a day seven days a week to transmit its news bulletins, with the aim of reinforcing a Francoist regime isolated during the Second World War.

As a result, Spanish radio experienced a change of course. Whereas previously it had been a relatively free carrier of news and information, it now became a *de facto* government service in an era marked by a lack of freedom generally. Government control of news output was to become increasingly evident throughout the following years, particularly by 1962 when television was successfully establishing itself as a mass medium. As a result of this practice, radio went through years of crisis which first affected its credibility with listeners as a source of information and later the audience figures themselves.[5]

Between 1945 and 1962, once *Radio Nacional de España* (RNE) had consolidated its position, the Franco administration (which incidentally had not been admitted to the Geneva Convention for the distribution of frequencies) authorised the establishment of new radio stations. These included the following: *Red de Emisoras del Movimiento* (REM), linked to the local and provincial branches of the only political party authorised in Spain, the Falange Española Tradicionalista (FET), the Fascist movement which Franco co-opted as the official face of the regime; *Cadena Azul de Radiodifusión* (CAR), also linked to the Franco movement; *Cadena de Emisoras Sindicales* (CES), belonging to the only official (that is pro-Franco) trade union in the country; *Cadena de Ondas Populares de España* (COPE), linked to the ecclesiastical hierarchy; and several other stations run by private individuals as a concession from the state. These last mentioned reflected the varying and overlapping viewpoints of the 'coalition of interests', the so-called 'families' such as the church, the military, the agricultural elite, *et al.*, who were institutionalised into the regime's elite structure. Finally, to cater for the needs of small localities and rural areas, the government also allowed small, low-powered stations of poor quality which were operated at parish level. In all, some 1,300 radio stations were in operation in Spain around 1962.

After this rather chaotic expansion, radio was restructured towards the end of the 1960s. The parish stations were abolished, resulting in a halving of their total number. The remainder were forced to renovate their equipment and adjust their frequencies. Market pressures and technical constraints led to the disappearance of many other stations. REM and CAR merged to form a new network, REM/CAR, which still enjoyed close links with the Francoist state. By the time of Franco's death in 1975 the number of stations in operation had fallen to 210.[6]

Despite this restructuring, however, government control of news and political output remained virtually unaffected. The period of 'limited liberalisation', initiated by the regime and personified by the then Minister of Information, Manuel Fraga Iribarne, was superficial and never looked likely to reduce significantly government interference in the broadcasting media.

The law which prohibited any news transmission different from that broadcast by the state service, *Radio Nacional*, remained in operation for almost 30 years. While some relaxation was initiated in 1964, when the non-state radio stations were allowed to broadcast local, and later regional, news items of their own choice, the control of state radio remained entrenched in the case of both national and international news stories up until 1977.

Government control of television fitted the same pattern. *Televisión Española* began transmissions on a regular basis on 28 October 1956. Legislation on the new medium had, however, predated its appearance by some considerable time, laying down a series of norms which placed the television services firmly in the hands of the state. For example, the royal decree of 24 January 1908, which laid down the legal framework for the radiotelegraphic service, declared that the state had a monopoly over 'the establishment and exploitation of all systems and apparatus applied to the so-called "Hertzian telegraph", "Ethereal telegraph", "radiotelegraph" and other procedures already invented *or yet to be invented*'.[7] The law on radio broadcasting of 26 June 1934, promulgated during the Second Spanish Republic, affirmed that 'the service of national radio broadcasting is an essential and exclusive function of the state'; while the *Reglamento* of the National Radio Broadcasting Service, put into law by the decree of 22 November 1935, proclaimed that among the broadcasting services of the state 'the establishment and exploitation of the [services] of the broadcasting of sounds *and images* already in use *or to be invented in the future*' had to be included.

In contrast to the press and radio, in which private interests had a stake during the Franco years, television in Spain was instituted as a state monopoly. It was to be financed out of the state budget with the help of advertising revenue, without recourse to the system of licence-fees common in other western European systems.

The legal framework of the state monopoly became in practice a governmental monopoly. The system of a priori censorship which was applied to the press and radio before 1966 affected television as well. In fact, during the early years of television, its news bulletins were little more than retransmissions of the radio services of *Radio Nacional*. More generally, programme content could not infringe a code of morals which, inspired by the Church, was excessively puritanical. Dubbed Hollywood films were particular victims of this 'profoundly moral tone of television'.[8]

During the entire period of the Franco regime television was organised and manipulated on classic authoritarian lines, with direct censorship of programmes and a patronage system of appointments – both controlled by the Ministry of Information. Tactical use was made of television, especially during the 1960s, to sway the nation's attention whenever it seemed to be focusing on internal, conflictual matters. For example, at times of political agitation, television would keep viewers' minds off politics by screening a football match, a bullfight or a popular feature film.[9]

> Television conveyed the image of a country serenely governed by a distant but all-caring and all-comprehending Caudillo. The viewers were never alarmed by strikes, terrorist actions or international disrespect for the regime. Such incidents did not happen, since they were never reported.[10]

This use of television was particularly important in a decade which saw the resurgence of an 'underground' trade union movement, student opposition and rapid changes in a society undergoing an industrial boom. In short, television under Franco did little to reflect the diversity and pluralism of Spanish politics and society. The medium was concerned to show certain personalities and events and overall to maintain and propagate the ideology of the regime among the masses. It was also used as 'a political stepping-stone for the ambitious members of the administration', including most notably Adolfo Suárez.[11]

THE TRANSITION TO DEMOCRACY

With the restoration of the monarchy after the death of Franco, a new era in Spanish politics began, which would have far-reaching consequences for society and, it seemed, for broadcasting. However, in spite of pressures for change, the restrictions on the freedom of information on radio lasted for another two years, that is, up to the end of 1977, a period which witnessed the gradual and careful dismantling of the Franco regime's structure 'from within' by the governments appointed by King Juan Carlos, which steered a careful path between a Francoist backlash and fears, voiced especially by the United States, of Communist Party influence as the leading anti-Francoist force during the dictatorship.[12]

Although it is fair to say that while the political restrictions remained legally in force they were rarely applied in practice, it is also the case that broadcasting staff acted extremely cautiously for fear of provoking a reaction in the unstable political climate. As freedom of information in the broadcasting media was still not guaranteed by statute, self-censorship became a normal part of the broadcasters' *modus vivendi* with the politicians. Such prudence was particularly in evidence during the period in which Carlos Arias Navarro was Prime Minister (early 1976), when it seemed as though the country was going through a stage of continuity rather than change.[13]

Navarro was succeeded by Adolfo Suárez, whose great advantage as a technician of gradual change was his knowledge of the Franco regime's bureaucratic apparatus, which he had gained in a variety of posts including civil governor of Segovia and director-general of radio and television, before becoming Minister of the Movement and finally Prime Minister. His first government did little to deal with the Francoist legacy in the broadcasting field, with the first steps being taken only a full 18 months after Suárez' appointment.

After several months of hesitation and vacillation a royal decree was promulgated on 22 November 1977 concerning 'the freedom of information on radio'. Encouraged by this legislation, radio stations gained first in credibility, then in the quality of their news output and, finally, in listening figures. A good example of the change in approach was provided by radio coverage of the abortive *coup d'état* of 23 February 1981. Spanish radio, particularly SER, rose to the challenge, providing an instance of socially responsible broadcasting which exceeded public expectations and was notable for its audacity.[14]

After 1977 the Suárez governments were very active in the broadcasting field, as can be seen from the amount of legislation that was introduced and implemented during the years of his premiership (July 1976–January 1981). While at first sight it would appear that private interests benefited from the changes introduced, in fact it is now clear that it was the state sector which was strengthened.

The first step was taken 20 days before the promulgation of the 'freedom of information on radio' decree. On 2 November 1977 another royal decree provided for the incorporation of the radio stations operated by REM/CAR, *Cadena CES* and *Radio Peninsular* (all linked to the defunct Franco regime) within *Radiotelevisión Española* (RTVE). Shortly after, on 5 May 1978, a 'trusteeship commission' was created for these networks and by means of yet another royal decree they were integrated into *Radio Cadena Española* (RCE) on 4 December 1978. As a result, the old broadcasting machinery created for the Franco regime was placed at the disposal of the new democratic state and its government. Given that no formula guaranteeing the independence of the broadcasters from the state was expounded, the new RCE tended to carry out the same function it had performed before the restoration of democracy. This is still the case today.

A further step towards the strengthening of the grip of the state sector in Spanish radio came with the setting into motion of the National Technical Plan for Broadcasting (November 1978). Under the provisions of this document not only was a state monopoly established over short and long wave frequencies, but in addition the former criteria regarding state participation in the ownership of networks and stations in the private sector were maintained by the government. Radio frequencies would be granted to private interests 'on condition that the state should dispose of at least 25% of the capital shares in the company receiving the concession ... a participation which has to be effective in all cases where the power of the transmitter exceeds five kilowatts'.[15] It could be argued that this condition, which had been enforced during the Franco dictatorship, should have been suppressed if the government had really wanted to liberalise radio broadcasting in Spain.

The impression that broadcasting was being liberalised during the Suárez premiership was largely based on the implementation of the Transitory Technical Plan of the Public Broadcasting Service in Modulated Frequency (18 June 1979). This opened up the way for the entry of private interests into the area of FM radio.[16] A total of 300 new licences for FM stations was distributed mainly among private businesses in part compensation for the state's monopoly control over short and long waves. These stations, however, are very low-powered and are mainly geared to local broadcasting. Many of them are still in the process of being established, while others have been operating for some time and some have even merged to constitute FM networks.

The euphoria of the private interests which greeted these concessions masked the reality of the situation: while the private sector was growing, so too was the state sector. Furthermore, as a result of the creation of a new political tier based upon Autonomous Communities, the various regional governments have been granted authority to set up their own stations and to allocate licences of their own accord (although in some Communities plans are still only at the drawing-board stage). The impression of liberalisation served to encourage the development of a new type of station: municipal radio. Town councils of all political complexions jumped on to the bandwagon and established their own FM stations without seeking any kind of authorisation whatsoever. Alongside these another type of station has sprung up – pirate stations established by private interests, the so-called *radios libres* (free radio). There are about 400 stations of the municipal and pirate type operating in Spain today.

When the new Spanish Constitution came into force in December 1978 the state had control of a chain of daily newspapers, a large number of radio stations and all television. The policy of the different governments during the period when *Unión de Centro Democrático* (UCD) was in power can be summarised as follows: first, do away with the state-run press, finally accomplished in early 1984; second, regulate state-run radio and television; and third, establish a legal framework for the development of private television in Spain, although this was done in a very timid and hesitant manner.[17]

The second of these objectives was attained with the passing of the law of 10 January 1980, the Spanish broadcasting statute.[18] 'The legislation was the product of consensus politics between the UCD and the Socialists and was fiercely opposed by the Communists and the Catalan minority in Parliament on the grounds that it did not contain sufficient safeguards for minority groups.'[19] This statute, the constitutionality of which is still discussed in Spain today,[20] represents to a great extent continuity with the past. As such, it meant the loss of an historic opportunity to create a television system which, although a state monopoly, would not be controlled by the government. Let us look at this statute in detail.

The preamble to the 1980 statute affirms that

> broadcasting, established as an essential public service owned by the state, is a primary means of information and of political participation for the nation's citizens, helps form public opinion, cooperates with

the educational system, aids the dissemination of Spanish culture ... as well as being a major means of ... making freedom and equality real and effective, with special attention paid to the protection of minorities and to non-discrimination against women.

The 1980 statute gave the public corporation RTVE the task of managing the lion's share of Spanish broadcasting. With the objective of securing greater administrative efficiency, the corporation was split into three companies: *Televisión Española* (TVE), *Radio Nacional de España* (RNE) and *Radio Cadena Española* (RCE), with the main difference between the two radio networks (apart from their historical origins) being that RCE has commercial advertising breaks. The statute has resulted, therefore, in the integration of the RCE network, created during the Franco dictatorship, within the RTVE. As a consequence of this, any hope of these stations being transferred into private hands disappeared. Thanks to the 1980 statute, the government gained control of over 300 radio stations (including a monopoly on short and long waves) as well as all of television.

Article 4 of the 1980 statute lays down the operating principles of the state broadcasting services regarding programming. These principles are the classic ones of public service broadcasting, including objectivity, truthfulness and impartiality with regard to news and current affairs output; the separation of news from opinion, the identification of those who give voice to the latter and their free expression within the limits of the Constitution;[21] and respect for political, religious, social, cultural and linguistic pluralism.

The main decision-making bodies of the corporation are the board of governors, the advisory council of each of the three companies and the director-general. The board of governors has 12 members, six elected by the Chamber of Deputies and six by the Senate among persons with relevant professional merits. A two-thirds parliamentary majority is required, a rule which was designed to ensure a certain degree of consensus among the different parties represented in Parliament regarding the appointment of the governors. In fact, however, the appointments are politicised, perhaps inevitably, given the nature of Spanish politics. It should be noted that the Board does not have the power to appoint the director-general of the corporation or any of the directors of the three constituent companies.

It is the government which has the power to appoint the director-general. While this is common practice in many other Western European systems, in Spain it is symptomatic of the politicisation of broadcasting for partisan ends. The inconveniences of this situation whereby the director-general and his subordinates are beholden to the government are fully illustrated by the fact that between January 1980, when the statute came into force, and October 1982, when a general election was held (the third after Franco's death), the RTVE had three director-generals, each holding office for an average of only six months. This was despite the statutory guarantee of a four-year term of office (unless a general election intervened). If it is remembered that the director-general has the power to appoint the directors ot TVE, RNE and RCE, as well as the regional representatives of the corporation and the directors of the state broadcasting centres, it is clear that it is very difficult to have any kind of managerial or professional stability. This is a direct consequence of the dependence of broadcasting upon the government. The workings of the 1980 statute sacrifice professional to political control.

The UCD government of Suárez had the task of supervising the implementation of the 1980 statute and in particular of putting the principles enshrined in the new legislation into practice. However, the UCD made a pact with the Socialist opposition regarding the appointment of the first director-general of the reorganised RTVE.[22] The person chosen, Fernando Castedo, a state lawyer and member of the UCD, had the unenviable task of laying the foundations of a broadcasting service which in theory was independent of the government. His term in office, which lasted only from January to October 1980, unleashed a storm of protest from centre and right-wing politicians who accused him of having handed television over to the opposition. When Calvo Sotelo replaced Suárez as Prime Minister, Castedo resigned in the face of relentless criticism from a variety of quarters. His resignation was greeted with indignation by the Socialist Party, which had none the less contributed to his downfall.

The second director-general of RTVE, Robles Piquer, was appointed by Calvo Sotelo. According to one commentator, Calvo Sotelo was looking for 'a man with experience in the public field, with a "vision of the state", a feeling for authority and conservative inclinations'.[23] Robles Piquer fitted the bill perfectly. His appointment was, however, highly controversial, because he was a relation of the conservative leader, Fraga Iribarne, who had been Minister of Information and Tourism during the Franco regime. The choice of Robles Piquer was 'the most blatant of political moves, designed to head off criticism from a powerful sector of UCD that television had become too liberal .... Regardless of his capacity, the manner of his appointment seriously undermined the neutral image of RTVE management ...'.[24] As the choice of Robles Piquer, unlike that of Castedo, was not the product of a bipartisan political agreement, he became the object of persistent harassment by the opposition.[25]

Under Robles Piquer a 'civil war' began in television, which persists to the present day. A hundred and eighty broadcasting staff signed a petition denouncing the manipulation to which, they alleged, Spanish television was being subjected.[26] This charge was met with a counter-petition signed by 182 broadcasters who defended the role of the director-general and argued that news output was pluralistic and impartial. The political parties joined in the battle. The transmission of a programme on the *coup d'état* in Turkey, just after the attempted *coup* in Spain, provided a motive for demanding Robles Piquer's resignation. This was given and a short time later, he joined the right-wing Popular Alliance party of Fraga Iribarne.

The last director-general appointed during the UCD period of government was Nasarre, whose candidacy was supported by the general secretary of the UCD, Iñigo Cavero. Nasarre was a journalist by profession, who had gained political experience in the opposition to Francoism. His period in office has been described as 'the peaceful transition'[27] and when it ended one of the Socialist members of the board of governors was prompted to declare that he 'was going to leave state radio and television in a better condition than he had inherited'.[28] Under his administration there was a limited but noticeable swing towards professional, and away from purely political, criteria in programming policy. His spell as director-general, generally appreciated in political circles, came to an end in compliance with the principles of the 1980 statute when Parliament was dissolved.

In short, as far as broadcasting under the Suárez and related governments was concerned, we can conclude by saying that after a certain liberalisation in the area of news output, all subsequent measures led in the direction of laying a firm foundation for a solidly structured state-operated broadcasting system, albeit with vague notions of public service broadcasting norms and guarantees. This policy in favour of the state radio and television sectors reached its apogee with the publication of the 1980 broadcasting statute. The retention of a state monopoly over most of broadcasting was a manifestation of the centralist and statist mentality inherited from the previous Francoist regime.

THE SOCIALISTS AND BROADCASTING

After the general election of 28 October 1982 which brought the Socialists into power with an absolute majority in Parliament (202 deputies out of a total of 350), there was considerable speculation about how the new government would handle the broadcasting issue. It is now clear that it is very difficult in the Spanish political context to relinquish control of a powerful mass medium. If the period under Suárez and the UCD administration was marked by an increase in the dominance of the state broadcasting sector over the private, then the present Socialist administration under the premiership of Felipe González is characterised by the exploitation of these media to the benefit of the government, the Socialist Party and the ideology they embody. The Socialists have not really had the will or the capacity to allow the broadcasters the independence to run radio and television on public service lines. This is particularly important in the Spanish context because, given the country's low level of newspaper readership, radio and television are the most important means of mass communication, with only 20 per cent of Spaniards regularly reading a newspaper.[29]

In the field of radio the Socialist government has continued to reinforce the position of the state sector, and in particular RCE, by acquiring the licences of those private companies who have ceased broadcasting and incorporating the stations into the RCE network. Statistics now show that for the first time in the 60-year history of radio in Spain the majority of stations are run by the state: 50.2 per cent of all medium wave and FM. If to this is added the state monopoly on short and long waves, as well as the 25-per cent controlling share in the ownership of the private stations and networks, it is evident that the state is by far the most important factor in controlling Spanish radio. Moreover, far from diminishing this predominance it is likely to be extended, since the government wants to encourage FM broadcasting by the RNE. At the same time the country's economic crisis and the competition for advertising revenue from the RCE stations may force some of the private stations to go out of business.

As far as news and political output is concerned, it is increasingly difficult to distinguish between news reporting and editorial comment, with the result that the statutory norms of impartiality and balance are being clearly breached. Even supporters of the Socialist government have admitted the lack of reform in this area. For example, in mid-1983, only six months after the Socialists' accession to power, the daily newspaper *El Pais*, which balances its general support for the government with occasional critical articles and comment, published an editorial on the media in which it was argued that the Socialists had done nothing to alter the practice of governmental control over television. The editorial stated that:

> the degradation of *Televisión Española* is already manifest at various levels, from government control over news to the division of its internal organisation into cliques, not to mention plans to extend advertising to increase the corporation's financial base .... the public corporation continues to serve personal, private interests in an almost exclusive fashion.[30]

The article concluded that the current situation under the Socialist government was in sharp contrast to the election promises in favour of a public service, pluralistic television system to the extent that the sincerity of these promises now had to be doubted.

An illustration of the attitude of the Socialist government towards political output was provided by an incident concerning the popular current affairs programme, *La Clave*. The director of this programme had repeatedly demonstrated his opposition to any form of censorship or control over the selection of participants during the previous UCD administration. However, his determination did not prevent one edition of the programme on the subject of administration under left-wing municipal councils being cancelled on the grounds that the director was ill, whereas in fact he was temporarily out of the country. The real reason for the ban was that one of the guests on the programme was a former alderman of Madrid who had been expelled from the Socialist Party for having denounced certain irregularities in Socialist municipal administration. Obviously the Socialists have been as unable as their predecessors to resist the temptation of interference in news and current affairs output.[31]

Socialist control of television has been criticised from a variety of quarters on grounds of bias,[32] lack of objectivity, manipulation of news[33] and staff witch-hunts.[34] The criticisms made by the Socialists when they were in opposition are now rebounding on them, as they repeat the practices and errors of previous governments in flouting the principles of the 1980 statute.

While direct censorship is no longer practised, the statute has not prevented the González government from removing from their posts within the RTVE news departments (and more generally) those who do not agree with the Socialist line. A simple lack of identification with the government's ideology has been sufficient for this sanction to be applied. The failure of the statute to guarantee the independence of the broadcast media from the government is shown by the fact that the legislation is rejected by many broadcasting staff, including many Socialist Party sympathisers. Government control is exercised via appointments. For example, Jose Maria Calvino was named as director-general of the RTVE following the advent of the Socialist government to power. Calvino 'was originally the PSOE representative on the board of governors. He would never have got the job without the complete trust of the government.'[35]

So far we have concentrated on the politics of broadcasting at the national level. However, since the Socialist election victory a new dimension has been introduced into Spanish broadcasting. The central government now shares responsibility for broadcasting with the governments of the 17 Autonomous Communities, with the result that broadcasting has become less of a nation-building tool than previously. The centralist state monopoly has been broken – to some extent – with the creation of regional channels. These regional channels were set up under the Socialist government in an attempt to respond to political pressures which have grown since the fall of Franco for greater regional autonomy. Their legalisation forms part of the government's policy of recognising a separate cultural identity at the regional level, while at the same time being committed to the maintenance of a unified nation-state with minimal devolution of power from the centre to the periphery.

As might be expected the actions of the different regional governments are as diverse as their political majorities. For the sake of simplicity they can be split into two groups: those where the Socialist Party is in power and those where government is dominated by other political parties, including those of a separatist (or nationalist) character. This second group includes the regional governments of Catalonia, the Basque country and Galicia which have created regional radio stations run by the Autonomous Communities themselves.

Unfortunately these stations reproduce to a great extent the same defects as the national, state system in their operations, especially with regard to their independence from the governing class. In general the new regional radio stations are very seriously influenced by the political outlook of the party in power. Many of them wish to free themselves from the legacy of centralised control of broadcasting and some even to reject centralism itself in favour of 'national identity'.

In our view the greatest danger about regional radio stems from the monopolistic restrictions placed by the regional governments upon the provision of broadcasting licences to private interests. In this regard the most restrictive actions have been taken by the regional authorities of the Basque country, followed by the Catalonian government.[36] These practices, which severely restrict the free flow of information and free enterprise, both enshrined in the Spanish Constitution, have resulted in the creation of regional monopolies over broadcast information. In view of the lack of guarantees regarding the independence of these regional networks *vis-à-vis* the regional governments, control of news and dissemination of political propaganda are to be expected.

The effects of the decentralisation policy in radio have not all been welcomed by the González government. In fact there has recently been a noticeable soft-pedalling, particularly in those regions controlled by the

Socialists. Various governments in the Autonomous Communities had already studied the viability of establishing regional radio (and television) networks, while in some regions the conditions for bidding for the licences had already been published. However, the results of the experiments in the Basque country and Catalonia demonstrated to the Socialist national government that regional radio reduced the listening figures of the central, state networks. This is one reason why in those regions with Socialist administrations there has been a policy volte-face, with attempts now being made to strengthen the functioning of the state sector, especially RCE, rather than setting up regional networks. As in other areas of policy, decentralisation of broadcasting has been only partly successful in buying electoral support in exchange for concessions to regional sentiments.

It is true that to a limited extent, which should not be overestimated, the decentralisation of broadcasting to the regions has introduced some flexibility into the television system which has traditionally been highly centralist, relayed from Madrid and in recent years beamed by satellite all over the national territory. The statute of 26 December 1983 established a third television channel, owned by the central state, though responsibility for its programming could be devolved as a concession to a region at the request of the regional authorities.[37]

The 1983 legislation allocates to the state the role of providing each Autonomous Community with the technical infrastructure required for transmitting the third channel's programmes. The law also affirms that in terms of programming the public service principles which in theory underpin the activity of the state channels are to be applied to the regional channel.

The third channel has been conceived as a mirror-image of the state system, but on a regional scale.[38] As such the statute lays down that ownership and control cannot be transferred by any means or in any form, wholly or partially, to a third party; private interests are allowed no say in the running of the channel. As a consequence, television remains closed to the commercial sector.

Other provisions of the 1983 statute of note include that which gives the central government the right 'to ensure that as many official declarations or communications as are deemed to be of public interest be broadcast' (Article 13) with a statement giving the origin of such broadcasts. Priority for broadcasting live international sports competitions is reserved for the RTVE, although provision is made for simultaneous translation in the language of the Autonomous Community (Article 16). In addition, the regional company is not allowed to secure exclusive rights over programmes so that these cannot be transmitted in another region (Article 15) or acquire exclusive rights over events of national interest (Article 16).

Regional television in Spain is still largely at the drawing-board stage. Although several regional governments have expressed an interest in establishing a regional channel, the obstacles have not all been removed by the 1983 statute. Murcia and Andalusia, for example, have so far not pursued their plans because of an alleged lack of financial support.[39] Only two regions have so far gone ahead: the Basque country and Catalonia. The Basque parliament set up *Radio Televisión Vasca* in March 1982,[40] while the Catalonian parliament created *Corporación Catalana de Radio y Televisión* in May 1983.[41]

Basque television (*Euskal Telebista*) began broadcasting on 19 December 1982, while the Catalonian channel started transmissions at Christmas 1983. Both are examples of great interest since neither regional government is controlled by the Socialists.[42] It is too early to say, however, whether regional television will be an effective competitor to the state dominated system.[43]

The 1983 law also protects the dominance of the RTVE by giving the corporation exclusive rights over all broadcast and transmission systems using cable, satellite or any other means for direct or indirect transmission of signals over the national territory. As far as cable is concerned, back in March 1970 the government gave the national broadcasting service the right to control cable services. In 1972 RTVE signed a contract with the national telephone company, a commercial organisation enjoying a monopoly in Spain, allowing the installation of test networks in Madrid and Barcelona. However, while the main cables were laid, the necessary connection to individual households was never made, with the result that the experimental systems were never used. While the possibility of privately run cable television services has been raised by various groups recently, this would require new legislation opening up broadcasting to non-state interests.

CONCLUSION

The history of Spanish broadcasting since Franco's death has revealed the difficulties involved in creating a public service system independent of government control. To a large extent the legacy of Francoism in broadcasting has remained intact, particularly with regard to partisan political control of appointments and news output. In our view the best hope for the future lies not in merely reforming the state services, but in opening up the system to new interests. The UCD would probably have established some form of commercial television service if it had remained in power. On the other hand, the Socialist government has been traditionally hostile to any type of television not under state control.[44] However, there are some signs recently that attitudes within the Socialist Party and government may be changing. González has made vague noises about the institution of private television in the near future.[45] The development of 'new media' may encourage the Socialists to allow new forces to participate in broadcasting. But, until then, broadcasting in Spain (and television in particular) remains dominated by state and government, as it has been for so long.

NOTES

The authors would like to thank Raymond Kuhn and Tim Rees (St Antony's College, Oxford) for their helpful comments on a first draft of this article.

1. General works on Spanish politics include: R. Carr and J. P. Fusi, *Spain Dictatorship to Democracy* (London: Allen & Unwin, 1979); D. Bell (ed.), *Democratic Politics in Spain:*

Spanish Politics after Franco (London: Croom Helm, 1983); C. Abel and N. Torrents (eds.), *Spain: Conditional Democracy* (London: Croom Helm, 1984); P. Preston (ed.), *Spain in Crisis* (London: Harvester, 1976).
2. C. Soria, *Los orígenes del Derecho de Radiodifusión en España* (Pamplona: EUNSA, 1974).
3. The most important shareholders of SER are the Garrigues and Fontan families. Recently the newspaper *El Pais* has acquired nine per cent of the shares in the network. SER has 118 stations of which 54 are on the medium wave and 64 on FM.
4. On the period in Spanish broadcasting see V. Soria, *Historia de la Radiodifusión española* (Madrid: Martosa, 1934).
5. A. Faus-Belau, *La radio, introducción a un Medio desconocido* (second adition) (Madrid: Latina, 1981).
6. The range of radio stations was as follows:

	Stations
Cadena SER (Private)	54
Cadena REM/CAR (Franco Movement)	47
Cadena COPE (Church)	44
Cadena CES (Official trade union)	27
Radio Nacional (Official)	21
Cadena CRI (Private)	5
Cadena RATO (Private)	4
Cadena Radio Peninsular (Official with a commercial orientation)	8
Total	210

The restructuring initiated in the late 1960s also meant that all the radio networks were obliged to set up an FM station alongside each medium wave station.
7. J. Sinova, *La gran mentira: el tinglado de la televisión al descubierto* (Barcelona: Planeta, 1983), p. 30.
8. R. Graham, *Spain: Change of a Nation* (London: Michael Joseph, 1984), p. 236.
9. P. Macia, *Televisión, hora cero* (Madrid: Erisa, 1981), pp. 19–20.
10. R. Graham, op. cit., p. 236.
11. Ibid. On Suárez's period at the RTVE see G. Moran, *Adolfo Suárez, Historia de una Ambicion* (Barcelona: Planeta, 1979), pp. 201–51.
12. For an analysis of this process, see P. Preston, 'The PCE in the Struggle for Democracy in Spain' in H. Machin (ed.), *National Communism in Western Europe* (London: Methuen, 1983).
13. During the government of Carlos Arias Navarro an information 'slip' could have cost SER the loss of several radio stations.
14. At the time of the assault on Parliament, SER was the only Spanish radio station broadcasting 'live' the swearing-in of Leopoldo Calvo Sotelo as Prime Minister in place of Suárez. When the staff covering the event were forced to abandon their transmission, the SER team left their microphones on in such a way that the broadcast could still be heard on the radio. In this way the state security forces were able to follow the events as they were unfolding inside the Chamber of Deputies.
15. Article 3, Section 1.3. On the National Technical Plan for Broadcasting see *Boletín Oficial del Estado*, 9 Nov. 1978.
16. See A. Faus-Belau, 'El happening de las FM', *Nuestro Tiempo*, No. 333 (March 1982).
17. In this article we have not paid much attention to the topic of commercial television. On this subject see E. Lopez-Escobar, 'Spain Waits for Private Television', *Intermedia*, Vol. 11, No. 6 (Nov. 1983). Graham argues that 'Had UCD survived another year, commercial television would probably have been introduced'. R. Graham, op. cit., p. 238.
18. Law 4/1980, published in the *Boletín Oficial del Estado* on 12 Jan. 1980.
19. N. Torrents, 'Cinema and the Media after the Death of Franco', in C. Abel and N. Torrents (eds.), op. cit., p. 108.
20. The constitutionality of this law is currently being debated in Spain. See Manuel Jimenez de Parga, 'La libertad de TV: ¿decisión u obligación? in *La Vanguardia*, 2 Jan. 1983.
21. See Article 20, Section 4 of the Constitution.

22. J. Sinova, op. cit., p. 61.
23. Ibid., p. 79.
24. R. Graham, op. cit., p. 238.
25. J. Sinova, op. cit., p. 81. The press joined in the criticism. See, for example, 'TVE, olor a podrido', in *Tiempo*, 12 July 1982.
26. Ibid., pp. 89–90.
27. Ibid., p. 96.
28. Ibid., p. 105.
29. N. Torrents, op. cit., p. 108.
30. *El Pais*, 17 July 1983.
31. *Cambio 16*, 24 Jan. 1983. Alfonso Guerra, deputy Prime Minister, is usually blamed for the manipulation of the RTVE for political purposes.
32. A few days before the regional election in the Basque region a Socialist Senator was assassinated by the terrorist movement, ETA. TVE went to great lengths to report and comment on this event. On another occasion Spanish television had a minute's silence during a news programme in memory of the fallen Senator.
33. See, for example, *ABC*, 26 March 1984 and *Cambio 16*, 12 March 1984. The Catholic Church has complained of television coverage of religious issues and of its own role in Spanish history. See *YA*, 15 May 1984.
34. *Tiempo*, 11–18 April 1983.
35. R. Graham, op. cit., p. 238.
36. Radio networks operated by the Autonomous Communities are already functioning in both regions. Broadcasting is expected to begin in Galicia in October 1984.
37. Law 46/1983, *Boletín Oficial del Estado*, 5 Jan. 1984.
38. *El Pais*, 8 Jan. 1984.
39. *ABC*, 16 May 1984 and *La Vanguardia*, 1 June 1984.
40. *Boletín Oficial del Parlamento Vasco*, 30 June 1982.
41. *Boletín Oficial del Estado*, 6 July 1983.
42. A recent study on audience figures for the regional channel in Catalonia shows that in many parts of the region it is more popular than either of the two national channels. See *Anuncios*, 12–18 March 1984.
43. For a generally sympathetic account of Basque television's new channel see J. Howkins, 'Basques Use TV to Speak Their Own Language', *Intermedia*, Vol. 11, No. 3 (May 1983).
44. E. Lopez-Escobar, 'Spain Waits for Private Television', *Intermedia*, Vol. 11, No. 6 (Nov. 1983).
45. *El Pais*, 12 April 1984.

Greece: A Politically Controlled State Monopoly Broadcasting System

Dimitrios Katsoudas

The history of Greece over the past five decades has included periods of German occupation, civil war, military dictatorship, democratic government and, most recently, Socialist administration. At one level the impression conveyed is of a political system which is subject to frequent and abrupt change. However, this picture is by no means comprehensive, because there are also present strong elements of continuity. In this article we examine the nature of the relationship between the state and the Greek broadcasting services from a historical perspective, tracing the close links between the two from the establishment of radio in the 1930s through to the present-day Pasok regime. The article emphasises the overriding continuity of this relationship despite attempts at reform, structural reorganisation and changes of government. The picture which emerges is of broadcasting being used and abused for partisan political purposes by successive governing elites.

FROM ITS BIRTH TO THE END OF THE DICTATORSHIP

Radio and television in Greece both started their lives during periods of authoritarian rule. Regular radio broadcasts commenced as late as 1936, the year in which General John Metaxas, with the approval of King George II, established a dictatorship. Television also came to Greece remarkably late (1966–69) and its advent coincided with yet another dictatorship, that of the Colonels.

The first law regulating the status of broadcasting in Greece (Law 4551/ 1930) appeared just after a private citizen, Ch. Tsigirides, established a radio broadcasting station in Thessaloniki, Macedonia. This legislation was, in effect, little more than the recognition of a privilege ceded to another private individual, E. Makoglou. This law, which essentially regulated the status of radio in Greece prior to its takeover by the state, was withdrawn following the enactment of the 'Obligatory Law' of 19 November 1935.

Another 'Obligatory Law' inaugurated the era of direct state ownership of the broadcast media, creating a *Service of Radio Broadcasts* in the form of a public corporation.[1] Immediately afterwards, on 27 November 1936, the German company, Telefunken, was given the right to back technologically the new state organisation. Signed during the period of the German occupation, the Telefunken contract was declared void soon after the German evacuation of Greece (12 May 1945). 1945 saw the birth of EIR (the National Broadcasting Corporation) which – in one form or another – is the organisation still existing today.

Greek radio essentially took its present form in the decade 1945–55. As the end of German occupation was followed by the period of the civil war, which ended as late as 1949, the authoritarian climate of its birth was perpetuated not only for the duration of the Metaxas Dictatorship (1936–40), but also for the long period of the civil war and its seemingly endless aftermath. In fact the legal provisions for the media were a direct reflection of the prevailing political situation.

The legal framework of broadcasting for the entire period from 1945 to 1975, that is, up to a year after the fall of the Colonel's junta, was Law 2312/1953, entitled 'For the Organisation and Functioning of Greece's National Radio'. (This legal document was subsequently slightly altered and received additions at various intervals until its final abolition.) According to the founding law, EIR 'has the exclusive right of establishing and operating radio stations'.[2] It is noteworthy that the operation of private broadcasting stations was not prohibited, but was allowed only 'under special permit', a condition which was in effect extremely difficult to fulfil. In fact, Law 2312 established what essentially was – and has remained ever since – a state monopoly for the broadcasting media.

This monopoly was none the less seriously challenged, and in fact jeopardised, by the existence of the *Armed Forces Radio Stations*. The paramount importance of the military, particularly after the successful subjugation of the Communist revolt in 1949, could not be ignored, especially as the media were considered to possess obvious significance for the 'fight against Communism'. Obligatory Law 1663/1951, which brought these military stations into formal existence and declared that their purpose was to 'enlighten' and 'educate' the public, was a *de facto* recognition of the military's role in Greek life, a recognition which laid the foundations for many misfortunes in the nation's subsequent history. It is characteristic of the situation at the time that O.L. 1663 continued to be in force (a *special* law) even after the enacting of the aforementioned Law 2312 (a *general* one voted by Parliament). The state radio service had no say whatsoever in the running of this para-state Leviathan which was operated, controlled and financed directly by the Ministry of National Defence. As the military stations turned out to be very popular with listeners, not hesitating to 'flatter popular taste', they diverted precious revenues from advertising away from EIR, thus depriving the national network of scarce and valuable funds.

O.L. 1663/1951 was later abolished and replaced during the Colonels' junta by Act 722/1970 of the then military government. This Act created what came to be known as Yened, the *Armed Forces Information Service*. Yened was to be 'under the command of the Chief of Staff of the Armed Forces' and its purpose was 'the national, moral, and social education, as well as the training, information and entertainment of, primarily, the armed forces and the public at large'.[3] It is clear that the nation was now faced with an unprecedented (as well as constitutionally unacceptable) situation in broadcasting matters.

EIR, in the meantime, tried to organise itself as best it could. It was divided, unlike Yened, into three stations, the third coming into existence early in the 1950s as a cultural station of limited transmission range. (It was audible at that time only in Athens and its environs.) The first station, not unjustifiably called 'National', was solemn and 'serious'. It broadcast plays, music of all but the most trivial kinds, presented the most extensive news bulletins and so on. The second station which, like the first, had nationwide coverage, was an altogether more trivial affair. It allowed a large amount of advertising daily, had a fair number of programmes sponsored by commercial companies and broadcast much popular music: Greek, western, or otherwise. The third was – and is – the equivalent of Radio Three in Britain. In spite of conscientious efforts on the part of all those working there, it never really managed to escape the accusation of elitism which was – more often than not – directed against it. Its lack of sufficient personnel caused it to transmit classical music and opera incessantly with few attempts to analyse the output and develop critical thought – as happened after the dictatorship, particularly with Manos Hajidakis as its director.

The dynamics of the rapidly developing post-war Greek society affected the broadcasting media too. A great number of progressive plays and discussions, produced by talented people with democratic sympathies, did manage to change the tone, if not the content, of some programmes. Yet it was impossible to forget that Greek broadcasting was born in sin, under a dictatorship, and the political climate, even after the end of the civil war, was one of latent – when not overt – authoritarianism. The political system of the time has been described by Nicos Mouzelis as one of 'repressive parliamentarianism'[4] and this atmosphere could hardly leave the media unaffected. In a period of violent anti-communism the latter could scarcely escape the temptations of propaganda through the careful manipulation of news bulletins and other 'information' broadcasts.

The administrative structure of the broadcasting media was carefully designed to ensure absolute governmental control. The board of governors in effect dealt only with questions of finance and appointments, whereas the director-general (a true autocrat) was the one responsible for decisions regarding programming and scheduling. Dependence on the government was absolute, as all board members were appointed 'for two years' service by Royal Decree issued on the proposal of the minister to the Prime Minister'.[5] The minister 'has the right to expel – for reasons justifying his act – any member of the governing board', while later – under the junta – the 'Prime Minister' could do so at his own discretion.[6]

It is, of course, self-evident that the appointment of the director-general – in whose hands almost absolute power rested – was always a clearly political choice. Appointment and dismissal followed an almost identical course to that of any simple board member. There was, it has to be admitted, an advisory board which 'examines complaints, the observations of the press and those of private citizens'.[7] This board, however, for all practical purposes became totally inactive and was formally abolished in 1964.

Governmental manipulation – then, as always – manifested itself predominantly in the news sector. Article 5, para. 2 of Decree 3778/1957 expressly stated that 'the Minister to the Prime Minister can ask for all programmes and their texts to be submitted to him for approval'. This established not only censorship in general, but a preventive *a priori* one in particular. There was even a 'Council of Coordination and Control of Radio Broadcasts' created by an Act of the Council of Ministers.[8]

It is clear that, with a structure such as the above (only the essentials of which we have presented), there was little ground for developing further legal restrictions under the dictatorship which was established in April 1967. The dictators could, and did, simply *use* an 'efficient' administrative and legal machine, perfectly suited to the exercise of their now overtly authoritarian rule. During this period, which saw the arrival of television, Yened grew and became a fearful competitor for EIR (now named EIRT).

Greece, like Israel, was 'unnaturally' late in introducing television. Many reasons can be put forward for this delay in the Greek case. The organisation of radio itself took a long time to complete; and the establishment of a television network benefiting from equally carefully designed 'arrangements' required a considerable amount of preparation and planning. In the meantime the country possessed such an enormous number of cinemas (about 500 in the Athens area alone), employing whole sections of the population in distribution and servicing, that it would have taken a courageous political will to deflate such a prosperous sector. Furthermore, the problem of choosing the company (and its nationality) responsible for installing television in a period of studious and careful balance in Greece's relations with various European countries must also have played a role in the delay. It is, of course, futile to argue whether one or any of the above factors *determined* the belated arrival of television in Greece. It could simply have been that the governments of the day just avoided the necessary financial investment. In any case none of the elected governments which preceded that of the junta seriously undertook the installation of a television network.

There was another problem. Greece's geography is such that it would have been necessary to construct a very great number of transmitters on many of its hundreds of mountains and isolated islands. On the other hand, the establishment of a television network for only Athens, Salonika and the flat parts of the country (which could have been done quickly) would only have aggravated a tendency the sad consequences of which the country is still paying for: emigration to the great urban centres – with television serving as just one more attraction for settling there. Even today radio services – particularly those in FM – scarcely reach many areas, and for television coverage to be complete hundreds of transmitters have still to be constructed. None the less, the percentage of those unable to hear or watch today is minimal.

When discussing Greek broadcasting in the period before dictatorial rule was established we should be careful to avoid equating even the most problematic democracy with autocracy itself. For the prohibitions, restrictions and legal arrangements in existence before 1967 could scarcely alter an undeniable fact: that to all intents and purposes Greece was still a parliamentary democracy. Not far away from the EIR and Yened studios a free press and Parliament transmitted their own – infinitely more credible – messages. The broadcasting media could be largely ignored as agents of information and enjoyed only to the extent that they offered acceptable entertainment. Last, but not least, the judicial guarantees for state employees offered security and a recourse to any unfortunate broadcaster who might violate the rules. This meant that dissenting voices could be heard without the fear of political persecution, particularly if a cultural pretext could be used in the appropriate programme. There were, of course, limits to this tolerance: direct opposition to major governmental policies on 'national' issues was not condoned.

All this disappeared under the Dictatorship, for not only were there hardly any true guarantees left for anyone who might, however tentatively, attempt to oppose it, but the whole situation was now vastly different. Left-wing intellectuals and musicians were either in exile or in prison. Conservative politicians and many Conservative intellectuals, when not also in exile, were almost equally suspect. Furthermore, there could not now be any external 'balance', for the press too was thoroughly controlled.

The Junta's media 'philosophy' was so simple as to defy analysis. This period of broadcasting was in fact in even sharper contrast to the level of economic, political and cultural development of the Greek people. Greeks started listening to foreign broadcasts, mainly the BBC and *Deutsche Welle* for news and information. Others simply developed a healthy incredulity which, unfortunately, they retain to this day (and, sometimes, not so unfortunately).

In such an environment the importance of the broadcasting media, and particularly the all-powerful newcomer – television, was paramount. For the healthy reaction described above was by no means general; and there were people whose cultural and educational background made it very difficult for them to resist propaganda.

This propaganda was simple, but no less dangerous for that. As in the case of many an authoritarian regime, the country was presented as an oasis – thanks to the timely military intervention. Democracy was not attacked in principle, but no efforts were spared in convincing the Greeks that *their* democracy was 'sick' and in danger and that, therefore, 'surgery' was more than ever necessary. Communism was, of course, the scapegoat and attacks against it were a daily occurrence.

In the cultural field, naiveté reigned supreme. Football reached its apotheosis, while bouzouki music was almost constantly broadcast. It was to be realised only after the fall of the Dictatorship that present-day populism among other things has its roots in exactly that period of Dictatorial rule, and that the authoritarian regime's use of broadcasting was more far-reaching in its effects than it was originally considered to be. Broadcasting during the dictatorial period created a certain type of undemanding audience: culturally, popular taste was flattered rather than improved. It should also be noted that during this period it made little difference whether the audience was following EIRT or Yened as both were controlled by the military, the former directly and the latter indirectly. In fact Yened-TV, less burdened than EIRT which possessed an excessively large administrative apparatus, was quick to plan, with a high degree of success, populist and often vulgar, but more often than not popular, and widely viewed programmes.

FROM THE COLLAPSE OF THE DICTATORSHIP TO THE PRESENT-DAY

The Turkish invasion of Cyprus – as well as the Junta's coup against Makarios that led to it – were characteristically first made known to the Greek people through foreign broadcasts. This is, perhaps, an excellent illustration of the authoritarian regime's 'information' strategy. It became apparent, therefore, that the restored democracy, among its many other duties, ought to create broadcasting media that would be free, pluralist and effective in their cultural and informative role. Alas, this was unfortunately not to be the case, for whereas the new Constitution of 1975 establishes a truly free press, and indeed guarantees that the press will be free from any state intervention,[9] it formulates an almost diametrically different policy *vis-à-vis* the broadcasting media:

> Radio and Television shall be under the immediate control of the State, and shall aim at the objective transmission, on equal terms, of information and news reports as well as works of literature and art; the qualitative level of programmes shall be assured in consideration of their social mission and the cultural development of the country.

According to one of the architects of these constitutional arrangements, the reasons which led to the above provisions were various: 'tradition, political objectives (centralism), technical reasons (non-availability of radio waves) and economic factors (by 'economic' meaning the dispersal of revenue, or lack of it, for the state media if private, independent stations were allowed to operate).[10] The 'technical' reasons, which had originally been accepted by the German Federal Court (German legal practice has a tremendous impact in Greece), were already considered outdated there well before the adoption of the new Greek Constitution.[11]

As for the economic reasons, the existence of a myriad of private stations in the USA, and more recently in Italy, testifies to the fact that their coexistence with the state media is not always contradictory. On the other hand, it remains true that in most West European countries administrative control of the electronic media remains outside the sphere of the market economy and its forces, and that they are controlled, in varying ways, by their respective governments. In fact, the relevant article of the Greek Constitution is simply denying the autonomous private right to create and control the electronic media, but does not proceed to forbid it, leaving this to the discretion of the legislature, if it so wishes. As Professor Dagtoglou writes: 'From the constitutionally accepted "direct state control" emerges the state power to define – with a formal law – if, and under what conditions, individuals and/or market forces shall be allowed the *privilege* of broadcasting'.

As was to be expected, 'the Formal Law' was quick in ruling that radio and television were to continue their existence under the direct control of the state, administrative and otherwise. 1975 was a year of frantic activity accompanied by a considerable wave of optimism. The Greek government asked for the submission of an advisory report from Sir Hugh Greene, the former director-general of the BBC. Others, such as Alan Protheroe of the

BBC News Service, Joan Spicer of the British Television Institute and Felix Haydenberger of Bavarian Television were similarly asked to submit their own reports in preparation for the drafting of a new statute.

Sir Hugh Greene studied the situation carefully and diagnosed that EIRT (as it was then still called) was characterised by a colossal and slow-moving bureaucracy, the need for every minute expense to be approved by the Ministry of Economics, a very bad financial situation, an inefficient and awkwardly 'spread' administrative structure, technological backwardness and a lack of adequately trained professional personnel.

His first advice was to change the legal form of EIRT from a state enterprise to an organisation managed by the state but functioning as a private limited company. Sir Hugh claimed that such a solution would, among other things, psychologically help the EIRT employees to work to the best of their abilities. In addition, he recommended extensive decentralisation and a new flexible and effective employment strategy.

Sir Hugh was very careful to suggest a pluralist administration for the institution, as free as possible from direct governmental intervention. Therefore he proposed:

- A fifty-member advisory body comprising representatives from political parties, local government, the Church of Greece, the press, the 'market', several 'free professions', students' unions, etc. His catalogue, as he was quick to point out, was by no means exclusive. This body would check all the activities of the institution and guarantee pluralism and objectivity. (Sir Hugh thought that the German 'trans-party' system of public control was proven to be inefficient);
- a board of governors, comprising a chairman and six members to be appointed *after previous consultations with the leader of the opposition* (my italics);
- a director-general to be appointed by the board of governors and *not by the government* (my italics);
- the gradual absorbing of Yened by EIRT so that by 1976 one single organisation would comprise both TV channels and all radio stations.

Sir Hugh also suggested in detail various changes in the form and content of news bulletins and, indeed, in the structure and personnel of the whole information service. He also recommended the introduction of extensive educational programmes, the upgrading of cultural ones and the 'Hellenisation' of the programme output.

His report was enthusiastically received by the Greek press and public, irritated and disgusted by years of governmental control and manipulation of the media. The low quality of 'populist' films favoured by the Dictatorship was also intensely attacked – at least by the educated classes.

Unfortunately other considerations prevailed. As television in particular was a new and therefore formidable weapon, even the new democratic government could not resist the temptation of using it. Besides, the long tradition of state control of broadcasting made submission to this particular temptation easier. Nevertheless it was impossible to ignore completely either the public outcry or Sir Hugh's ideas. The government tried, therefore, to make the best of both worlds. But in all essentials the great opportunity which the restoration of a legitimate, wider and infinitely more pluralist democracy had offered was lost.

At the end of November 1975 the new legal framework for broadcasting (Law 230) came into existence.[12] Like its predecessors of the pre-dictatorship period it summarises admirably the politics of broadcasting in Greece – admirably but not quite as clearly. For the constraints of anti-communism were no longer present and governmental control had to be skilfully combined with liberal rhetoric. Indeed, some of this was even honest, since the restrictions as they were then applied, although betraying a profound conservatism, could not easily be labelled 'authoritarian'. It must also be taken into consideration that the all-powerful opposition press was probably causing the government considerable anxiety and television was seen as a means of counterattacking.

Several of Sir Hugh Greene's proposals had been accepted. Law 230 *did* abolish EIRT and, in its place, created – as Sir Hugh had suggested – a limited company, ERT (Hellenic Radio and Television), whose one shareholder was the Greek state.[13] Yened was temporarily retained but, it was stated, 'it shall merge with ERT when the necessary economic, technical and organisational conditions are ripe'.[14] It is characteristic that in Parliament the government had originally introduced the bill with the words 'it *may* merge' and it was the outcry of the opposition that led to its removal. The merger, it was optimistically suggested, would come after two years. In addition, the three basic administrative units suggested by Sir Hugh were now established: a director-general, a board of governors (with seven instead of the proposed six members) and a 'General Assembly'.

However, as a former news director of ERT observed, the government ignored the most basic suggestions of the foreign expert: 'The political power threw away the advice of foreign experts, with the same ease with which it had invited them to offer their advice.'[15] Whereas, for example, Sir Hugh believed that 'maximum decentralisation should be a major objective', the law concentrated most effective power in the hands of the director-general. In place of Sir Hugh's 'fifty-member body, representative of the nation at large', the law created a twenty-member General Assembly where governmental representation was in an overpowering majority and very little expertise was involved. Sir Hugh, as we saw, was explicit about the board of governors – it would be appointed by the Prime Minister (or the President of the Republic) after previous consultations with the leader of the opposition. In similar vein he had suggested that the board of governors would appoint the director-general. The law, on the other hand, finally ruled that the board of governors 'shall be appointed following *the decision of the Council of Ministers*'[16] and that 'the director-general and the two assistant general directors (unforeseen by Sir Hugh) shall also be appointed following the decision of the Council of Ministers'.

The letter, but not the spirit, of Sir Hugh's proposals had been partially retained. Th. Karzis draws one's attention to a 'detail' which caused Alan

Protheroe to protest. The law, in one of its liberal verbal 'outbursts', states that 'ERT broadcasts shall be permeated by the democratic spirit, a feeling of cultural responsibility, humanism and objectivity and they shall be *adjusted to Greek realities*' (my italics). To anyone who knows Greece at all 'Greek reality' is an excellent friend in need – a useful way of saying that one is not obliged to abide by the letter of what has been arranged. Alan Protheroe was quick to grasp this point, since in his own report he wrote:

> I also realise – and I sincerely hope that, at this point, I shall not be misunderstood or be considered arrogant – that these words, 'Greek reality', may in many cases be transformed into something like an excuse, a 'reason' for not reaching decisions and for the postponement of much needed change ....[17]

It is interesting to pause for a while and look at exactly how the law ensures tight governmental control of ERT (for Yened, as long as it remained administratively in the hands of the Defence Ministry, there could be no question of objective output). The director-general and his two assistants are not only directly appointed – and dismissed – by the government, but their qualifications are so vaguely defined as to allow the government to choose from among a very wide range of personalities, all of them more or less willing to serve its interests.

They must simply be 'well known' and be 'capable of contributing to ERT's aims through their special knowledge and experience'.[18] But people 'well known' enough for their expertise in broadcasting were scarce and, indeed, probably not particularly *wanted* either. In fact ERT director-generals in the course of the last nine years have been with one exception journalists and – more often than not – have found the task impossible, realising that there was more governmental control and censorship than even they had imagined. All in all, there have been no fewer than six director-generals of ERT since 1974, a situation which in itself testifies to the political and administrative problems faced by the incumbents.[19]

There is an obvious contradiction in the role of the director-general. He is, on the one hand, a complete autocrat of ERT, since not only the law but also ERT's internal statutes give him almost dictatorial powers. He can appoint and dismiss personnel, approve expenses – for considerable amounts of money – and he introduces to the board of governors anything which he considers to be in need of approval. The board accepts or rejects on the basis of his suggestions. However, on the other hand, the director-general is at the absolute mercy of the government since his appointment is clearly a matter of 'political will' on the part of the latter and he can be dismissed before the end of his term 'following a decision by the Council of Ministers' which, in Greece, means simply the Prime Minister.[20]

Obviously it becomes increasingly difficult to find a personality willing to sacrifice him/herself and, the more unsteady the post becomes, the more difficult it proves to find a director-general. Any incumbent faces another contradiction: he is the obvious target of the press and, through it, of the public at large. The public is virtually outraged at the lack of objectivity in the media. However faithful to the government, the director-general is invariably making concessions to public demands, allowing occasional anti-governmental 'messages' to pass through. This has offended the government more than once. Similarly, when public tolerance runs out, it is easy for the government to hold the director-general responsible and, therefore, through his dismissal, to whitewash itself of all responsibility. It is for reasons such as the above that most ERT heads have lost their post before they even had full knowledge of ERT's labyrinthine building in Ayia Paraskevi.

The board of governors becomes even more void of power when observed closely. Contrary to all accepted practice, the governors do not have the power to elect their chairman and vice-chairman, who are both *nominated* by the government 'by the same or similar decision'.[21] Their qualifications are as vaguely defined as those of the director-general and, more often than not, their only knowledge of ERT affairs is acquired through the director-general's reports. Most board chairmen disappear from the public eye soon after their appointment. There was recently, however, a notable exception, namely, Professor Constantine Beys who alone managed to come to the fore through frequent interviews with the press. However, he has been subsequently replaced as the law, in this case, also allows the replacement of any board member *before* the end of his/her term.

The General Assembly is, on closer inspection, even more of a caricature when compared to Sir Hugh's ideas. As we have already seen, it comprises twenty, instead of the proposed fifty, members and it is deliberately designed to be innocuous. Such people as general directors of ministries, university rectors, the President of the Council of State and that of the Athens Academy are members, while the Director of the Bank of Greece acts as the chairman.

Members of the General Assembly 'express their views on programming and on the output of the entire ERT organisation'. There is a faint vestige of pluralism: membership includes three representatives of the opposition. Like the other members, they can demand a meeting of the General Assembly, although the actual holding of the meeting is left to the discretion of the government. In fact, General Assembly meetings give the impression that the ERT is, after all, run democratically, since press headlines emphasise opposition views and protests. But protesting, or rather the right to do so at a meeting, cannot be equated with actually changing the course of the institution. The opposition cannot even successfully determine the course of the Assembly, let alone the entire administrative apparatus of the ERT.

THE *SUI GENERIS* CASE OF YENED

It is important to remember that, until almost recently, the military retained their own broadcasting and television system which, as we saw, was unified towards the end of the 1960s in what came to be known as Yened. The importance of Yened was dramatically enhanced with the advent of television, for if one can certainly ignore one of the four major radio stations it is difficult to do likewise with one of the two television networks. The Yened channel grew under the dictatorship and, without any of the reservations or traditions of 'quality' of the state organisation, it managed to leave the latter lagging far behind it in popularity. This was surprising for it lacked both the technical means and – to some extent – the money to progress. Why then was it so successful in attracting audiences?

It is interesting to follow Roviros Manthoulis, a television specialist who was among those most responsible for the amelioration of ERT programmes after the Dictatorship. Manthoulis[22] asks the question: what contributed to Yened's popularity? His answer could be summarised thus: facing the well-intended but then 'colourless' EIRT programmes, Yened chose a 'quantitative' approach. Yened in fact did possess a programming policy whereas EIRT had none. In its effort to win viewers and nothing else – and to maintain its revenues from advertising in order to cover programme costs – Yened, without even a sign of cultural consciousness, followed the system of the commercially successful networks in other countries and, most particularly, America; it constantly offered 'light' programmes bought mainly from American commercial networks. There has been no commercially successful American serial which Yened has ignored. Simultaneously, the entire stock of Greek Finos-Films (popular Greek films, mainly comedies) was bought and Greek serials, in the same vein, were rapidly ordered.

The merging of Yened with ERT (as the state broadcasting company came to be known after 1975 when Law 230 was enacted) was, of course, predicted in that law. The long functioning of Yened, parallel to that of EIRT and later, ERT, was unquestionably illegal – as Professor Dagtoglou, architect of Law 230/75 has shown.[23] It was 'an instrument of the armed forces, ill-suited to their constitutional position and the democratic, parliamentary nature of the country'.[24] What is, indeed, strange is the fact that there was no haste in abolishing it. Informed public opinion and the press demanded its immediate dismantling and merging with ERT. However, the critics of today tend to forget that in 1974–75 the situation was totally different. The military *surrendered* power to the civilian government, the latter did *not*, after all, acquire it by force. The dismantling of Yened would have been a serious blow against military pride. Furthermore, the overall situation was extremely dangerous, as Greece was almost about to go to war with Turkey. Nevertheless the *real* question remains: why did the New Democracy government not respond to public opinion – and its own law – and proceed with the merger? The answer probably is that once established and with its own Defence Ministry links, Yened became a sort of *fait accompli*.

After 1975 Yened was in any case little more than a shadow of its previously strong military self and competition with the rapidly changing ERT made the military channel more 'radical', 'progressive' and 'culturally minded'. All in all, apart from its name (and the obvious breach of the law), for the non-legally minded viewer, the existence of Yened was no more offensive than that of ERT. Nevertheless the functioning of Yened was unconstitutional, as Professor Dagtoglou has made clear:

> The merging of YENED with the new ERT, due for completion in the

course of two years 'if the necessary economic, technical and organisational preconditions are ripe' entails, in view of the unconstitutional nature of YENED (even more pronounced under the 1975 Constitution) that the government shall *create*, during the years 1976–77, those conditions [his italics].[25]

Yet essentially, nothing was done until 1981 when New Democracy lost power to the Socialists (Pasok). A draft law hastily prepared just after Greek EEC entry, and which was turning Yened into a public corporation but with strong connections with the military, was violently opposed. The Yened personnel this time rose in protest and openly declared that it was, after all, high time to abolish the military network. When in opposition, the Socialists had protested strongly against the continued existence of Yened. The time was now ripe for a change, and before a year elapsed ERT-2 came into existence. The, till then, military organisation was renamed ERT-2 and became 'an autonomous public service under the minister to the Prime Minister'. Under the Socialist government ERT-2 has become essentially a Pasok channel. Even more than ERT-1, where one often encounters certain traditional restraints, the former military channel has moved from favouring the *government* openly and unashamedly to favouring the *party* and a certain ideological approach.

BROADCASTING AND POLITICS IN GREECE: TOWARDS A CONCLUSION

It is worthwhile to pause and consider the actual *use* to which a state-controlled (and essentially state-run) broadcasting system has been put over the years. We have briefly indicated the nature of post-war, and particularly post-civil war, use: relatively naïve, patriotic, hailing the 'traditional values' of the nation and the 'glorious exploits of the Greeks'. There was little political *ideology* in the modern sense. Nationalism, such as it was, appeared rather innocuous and basically non-aggressive: the Greeks were 'great but wronged'. There is tremendous appreciation of their cultural contribution but, politically, they meet with little understanding. Communism is all around – and dreadfully dangerous. Democracy is precious, and only the Greeks enjoy it in the region. The monarchy is an element of continuity and, why not, *éclat*.

Were it not to sound like turning things into a '*reductio ad absurdum*' such would be the basic political undertones of radio broadcasts in the 1950s. For a considerable number of Greeks pressure for freeing the media from tight government control existed – but was not overwhelming. People read the newspapers of their choice and they were seemingly resigned to the fact that the radio was the voice of the government. The centre government which succeeded the right in power in 1963–64 almost unhesitatingly accepted that principle.

In spite of sparse resources, many programmes were enormously respected. The tone of cultural programmes was lofty, 'Europeanisation' an ideal, and artistic or social populism almost completely absent. When not governmental, broadcasting – at least in its cultural aspects – could often be 'national'. During the dictatorship period, however, the political element was turned into sheer propaganda while culturally an almost completely different set of values (apart, of course, from the usual 'national' ones) prevailed.

The fall of the dictatorship led to a change in the broadcasting field. As expected, the desire for totally free expression was paramount: seven years of silence fed it with an almost Protean power. However, Law 230/75 while abiding to the principle of objective and impartial information was in fact a conscious attempt to manipulate the media. Whether a reaction to the predominantly centre-left press or otherwise, it was an erroneous and ultimately costly political decision. The politics of broadcasting could no longer count either on the consensus or, indeed, the apathy of the electorate. The dictatorship had radicalised the country in more than one way.

Having made their political decision, the Conservative government adopted what the first minister responsible for broadcasting, called the 'principle of neutrality'. Mr Lambrias admitted:

> It is a dangerous principle, for it means that broadcasting is 'national', and does not favour parties – or propagate ideologies. It never attacks opposition parties and refuses to advertise the Conservative party's activities. Characteristically, the first New Democracy (ND) Congress in Chalcidiki was not given any but the most casual coverage.[26]

Constantine Karamanlis, then Prime Minister, expressed the view that 'party' politics in television 'divide the nation'. But, as a political analyst mildly put it, 'ND's distinction between party politics and governmental policies was seriously flawed .... Time and again the channels presented ND's governmental activities, and various ministers explained in long monologues their aims and the effects of their policies'.[27]

The press was furious, while the public did not appreciate the fine and subtle distinctions inherent in the so-called 'principle of neutrality'. For them it meant silencing the opposition – except in electoral periods when the broadcast media were extremely fair, allotting considerable time to all parliamentary parties. It is a pity that such short-sighted policies were followed for – after 1974 – programme output was markedly improved. The general tone and cultural atmosphere of broadcasting was now quite liberal and – apart from governmental activities – there were few attempts at propaganda. Indeed, quite often, the Conservative press complained of 'the extensive penetration of Radio-TV by "Communists"', an allegation which proved to be surprisingly accurate after the advent of Pasok to office.

During the electoral campaign of 1981 which brought Pasok to power, a cleverly designed poster invariably attracted public attention – and sympathy: 'PASOK wants to and *can* liberalise television'. In fact few electoral promises have been so blatantly ignored. Essentially the change-over to a Socialist government was even more detrimental to the objectivity of the broadcasting media.

There were many changes introduced. Some were positive. For example, the 'principle of neutrality' was completely abandoned. Opposition statements were aired (although not always in their complete form) and party congresses and important rallies televised. Opposition leader Averoff spoke twice 'to the nation'. Representatives of local government and youth movements, as well as people in remote villages, were frequent television guests. But the true face of 'Socialist' television soon became apparent; serials, commentaries, discussions and interviews, all aimed at nothing less than the propagation of a given ideology – in this case – Marxism.

The introduction of party politics, incomplete and 'edited' as it was, served only as a smokescreen for a propaganda campaign the like of which would have made even the dictatorship blush. The main targets of this propaganda were the 'Right', 'Imperialism', 'Capitalism', the Church (now less frequently than in the early months), the Americans, occasionally Western Europe and every single EEC country in particular. Western Europe faces 'a crisis of the system' and the EEC is 'constantly finding itself at a dead-end'. Endless Pasok meetings or party talks occupy a predominant place (often the first) in news bulletins whose contents, not unusually, could easily be labelled 'Mr Papandreou's day'. Dissenting voices are heard as, for example, in discussions on 'Marxism', 'productivity' and so on, but in the former, three out of the four discussants were Marxists, while in the latter, only one out of a total of seven was a free-marketeer. 'Peace' was discussed with three pro-Soviet and one mildly pro-Western discussant. These examples, it should be noted, are by no means exceptional.

Governmental 'replies' are often broadcast before one has heard who exactly has accused the government. In the 1984 European elections campaign, time was lavishly offered – to the Socialist government's credit – to even the most insignificant contestants. In fact, almost nowhere in Europe is television more open in electoral periods than in post-dictatorial Greece. But the leader of the opposition's speech in Patras was inexplicably postponed for an hour so as to coincide with a popular Greek comedy on the other channel. His other speech in Salonika was not announced in the widely viewed Saturday afternoon news (it was to be given on Saturday night) and, just before it was televised, a lengthy 'answer' of the governmental representative was given – to an audience who had not yet heard the speech! Socialist television is mainly, as *The Times* observed recently, 'rewriting Greek history and whitewashing the Left over its role in the civil war.... An air of vindictiveness and of the revival of old passions pervades it'.[28]

Certain positive trends were for a time visible. After the European elections, governmental abuse of broadcasting was considered by even the most dedicated pro-Pasok newspapers – and most voters too – as unacceptable. 'We are tired of hearing that television was bad under ND, for it is now markedly worse' is the tone of many a pro-government columnist. Discussions were more balanced and news bulletins less one-sided. Pasok seemed to be realising the dangers of overt manipulation. However, the election in September 1984 of Constantine Mitsotakis as the leader of ND, coupled with Papandreou's strong personal dislike of him, has once more led the government to exert pressure on the broadcasting media. Old habits die hard in Greece. There is, moreover, little sign of change elsewhere. The 'new media' of cable and satellite have had as yet no impact on Greece, while the advent of a commercial television channel is only now being considered within the ranks of the New Democracy as it adopts a neo-liberal economic approach. The hold of the politically controlled state monopoly over broadcasting will not be easily shaken.

NOTES

1. O.L. 95/1936.
2. L. 2312/1953, Article 2.
3. Act 722/1970, Article 101.
4. N. Mouzelis, *I Ptosis ton Dictatorion* (Athens: Papazisis, 1975).
5. Act 3778/1957, Articles 6 and 3.
6. Act 745/1970.
7. Law 2312/1953, Article 12.
8. Act 85, June 1959.
9. 1975 Constitution, Article 15.
10. P. Dagtoglou, writing in *Nomikon Vima*, Vol. 29, p. 270.
11. See, for example, Lerche, *Rundfunkmonopol ...*, 1970.
12. Law 230, 27 November 1975.
13. Law 230, Article 1.
14. Law 230, Article 4.
15. Th. Karzis, *I Elliniki Tileorasi* (Athens: Kaktos, 1981), p. 88.
16. Law 230, Article 10.
17. Alan Protheroe, *News and Current Affairs Broadcasting in ERT TV: Report and Recommendations*, in Th. Karzis, op. cit., p. 35.
18. Law 230, Article 12.
19. P. Bakoyannis, appointed in the summer of 1974, resigned before the elections due for November of the same year following a disagreement with the government about television coverage of those elections. He was replaced by another journalist, J. Lampsas, who lasted from the end of 1974 to late 1977. His successor, the sole non-journalist, K. Hondros, kept the post until his death in 1981.
    Since the 1981 Pasok election victory the director-generals have included G. Romeos (late 1981 to early 1984), D. Kassimis, who was dismissed after the European elections of June 1984, and the present incumbent, Vassos Mathiopoulos. All three have been journalists. With the sole exception of Hondros (and the present director-general), all the others were dismissed following disagreement with the government over an aspect of policy. It is a matter of speculation what the fate of Mathiopoulos will be.
20. Law 230, Article 12.
21. Law 230, Article 10.
22. R. Manthoulis, *To Kratos tis Tileorasis* (Athens: Themelio, 1981).
23. P. Dagtoglou, *Radio-Television and the Constitution* (Athens: Sakkoulas, 1978), p. 31.
24. T. Doulkeri, *Radio and Television: Their Legal and Social Problems* (Athens: Papazisis, 1979), p. 78.
25. P. Dagtoglou, op. cit., p. 166.
26. Interview with the author.
27. J. Loulis, *The Athenian* (Feb. 1984), p. 14.
28. *The Times*, 6 June 1984.

The Politics of Cable and Satellite Broadcasting: Some West European Comparisons

Kenneth Dyson

The history of modern Europe is littered with examples of the way in which technology can decisively influence politics: artillery, railways, telephones and nuclear power come immediately to mind. One of the striking areas of technological innovation in this century has been communications. 'Off-air' radio and (later) television broadcasting were clearly communications technologies of enormous political and economic potential, associated with the emergence of a mass, and apparently captive, national audience. In the 1970s it became clear that communications in general, and broadcasting in particular, were about to undergo further major (indeed a set of) technological transformations. Satellite communications and 'broadband' cable indicated a 'third age of broadcasting', as part of a new 'wired society' in which there would be a massively expanding market for information.[1]

As far as West European politics is concerned, the new communications technologies had two major features: the rapid breaking down of the barriers between broadcasting policy and industrial policy, as economic and commercial issues gained momentum; and the opening up of strongly national telecommunications and broadcasting markets, as industrialists and broadcasters saw the possibility of, and need for, new European-wide markets. Broadcasting was subsumed in the information technology revolution and in the efforts of European governments individually – and, to an extent, collectively – to capture rapidly expanding international markets for information, entertainment and electronics.

In the early 1980s cable and satellite television captured the imagination of governments, industrialists, broadcasters and film producers. Governments of very different political complexions presented communications and broadcasting as glamorous areas for investment and growth; they invested considerable political prestige in various new projects, notably to capitalise on indigenous expertise in telecommunications and aerospace. Yet the political processing of the new policies proved difficult and time-consuming in all states. Clear, bold political strategies dissolved into a confusing picture. Cable and satellite television appeared as highly speculative investments, their economics fragile and their technologies complex, changing and competing. Market research into potential consumer demand for additional entertainment and new interactive services yielded inconclusive results, whilst technological change, notably in optical fibre cable and in satellite transmission capacity, altered the balance of advantage amongst rival communications systems. In addition, the availability of sufficient high-quality programming to justify consumer investment in, and subscription to, the new technologies emerged as a major constraint.

The politics of cable and satellite development has revolved around the age-old questions of who controls the technology, for what purpose and by which means. Some governments attempted to give clear answers. For example, in Britain investment in the new media technologies was to be led by the private sector, exploiting the market for entertainment; government's role was to encourage competition. In France, by contrast, the state was to play the leading role, thereby ensuring that France entered the new industrial age on time and that her aerospace and telecommunications industries had a major presence in key world markets.[2] In practice, governments discovered that the purposes to which the new communications technologies could be applied were complex, ambiguous and often controversial. These various purposes kindled the enthusiasms and anxieties of a large range of groups, each of which sought to influence public policy, often exploiting privileged access to a ministry.

Cable and satellite technologies could serve three main purposes. One is that they offered the possibility of a wider range of television programmes, of specialised programming (narrowcasting) and of stimulating a new generation of independent producers. Already the huge growth of the video cassette recorder (VCR) market had indicated a desire for greater personal choice in viewing. The home was becoming a TV-based entertainments centre, and a commercial struggle was on, particularly with the United States and Japan, to see who could establish the dominant technological format.

For some, the central feature of the new media technologies was freedom of choice, a liberation from the constraints of scarcity of wavelengths that had been associated with traditional 'off-air' broadcasting. The liberal promise of a new openness of communications internationally and of greater choice individually was given strong political expression in France by Jacques Chirac (mayor of Paris and leader of the main opposition party, the RPR) and in West Germany by Christian Schwarz-Schilling, Federal Minister of Posts and Telecommunications in Bonn's Christian Democrat–Liberal coalition. This liberal promise, as much as any pressures from technology and commercial lobbies, played a major role in encouraging governments to embrace cable and satellite technologies. There were, nevertheless, important voices urging caution. Helmut Schmidt intervened personally in 1979 to block the cable plans of the Federal Post Office, believing that 'more would mean worse' and advocating a 'television-free' day each week; his political party, the Social Democrats (SPD), feared the political implications of private commercial television, operated by publishing groups close to the Christian Democrats. Gaston Deferre, a veteran Socialist politician and Interior Minister in Paris, saw a serious political threat if cable television fell into the hands of right-wing local authorities, whilst the Dutch Minister of Culture, Eelco Brinkman, a Christian Democrat, expressed fears about standards and about the quality of family life in the new age of broadcasting.

The other two purposes of cable and satellite technologies were even more closely bound up with economic and industrial strategy. Technologies that can promise 'modernisation' (particularly when there is a 'knock-on' effect to the wider economy), 'international competitiveness' and 'jobs' have immense political appeal, especially in a period of protracted economic recession. In the first place, the new technologies would provide a major stimulus to the electronics and aerospace industries. Telecommunications was emerging as a strategic industrial resource in world markets; national telecommunications authorities were increasing their investment rates whilst, in 1983–84, the European Community began to show an interest in an integrated telecommunications policy in order to build a stronger European industry. The French government was still mesmerised by the mission to overcome France's technological backwardness in telecommunications as well as keen to exploit her European lead in space technology. Success of the newly nationalised electronics corporations, notably CGE and Thomson, was also a major consideration for a French Socialist government. The British government was pressed to take advantage of a British lead in European optic fibre development and to act to make up for a lost lead in space technology since the early 1960s.

Second, well-tested coaxial cable or the newer optical fibre cable could create a broadband 'electronic grid', carrying not just more television channels but a whole range of interactive communications services, from video-conferencing and videotext to tele-banking, tele-shopping and home security services. Lord Weinstock of GEC has spoken of an 'electronic motorway system' and Kenneth Baker, the British Minister for Information Technology, of a new industrial revolution equivalent in significance to the earlier railway and telephone revolutions. In 1983 the French Industry Minister (and now Prime Minister) Laurent Fabius referred to France's ambition to be 'the third electronic nation of the world' (after the United States and Japan). Schwarz-Schilling presented his plan to cable Germany at the rate of one billion DM per year as a major contribution to the new coalition's aim of expanding long-term employment. Yet he had to revise downwards his estimate of jobs created per one-billion DM investment from 'up to 23,000' to 13,900–14,400. In a paper for the National Economic Development Council in 1984 British Telecom indicated that an annual investment of £350–£400 million in cable television was likely to create only some 6,000 permanent jobs. The German Trade Union Federation (DGB) argued that broadband cable was in fact likely to lead to a massive loss of jobs in the service sector; cable was attacked as an assault on 'the mind, bank account and job' of the employee. Furthermore, by facilitating home-based working patterns cable threatened employee solidarity and hence the effectiveness of trade unionism.

Given these complex facets of the new media technologies, a kaleidoscope of positive and negative, politicians throughout Western Europe found it difficult to gain a clear and steady grasp of the issues. In common they had many difficulties. First, they had to master the new technologies – to learn a language including such terms as 'fibre optics', 'coaxial cable', 'broadband', 'tree-and-branch', 'switched-star', 'interactive services', 'narrowcasting', 'transponders', 'decoders', 'dishes', 'C-MAC' and 'E-PAL', 'headend' and 'churn rates'.

At first glance cable and satellite television could seem deceptively simple technologies. Cable television is a communications system that delivers television programmes and, in modern broadband systems, a wide range of telecommunications services via a cable which is normally laid in the ground in ducts. Broadband cable (that is, one able to carry a wide portion of the spectrum) may be either the tried-and-tested coaxial (with a copper conductor) or the new optical fibre (which, by using light pulses through a thin core of glass, can carry limitless bandwidth, is immune to interference from outside signals and has a very low loss of signal power).

Satellite television may be transmitted either via medium-powered satellite to cable operators for distribution over the cable network or via Direct Broadcast by Satellite (DBS) to small dishes attached to individual homes. In geostationary orbit some 22,300 miles high above the equator a DBS satellite requires powerful transponders to receive and transmit signals. Medium-powered satellites like the European Communications Satellite series are complementary with cable, helping to enrich the diet of programmes. By contrast, DBS is competitive, with the particular attraction being that it becomes available nationwide to a large proportion of the population the moment it starts to operate.

The language of the new media does in fact hide a speed of technological change that is continuously altering technological and political assessments. Past decisions, for instance, about the type and power of satellites, are rapidly overtaken by new developments. Thus in a report on DBS in 1984 Gérard Théry, former head of telecommunications (the DGT) in the French Ministry of Posts, concluded that major improvements in the effectiveness of receiving equipment for satellite transmissions had cast doubt on the need for the high-powered and very expensive satellites already planned for DBS. In 1982 the political spotlight fell on France's 'over-ambitious' plan to cable France with optical fibre cable; by 1984 the focus of criticism had shifted to the macroeconomic and technological costs of Schwarz-Schilling's plan to cable Germany with 'old-fashioned' coaxial cable.

West European policy-makers were also attentive to American experience of cable, for the United States had a well-established cable television 'industry'. In 1983 more than 40 per cent of American homes were cabled, with 'cable' homes spending some 16 per cent more time watching television. Much could be learnt about the nature of the market (usually younger, affluent families with children and a video); about the importance of satellite transmissions for programming of local cable systems; about the importance of marketing the 'tiers' of programmes in order to achieve a sufficiently high take-up rate for profitability (around 30 per cent) and to overcome a potentially high turnover of subscribers (the 'churn' problem); about how bidding wars for new franchises can produce extravagant promises and poor profitability; about the difficulty that DBS has in establishing itself once a cable television industry is in place; and about the emergence of a *de facto* DBS as viewers buy their own large dishes to 'pirate' existing satellite transmissions. Perhaps most strikingly, the demise of channels like *CBS Cable, Satellite News Channel* and the *Entertainment Channel* revealed the dangers of hyper-expansion and helped inject a note of caution, notably amongst the financial institutions after 1982. By 1983–84

CBS, Western Union and Rupert Murdoch's News International were abandoning or deferring their DBS plans for the United States.

The formulation of public policy in Western Europe for cable and satellite television took place, then, against a background of conflicts of priorities (for example, entertainment versus interactive services, defence of national identity versus freedom of communications), of rapid technological change and of the 'shake-out' in the American industry. The policy process revealed alternative faces of confidence (for example, in French space technology) and uncertainty (for instance, about France's DBS plans). Overall, the impression was of enormous complexity, as a range of forces collided and converged, of turbulence confronting policy-makers, of a mixture of bold plans with confusion in government about the future of broadcasting as part of sweeping changes in larger communications systems. It was clear that a radical redefinition of the purposes and forms of regulatory policies for broadcasting was necessary. If politicians were prepared to ignore such a need, external threat from European neighbours (for example, Luxembourg) or the United States and Japan served to awaken them.

Cable and satellite television were raising new issues that crossed the boundaries of traditional policy communities in telecommunications, industry and broadcasting. They were generating new, rather loose policy networks, characterised by a nucleus of committed actors (whose professionalism, time and money were invested in the technology) and mobile actors (who were seeking to find the most promising niche in new media markets).[3] An electronics conglomerate like Thorn-EMI could encompass cable television operation, cable programming (the premium movie-channel *Premiere*) and a role in DBS programming; whilst a national telecommunications carrier like British Telecom embraced cable-laying and operation, programming and DBS manufacture. In Germany the press, a traditional lobby for private commercial television, sought a programming role in satellite transmission and in the four pilot cable television projects; in Britain Robert Maxwell's publishing company, Pergamon Press, sought to acquire the cable television interests of the largest cable television operator, Rediffusion. In short, the policy process was strikingly fluid; actors' perceptions changed in line with a fast-moving situation. Questions of political and industrial strategy were entangled with the engineering problems of technologists and the managerial and marketing problems of commercial organisations which have to sell cable and satellite television to the public and to advertisers.

CABLE TELEVISION IN WESTERN EUROPE

In Western Europe there are two major conceptions of cable: first, as an entertainment system, an optional luxury good that is best provided by private firms within a framework of public regulation; and second, as an advanced broadband communications system, a functional requirement for the whole economy and hence placed under the direct control of a national telecommunications authority. In Britain cable television has been associated with private ownership and finance and predicated on commercial judgements, while in France and Germany it has been linked with public-sector investment that is prepared to anticipate need even though existing demand is unclear.

In Britain the decisive political breakthrough came with a report from the Cabinet Office's Information Technology Advisory Panel in February 1982. The ITAP report reflected the values of Thatcherism – more market, less state, more competition, less regulation – and, in advocating a reliance on entertainment services to finance the new 'wired society', threw overboard the hostility to cable television voiced in the Annan Report on the Future of Broadcasting in 1977.

Lord Hunt's committee on cable expansion and broadcasting policy reported in September 1982. The Cable Authority proposed by Hunt was a central feature of the Cable and Broadcasting Act of 1984. It was to grant licences on the basis of very general criteria (the Act spoke only of 'a proper proportion' of British/EEC programming) and to supervise programmes 'with a light touch'. An attempt was made to give momentum to cable television in two ways: after assessments by the Economist Intelligence Unit and recommendations from 'the three wise men', 11 interim franchises were awarded in November 1983 ('new-build' systems); and 11 existing cable operators, notably Rediffusion, were granted temporary licences to 'upgrade' their systems.

The enthusiasm for developing the new cable television systems was then dissipated by legal snags that meant that licences were not issued till summer 1984; by a major change in the economics of cable with the phasing-out of capital allowances in the 1984 budget; and by longer-than-expected lead times in the development of the switching technology. Having given priority to private-sector investment in cable, the government did not do enough to reassure cautious financial institutions. Having rejected British Telecom's view that it should develop an integrated national electronics grid, the government protected its profitable telephony services by not offering them as an inducement to cable operators. Finally, having given the go-ahead to private cable operators, the government protected the BBC and IBA by giving them exclusive control of broadcasting major national events. In short, a dynamic strategy launched from the centre fell foul of the fragmentation of responsibilities in the field of communications. The Home Office and the Department of Trade and Industry remained strongly influenced by powerful vested interests.

The French approach to cable television was more comprehensive, determined and imaginative. The bold cable plan of November 1982 had its roots in the diagnosis of French technological backwardness contained in the Nora Report of 1978 and in the ending of the state's legal monopoly of broadcasting with the Law on Audiovisual Communication of July 1982. As presented by the Socialist Industry Minister, Jean-Pierre Chevènement, cable television was part of a grand industrial design to wire every household to a national network, using optic fibre cable and switched-star technology. By 1992 six million French homes were to be wired at a cost of 12 billion fr. In 1983 a *Mission sur la Télédistribution* was established under a Socialist deputy, Bernard Schreiner, to revive 12 earlier cable experiments and, more significantly, to encourage and stockpile 2,000 hours of French programmes for the new channels.

Then, after a period of reflection and bitter argument, the French cabinet took a series of major decisions on cable television in April 1984. Although the pace of cabling was slowed to take account of tighter budgetary constraints and the need to develop an indigenous production capacity, the state-led national approach remained: the national posts and telecommunications authority was to construct and own the network and control all transmissions; in return it was to play the major financing role; public and private interests were to have equal influence in the local cable television systems, but initially private companies were to be limited to only one network; a limit of foreign programming to about 30 per cent of the total was designed to frustrate proposals, like that of Chirac for Paris, to run entire foreign channels; whilst, in order to develop the French programming industry, one-third of cable television revenues was to be used to finance original programmes. The French approach to cable indicates: the capacity for bold, resolute plans to survive intense factional in-fighting within central government (especially from the DBS lobby and from the pay-TV lobby grouped around the new off-air fourth channel *Canal plus*); the clear priority attached to industrial policy; the greater prestige of the DGT than of French public broadcasting; and the influence of the cinema lobby in France.

The West German approach to cable television combines certain features of Britain and France with its own distinctive approach. Given the fragmentation of responsibilities in a federal system – with telecommunications a federal matter and broadcasting/cultural policy a *Land* (state) concern – the possibilities for delay and frustration were even greater than in Britain. A party in power at one level could seek to undermine the efforts of a party in power at the other level. At the same time there were certain similarities with France. In both cases a political party had just returned to national political power after many years in opposition (the CDU/CSU since 1969; the French Socialists since the 1950s). The French and German governments, although very different in political complexion, harboured strong resentments against public service broadcasting organisations through which, they believed, injurious party political influence had been brought to bear against them in the past. Also, despite early talk of greater competition and deregulation in telecommunications, cabling was seen in Germany as essentially a national investment programme, controlled and financed by the Federal Post Office.

Influential Social Democrats saw broadband cable as a Trojan horse for private commercial television, provided by interests close to the CDU/CSU. Hence in 1979 the Schmidt cabinet blocked Post Office plans to cable 11 German cities. Despite this 'blockade' of cable two developments took place: the decision by the heads of state governments in the Minister-Presidents' Conference to hold four pilot projects (with Berlin, Dortmund, Ludwigshafen and Munich as sites) and the appointment of a new media enthusiast as Federal Post and Telecommunications Minister by the new CDU/CSU/FDP coalition in 1982. Although the decision to hold pilot projects was taken in 1978, the first two did not come into operation till 1984, in part because of SPD procrastination. More significantly, Schwarz-Schilling announced in 1982 a plan to cable 50 per cent of German homes by 1990 at a cost of one billion DM a year. It was also emphasised that priority in investment would be given to those states that created a clear legal basis for more diversified programming.

The first major casualty of the 'unblocking' of cable was the unitary structure of broadcasting. Broadcasting was a state prerogative, organised by *Land* law and treaties, with a shared second channel (ZDF) and collaboration of the various regional stations in ARD. Now, both for ideological reasons and to attract the new federal investment, CDU *Länder* began to draft their own new media laws to encourage private programming. They also sought to encourage a private German consortium for a new satellite channel. Faced by this pressure, and by pressure from SPD local authorities which wanted the new cable investment, SPD *Länder* governments began to press for an adaptation of SPD policy away from outright opposition to private television towards a concern for effective social control. That adaptation took place in 1984, just after the poor starts by the Ludwigshafen and Munich projects and as the Federal Audit Court issued a highly critical report on Schwarz-Schilling's cable plan (for its underestimate of costs and overestimate of take-up rate). Schwarz-Schilling was criticised not only for a cable enthusiasm that bordered on the naïve and arrogant, but also for overinvestment in the old-fashioned coaxial cable, again an expression of unwillingness to wait for, or press German industry to provide, optic fibre cable. Yet the problems of processing cable policy in Germany went far deeper than Schwarz-Schilling. They were rooted in a constitutional division of responsibilities between telecommunications (federal) and broadcasting (*Land*), making unified political direction in the new policy network difficult, if not impossible.

In the case of the Netherlands the problem of unified political direction in the cable policy network had its main basis not in the territorial distribution of powers but in divisions within the governing coalition of Christian Democrats (CDA) and Liberals (VVD). The Netherlands has one of the most regulated broadcasting systems in Western Europe, with only two national channels, broadcasting about six hours a day and advertising restricted to two ten-minute blocks. Neither channel is the exclusive preserve of any one broadcasting organisation: the eight broadcasting organisations represent the ideals of different social and religious groups and, along with the 'neutral' Netherlands Broadcasting Foundation (for news and sport), guarantee a serious-minded programming. Similarly, Dutch cable systems cannot originate programmes (although they do offer Belgian and German channels and, since 1984, Rupert Murdoch's *Sky Channel*). Nor can they carry advertising or pay-TV. Yet during the 1980s technological and political forces for liberalisation gained momentum. The popularity of pirate broadcasting between 1979 and 1981 indicated substantial public demand for new programming. Also, with 65 per cent of the population cabled, the Netherlands had the second-most extensive cable system in Western Europe (after Belgium). The cable system was under-utilised and easily accessible for new programming. By 1983 there were pressures for a third national channel, for more broadcasting time for the existing channels and for a subscription satellite channel. As far as interactive services were concerned, the Dutch government remained cautious – despite its reputation as a model of telecommunications with the opening of the world's first computer-controlled telephone exchange in Rotterdam (1971), the presence of a major optical fibre cable manufacturer in NKF-Kabel (a subsidiary of Philips) and Philips' collaboration with AT & T on digital switching equipment. The most advanced cable technology was tested in two long-term experiments (in Geldrop and in three Limbourg towns) where it became clear that full interactive services were unlikely to be financially viable till the mid-1990s.

Just how controversial broadcasting could become had been shown in 1965 when a Dutch government had fallen on the issue of introducing television advertising. The form in which the government of Ruud Lubbers (a Christian Democrat) attempted to heal the divisions within the coalition only opened up a serious divide between cabinet and Parliament. When Brinkman, the Christian Democrat Minister of Culture, presented his controversial White Paper on Broadcasting in August 1983, it was clear that the smaller Liberal Party had won major concessions. Christian Democrats, who unlike many of their German equivalents were strong supporters of public broadcasting, were disappointed that the proposal for a third 'conventional' channel was rejected. The intention was to leave the field clear for a subscriber satellite channel, to be operated only by new commercial organisations. The satellite channel was to have a 'reasonable' Dutch content (Brinkman spoke optimistically of 20 per cent). Satellite broadcasting was to be allowed into the Netherlands as long as it originated with a company registered there, was not compiled specifically for Dutch audiences and did not contain advertisements aimed solely at the Dutch market. The major concession to the traditional broadcasters was that the two national channels were to be given more broadcasting time. Overall the major winner seemed to be the commercial organisations with an interest in the satellite channel – *Euro-TV* (a subsidiary of the Belgian publishers Dupuis) and the Dutch publishing groups Elseviers and VNU. However, in Parliament Christian Democrats combined with the Labour Party to reject both the proposal that there should be no third channel and the view that only new commercial organisations should play a part in the new satellite channel.

What has come out most clearly from this survey of policies for cable television is how the character of the policy network is shaped by whether constitutional factors (like German federalism), coalition factors (as in the Netherlands) or bureaucratic mores (such as the British style of negotiation with groups) facilitate or, more likely, impede a unified political direction of telecommunications and broadcasting. Pronouncement of a bold governmental plan, whether state- or market-orientated, is one thing; being able to achieve unified political direction is quite another. In France, at least, policy-makers are able to take seriously the idea of a unified communications policy, of which the cable plan is a major part.

Two other important influences on the policies for cable television are closely related: the technology already in place and the structure of interest group politics. Thus in the Dutch case cable penetration was high (65 per cent) and the cable-operating industry well established. Correspondingly, debate focused on how to use the surplus capacity, in other words, on satellite programming. Britain too had a strong Cable Television Association and in Rediffusion the largest private cable television operator in Europe. The Cable Television Association was stirred to action not just by the new technologies but by the many loss-making older relay systems that were having to be closed. The number of British households linked to cable television fell from 1.6 million to 1.3 million between 1980 and 1984. By arguing from its strengths (for example, technological experience) the Cable Television Association was able to exert influence on the ITAP report and, hence, on the general direction of policy in Britain. More problematic, but highly important, was the relationship between the VCR market and cable television. The British VCR market was the first to mature, in large part because of the strength of the television rental sector: by 1984 some 40 per cent of homes with a television had a VCR. It remained unclear (and a factor of uncertainty) whether this high penetration by an alternative technology offering variety of programme choice was an indicator of a potentially weak market for cable television or (along with home computer sales) of an enthusiasm for any new technologies that promised to enrich the home as an entertainment and learning centre. In contrast to Britain the relatively low penetration of VCRs in the United States (19.2 per cent of homes with a television) seemed explicable in terms of competition from an established cable television industry. Official attitudes towards VCR could also be influenced by the fact that Japan had established the dominant technological format in this market. In France the VCR market remained weak, in part because it attracted a heavy luxury goods tax and in part because of ingeniously difficult import arrangements. Cable television was more clearly 'in the national electronic interest'.

The character of the cable policy network was also closely related to the prestige of national telecommunications authorities and public broadcasting organisations. The success of their lobbying was closely related to government's perception of their past performance, a perception that was in turn influenced by the extent to which the political ideology of government favoured state or market. In France the reputation of the DGT was stronger than that of public broadcasting. Lobbying for cable by the DGT was strengthened by their success after the mid-1970s in giving France a world lead in digital switching technology (as well as in electronic telephone directories, new video telephones and data transmission services). They were in a strong position to make similar claims for optic-fibre cable and to compare their record with American experience which showed how private franchise-holders were likely to back down from earlier ambitious plans. By contrast, the public broadcasting system was attacked for lack of choice, poor quality programming and governmental control. The French Socialist government lifted the broadcasting monopoly of the latter but not the telecommunications monopoly of the DGT. British Telecom had greater difficulty in making out a case for its past success and confronted after 1979 a government that favoured the market. By the early 1980s British Telecom was burdened with huge amounts of obsolete equipment, the relatively poor performance of British telecommunications manufacturers in developing digital switching systems (System X) and a legacy of underinvestment. Its investment on a per capita basis was well behind France and, especially, Germany. A Conservative government was unlikely to inject state aid to overcome so formidable a problem. The solution was deregulation of telecommunications: licencing of Mercury as a new private carrier, provision that cable television operators could also be cable providers, privatisation of British Telecom and creation of a new regulatory authority.

An important factor in generating bold (albeit different) cable plans in Britain and France was a perception of technological backwardness. France approached cable in the way that it had earlier tackled a telephone system whose penetration in 1974 had been behind Spain and Greece. Germany's sense of urgency grew with the successes in world telecommunications markets of the French firm CIT-Alcatel and the Dutch giant Philips. Yet the factor of technological backwardness was not always present in Western Europe. The Netherlands could claim to be a telecommunications model and could afford to adopt a low-key, incremental approach to cable technology. As we shall see in the case of satellite television, external commercial threat was matched by internal challenge from within Europe, particularly when a Dutch firm like Philips entered joint ventures like that with AT & T to market advanced telecommunications equipment.

SATELLITE TELEVISION: THE EUROPEAN DIMENSION

With satellite broadcasting the European dimension of the new communications technology was even more apparent. Indeed, by comparison, cable television seemed to provide 'an electronic Maginot-line', enabling governments to continue to control viewing. Satellite broadcasting has little respect for frontiers. The Broadcasting Commission of the German Minister-Presidents' Conference estimated that by 1988 there would be up to 30 European-wide programmes. These satellite programmes presented an external threat in various forms: that extra programming would lead to an American 'colonisation' of the media; that failure to agree common European technical standards for satellite transmission and receiving equipment would lead to a lack of competitiveness with American and Japanese equipment manufacturers; and that the development of internationally competitive European broadcasting and telecommunications would be further frustrated by a labyrinth of national broadcasting regulations.

European-wide regulation and promotion of satellite television was of interest to three bodies: the European Broadcasting Union (which was particularly concerned about common technical standards); Eutelsat, established by the European Space Agency to manage international satellite communications in Western Europe (with its own ECS programme, the first of five being launched in June 1983); and the European Community (with its interest in 'a common market for broadcasting' amongst the ten partners). The issue of common technical standards was of major commercial significance, and in 1983 the EBU accepted the sophisticated C-MAC picture system for DBS (developed by the IBA) as a European standard. Yet uncertainty remained as the French and German governments seemed to prefer a picture system more compatible with their cable plans. In 1984 the two largest manufacturers of television sets in Europe, Thomson of France and Philips of the Netherlands, agreed to work to a modified MAC system. Equipment manufacturers sought larger markets through common standards, whilst governments hesitated at the prospect of opening up their national telecommunications markets. As a consequence decisions about DBS were delayed.

As far as the European Commission was concerned, satellite (and cable) television had two aspects: as developments affecting the internal market (specifically, competition and harmonisation policies) and the European programming industry. In a 500-page discussion paper (intended as the basis for a later draft directive) of 1984 the Commission emphasised 'free competition' amongst broadcasting organisations and 'free access' to all member states. Common rules were envisaged for three main areas – copyright, standards (notably protection of minors) and advertising (which, unlike some member states, the Commission saw as centrally important for financial viability). If the search for common rules came up against widely differing national views about broadcasting, consideration of aiding the European programme industry was hindered by the budgetary crisis of the Community. The BBC took the initiative on the issue of American colonisation, arguing that broadcasting was an important industry (in Britain alone employing some 60,000 and worth £1.5 billion a year) and that it must be aided not just to stem a tide of cheap American imports, but also to sell itself more effectively in non-European markets. Specifically, the BBC argued for a European Film Board Fund, combining EC industrial funds with private funds and concentrating on aiding European programmes designed for audiences in more than one EC country.

Satellite broadcasting in Europe is extremely complex, involving different types of satellite and different scales of collaboration – from national telecommunications satellites and European Communications Satellites to DBS. National and ECS satellites are multi-purpose and low-powered, more suitable for feeding cable systems. DBS is distinctive in the sense that the satellite is heavy, single-purpose and very costly – to build (it needs at least two satellites to ensure a constant service), to launch (with heavy insurance cover), to run (with high programming costs) and to link up the viewer (who needs an appropriate dish, amplifier and de-scrambler). Two major issues have faced national policy-makers: how to use the ECS channels as they become available; and whether and how to build DBS satellites and, if so, how to programme them.

DBS has particularly excited British, French and German policy-makers and, as we shall see a little later, Ireland and Luxembourg. In the case of Britain, France and Germany the interests of the indigenous aerospace industry have been central to DBS policy, particularly British Aerospace, France's Aérospatiale and Germany's Messerschmitt-Boelkow-Blohm. Aérospatiale and M-B-B had been involved in various collaborative ventures since the 1950s (aircraft, missiles and helicopters). In 1979, in the heyday of political cooperation between Helmut Schmidt and Giscard d'Estaing, they agreed to establish a joint company Eurosatellite to manufacture and sell high-powered DBS satellites, with first broadcasts in 1986. Other shareholders were Thomson of France, AEG-Telefunken (now ATN) of Germany and Etca of Belgium. Orders were placed for three systems, each providing three extra channels and to be launched by the European Ariane rocket: *TDF-1* (to be launched in October 1985) for France, *TV-Sat* for Germany and *Tele-X*, a Nordic television satellite with one channel each for Finland, Norway and Sweden.

In France itself *TDF-1* became the focus of a major controversy. Support came from CNES, the prestigious national space agency, and from Georges Fillioud, the Minister of Communications, who spoke of the competitive threat from Japan (with its first DBS launch in 1984), the United States and Luxembourg (the American satellite company Coronet had based itself in Luxembourg and was attempting to produce a low-cost rival to DBS). Opposition emanated from the DGT, which argued that it was technologically obsolescent, excessively expensive and 'anti-cable', while DBS was also rejected by Eutelsat in favour of medium-sized satellites. *TDF-1* was kept alive, but Aérospatiale and M-B-B decided in 1984 to invest in a new family of medium-powered, multi-purpose satellites, the Spacebus project (evoking the European Airbus project on which they were also working). Matra, Aérospatiale's state-controlled rival, had been in a collaborative venture (Satcom International) with British Aerospace to build lighter satellites (*Eurostar*).

Britain's approach to DBS was a mirror-image of that to cable television: in contrast to the heavy governmental financial support in France and Germany, the British government insisted that there must be no direct governmental financing of DBS. In practice the idea of a new, privately-financed competition in broadcasting from space gave way under the pressure of circumstances. The government accepted the IBA's view that 'a relative monopoly' for BBC and ITV was necessary to meet 'the chilling economics' of DBS. A central factor in Britain's DBS policy was the commitment of the Department of Trade and Industry to the success of United Satellites, a consortium that it had put together from British Aerospace, British Telecom and GEC-Marconi. In order to establish its *L-Sat* as a force in world markets, the department pressed for the launch of a DBS system (eventually three satellites) in 1986. Yet the fate of that system was left to the commercial judgement of future participating broadcasting organisations. The Home Office authorised the BBC to operate two DBS channels and then, in October 1983, announced that the independent television sector could also have two channels (of which at least one should go outside the existing ITV companies, contrary to the view of the IBA).

As with cable, the British government wanted to use the new technology to inject new blood into broadcasting, 'a third force' of commercial non-broadcasting organisations. The BBC had shown interest in subscription DBS as a way out of the blind alley of reliance on the licence fee, whilst the IBA had been distracted by a recent round of franchising ITV companies.

By 1984 both BBC and ITV were pressing for security as a condition of their participation, pointing to the huge cost of the project (£400 million) and the failure of the government to issue technical specifications for receiving equipment (a delay caused by the government's hope for European-wide agreement to the C-MAC system developed by the IBA and opposed by the BBC). The all-important receiving equipment was unlikely to be available for 1986–87 or at a low enough cost.

DBS in Britain is a case study of how technological/industrial crisis can generate neo-corporatist behaviour. Faced by the BBC's unsuccessful talks with Thorn-EMI about cost-sharing, and the threat of the BBC's withdrawal, government was subjected to strong industrial pressures to 'orchestrate' the various interests involved: the pressure came from United Satellites and from equipment manufacturers (notably Mullard, which was represented in ITAP). Accepting that DBS was 'a high-risk, high-cost venture', and that indecision was dissipating an early technological lead in DBS standards, the government opted in 1984 for a consortium approach. A tripartite working party was established with representatives from the BBC, the IBA and the Independent Television Companies Association (the chairman of the latter's cable and satellite working party), under the chairmanship of the same 'honest broker' who had brought together the various parties in the troubled System X project. The working party was part of a wider attempt to involve the United Satellites partners and equipment manufacturers in talks with the broadcasting organisations. Each participant demanded its price: the BBC that its participation should represent at least 50 per cent of the project; the 15 ITV companies that the IBA would at least not be obliged to re-advertise their franchises in 1989, whilst the IBA pressed the case for the ITV companies' extension of franchise to 1997. The working party's conclusions embodied these demands and were fed, as amendments, into the Cable and Broadcasting Bill. The 'new blood' was confined to a 20 per-cent share, was restricted to a British/EEC connection and was to be recommended to the government by the IBA as the spokesman for the commercial sector. In 1984 the government selected Thorn-EMI, Granada TV Rentals, the S. Pearson group (including Goldcrest Films and the *Financial Times*), the Virgin Group and an outsider, Consolidated Satellite Broadcasting (formed by a few independent producers). The three major parties began a series of meetings to construct a DBS consortium, to share out the stake amongst the 'third-force' companies and then to negotiate with United Satellites.

Irrespective of the difficulties of DBS, the speed of development of satellite broadcasting was opening up major conflicts about the use of new channels. In the German case these conflicts were strongly domestic. In order to assist his cable plans and to give impetus to private commercial broadcasting, the German Minister for Posts planned 17 to 19 satellite television channels by 1990. Fifteen would feed directly into cable. Six channels were to be rented from the *Intelsat 5* communications satellite (with the exception of a channel for ARD, these were to be allocated to specific states); seven from a new all-German satellite, *DFS Copernicus*, to be built by a German consortium including Siemens and M-B-B; and two from the

ECS2. In addition, *TV-Sat* would provide from 1986 two to four DBS television channels. The major conflicts surrounded the allocation of channels on ECS2 and *TV-Sat*. From the telecommunications perspective, Schwarz-Schilling was anxious to enrich the new cable network and entice customers, if necessary by foreign programming. The Minister-Presidents' Conference was divided about private commercial broadcasting on party lines but, in its concept for restructuring broadcasting of October 1984, united in its support for a German (and European) programming solution. It could agree that ARD and ZDF, the main public broadcasters, should share one 'Eastern' channel on ECS2 (mainly to serve cable in Berlin and one channel on *TV-Sat* (here ZDF planned to develop a European programme embracing theatre, films, concerts, sport and current affairs). Lothar Späth, Minister-President of Baden-Württemburg, pressed strongly in favour of a role for the public broadcasting organisations in breaking out of German provincialism by developing a European cultural channel genuinely reflecting the EEC. The ZDF was notably keen to break out of its one-channel ghetto, and by 1984 had already developed a music channel and a channel of rescheduled programmes (ZDF2) for the pilot cable projects. It was also able to agree about the allocation of the *Intelsat 5* channels. A state treaty seemed, nevertheless, a remote prospect. Led by Bernhard Vogel, Minister-President of Rhineland-Palatinate, the home of the first pilot project (Ludwigshafen), the CDU Minister-Presidents attempted to construct a private consortium for ECS2's 'Western' channel. The consortium that emerged was notable for its exclusion of Bertelsmann (a liberal publishing group) and *Westdeutsche Allgemeine Zeitung* (an independent newspaper): it was centred on the conservative publishing groups of Springer, Bauer and Burda and on the *Programmgesellschaft für Kabel- und Satellitenrundfunk* (PKS), financed by the cooperative banks. WAZ and Bertelsmann, respectively the largest German regional press and the world's largest publishing house, decided to pursue an independent path, Bertelsmann teaming up with Radio Télévision Luxembourg initially in a new German-language 'off-air' programme *RTL Plus*. Also controversial was the allocation of *TV-Sat* channels amongst the states and the decision about just how many of these channels were to be for television.

The new satellite channels were major assets, and individual European countries were bound to seek commercial and cultural advantage from new international media. With a satellite footprint into Britain, the Netherlands, Denmark and parts of Sweden, Ireland was tempted by a commercial approach. The Irish government invited some 15 groups (of which only four were Irish) to submit proposals for the five channels allocated to Ireland. But right at the heart of the new media maze stood Luxembourg, a small state occupying a strategic position and with a media tradition symbolised in Radio Télévision Luxembourg. Its internationally recognised orbital position gave it a satellite footprint covering a huge area of Western Europe, whilst its government proclaimed the importance of the principle of the free flow of information. The Prime Minister, Pierre Werner, took personal charge of communications policy which was pursued in a highly centralised and secretive fashion. The German government was suspicious, the French government hostile, whilst Peter Glotz, general secretary of the German SPD, spoke of Luxembourg's 'declaration of war' on West German public broadcasting. In Germany the breakthrough was made in 1984 with *RTL Plus*, an 'off-air', German-language, commercial channel directed at the Saar, Rhineland-Palatinate and parts of North Rhine-Westphalia. Luxembourg started with the idea of its own fully independent DBS satellite (*Lux-Sat*) but, daunted by the huge costs, pursued two other options: a French-language channel and a German-language channel on France's *TDF-1* (agreed in 1984), and support for the efforts of an American company Coronet to raise capital for a private-enterprise telecommunications satellite (the GDL project). The GDL project was attacked by the general secretary of Eutelsat as 'an anti-European initiative', threatening 'ruinous competition' with Eutelsat's programme, while the French Minister of Posts and Telecommunications spoke of Luxembourg's 'Coca-Cola satellite' assaulting 'our artistic and cultural integrity'.

France sought to pre-empt Luxembourg by its own early initiatives in spreading French culture through Europe by means of international distribution to cable systems of the new *Canal plus* from November 1984 and via TV5, a satellite channel providing an amalgam of French-language programmes (taken by the German pilot cable project in Munich). The BBC and ITN began to study the feasibility of satellite-delivery of a 24-hour news channel for European cable operators (covering the main European languages). The BBC, in conjunction with Harold Holt and a merchant bank, established a company to explore the possibility of a European music channel, beaming live opera, concerts and theatre across Europe; Thames Television decided on its own satellite channel via ECS, whilst the cable and satellite working party of ITCA explored a collaborative channel for European cable operators. The possibilities for international collaboration were revealed in the Eurikon project; several European broadcasting companies (notably in the Netherlands, Ireland, Switzerland and Spain) sought to offer a genuinely European news, current affairs and financial service via ECS.

The need for urgent action by European broadcasting organisations was indicated not just by the entrepreneurship of Luxembourg, but also by the arrival on ECS in 1984 of Rupert Murdoch's commercial, advertising-based *Sky Channel* and of *Music Box*, the first music channel put together by the Virgin Group, Yorkshire Television and Thorn-EMI. By the autumn of 1984 *Sky Channel* was available in 'upgrade' British cable systems, in the German pilot projects in Ludwigshafen and Munich, in a major Paris hotel, in Finland, Malta, the Netherlands, Norway and Switzerland. Major advertisers like Philips were beginning to show a new interest in Western Europe as one market by buying time on *Sky Channel*.

CONCLUSION

Perhaps the most striking impression from this attempt to offer a portrait of the new broadcasting technologies is the strength of particularism in Western Europe. Western Europe is likely to remain a series of separate markets for cable and satellite programming – but with the major difference that (even allowing for the multiple sound channels on future satellites) the broadcasting markets are likely to be increasingly defined by language groupings (notably English, French and German) rather than national boundaries.

At the same time the force of external commercial and cultural threats from Japan and the United States was helping to break the mould of particularism. American equipment suppliers (like Oak Industries and General Instruments), programmers (like Home Box Office), cable system operators (like Cox Cable and American Television and Communications) and satellite companies (like Coronet) were keen to capitalise on their experience in Europe.

This threat was most keenly felt in France. During 1983–84 French governmental views were strongly influenced by two developments: the joint venture in digital switching equipment between Philips of the Netherlands and American Telephone and Telegraph; and the launch of Japan's first DBS satellite, sparking off a fear that Japan's early lead in satellite television could lead her to sweep Europe with sales of domestic reception antennae. Confronted also by the factor of new domestic budgetary constraints, the French government took the initiative to promote wider European collaboration in telecommunications, seeking industrial alliances across frontiers and government encouragement of common technical standards and collaborative research and development. Examples include the talks with British Telecom about a reciprocal opening up of their national markets for digital telecommunications equipment, the Spacebus project with Germany, and the proposed videocommunications link between EEC capitals. Otherwise, the perception that fragmentation into closed national telecommunications markets, duplication of research and development and lack of common technical standards constituted a major industrial handicap was strongest at the levels of the European Commission and some individual companies.

Even so, the French and German governments remained cautious about opening their national telecommunications market to foreign equipment manufacturers, except on the basis of a broad European collaboration and on the principle of reciprocity. In 1984 the French government opted, correspondingly, to keep foreign suppliers out of its new cable investment. In Germany as well as France the emphasis on public investment in cable made it difficult for foreign suppliers to break into national markets. By contrast, the new emphasis on deregulation and competition in Dutch and British telecommunications offered opportunities to foreign suppliers. The difference between the two cases was that the Netherlands was deregulating from a position of strength in telecommunications: a Dutch company like NKF-Kabel saw greater opportunities in the British cable market than in any other in Western Europe.

A second clear impression from this comparative survey is the fragmentation of decision-making and the way in which rapid technological change causes strains in policy formulation. One might note the conflicts between the Department of Trade and Industry and the Home Office in Britain, the former complaining that the latter was crippling cable television by attempting to over-regulate it, and how both were taken by surprise in 1984 when the Chancellor announced the phasing out of capital allowances, thereby sharply changing the economics of cable television. Outside Luxembourg France has come closest to realising that all forms of communications are related and should be treated as such, and that it is important to link the cultural and industrial aspects of communications. Even so, the idea of a coherent communications policy has something of a dream-like quality when measured against the complexities of the technologies and the constitutional and political factors that underpin the distribution of powers in modern liberal states. Perhaps it is more important that a bold idea should be widely shared and nurtured at a central political point and that those who nurture and share that idea should have a clear, yet flexible political strategy for its realisation. Here we enter the realm of the political sociology of ideas.

A third strong impression is that West European governments and broadcasters have been facing an increasingly turbulent environment. Public service broadcasters and their defenders have tended in the past to react to new technologies with cynicism: to video in the late 1960s, and then to teletext and cable television in the 1970s (the Annan report's strictures on 'the ravenous parasites' of pay-cable television are archetypal). They must now recognise that Western Europe is moving inexorably towards 'the wired society' as part of general changes in the communications structure. In broadcasting, as well as in telecommunications, there are major new opportunities for entrepreneurial talent, not least in European-wide ventures (like cultural, current affairs and movie channels). Although new developments present a severe test for public broadcasting organisations, they start with the advantages of managerial and programming experience. The race is likely to be won by those companies that can develop an imaginative and distinctive programming philosophy. To the question 'will industry be given a greater role through advertising and sponsorship?' the answer is probably 'yes'. Entrepreneurially-minded people in the BBC and Germany's ZDF are already seeking out new partners with whom to collaborate.

The question 'will the viewers pay more for new channels or will the standards of programmes deteriorate?' is clearly a major one for policy-makers. Regulatory policy-making for cable and satellite broadcasting must take account of three considerations: the rationale for regulation provided by the nature of 'off-air' broadcasting is eliminated; the context of regulation is confused and imperfectly controllable (if controllable at all), indicating the need for redefinition of its purposes; and the need for flexibility and support for new ventures, given that early participation in new markets is likely to be crucial for eventual success. The attempt to maintain programme standards by regulation in the form of import quotas (as in France) or of concern for public order, decency and good taste may be well-conceived and worthy. It is, nevertheless, an inadequate response and, standing alone, likely to frustrate the promotion of a European industry. The major need is to shift the public debate about cable and satellite broadcasting from the nature of their technology as communications-delivery systems to programming. Programming is the industry on which the success of cable and satellite television depends. The central issue for broadcasters and policy-makers is protection of the right of the artist to speak to the audience in a broadcasting age when attention to 'the ratings' deflects attention to the short term and to fostering imitation rather than innovation. An aim of public policy must be to ensure that the major functions of European broadcasting are *better* accomplished with the new media – the functions of articulating social concerns, fostering the investigative values and insights of the documentary and encouraging dramatic values. Whether by national initiative (witness the programming activities of the *Mission sur la Télédistribution* under Bernard Schreiner and the French cable regulations of 1984) or by EEC action (witness the BBC's proposal for a European Film Board Fund), European public policy must do much more to stimulate creative talent. That process will be encouraged the more European broadcasters see Europe as a single broadcasting market. It will also be encouraged the sooner that individual governments recognise the potential of broadcasting markets in the age of cable and satellite technologies.

In the absence of greater initiative the prospects are bleak. Programme production is expensive because of the time involved and because it is a creative process; the programme costings of cable operators in Britain and Germany are very low indeed. If the result is a diet of derivative, predictable output, American programming is likely to prove both cheap and easily available in large quantity. A European-wide programming policy, based on a distinctive programming philosophy, is a crucial area for EEC and EBU action. The issue of programming philosophy and of a genuinely European concept comes to a head in the DBS projects. Here is the opportunity for 'a European superstation in the sky', carrying not just a distinctive European news service but also live sport, theatre and concerts from all over Europe. In 1987 the new powerful Olympus satellites of the European Space Agency will provide a channel for the first pan-European DBS service.

The sense of urgency is not (or should not be) affected by the downgrading of forecasts for cable television penetration. In 1983 CIT Research forecast that by 1992, 27 per cent of West European households would be linked to cable television; in 1984 that forecast dropped to 19.5 per cent. After the British budget of 1984 the accountants Deloitte concluded that cable television in Britain was under threat. Even if some of the new systems in Britain fail, and if the four German pilot projects prove a disappointment, Britain will have its 'upgraded' systems as models and the German Bundespost's cable network will be at the disposal of *Land* governments. It is clear across Europe that cable television systems are fragile; they are in need of nurturing, either by public investment in the infrastructure (as in France and Germany) or by 'sheltering' private investment (by flexible tax rules, including very generous capital allowances). The financing of the system is also eased if cable television is integrated with the range of telephony services. Against this background, the 'revolution' in the communications structure, and in broadcasting in particular, is likely to take place over a longer period of time than was envisaged in 1981–82. The major impact on the public broadcasting organisations will take place in the 1990s rather than the 1980s. Yet the broadcasting organisations and public policy must change rapidly during the 1980s if their corporate identity, and European cultural identity, is to have much meaning. The responsibility lies squarely on the shoulders of trans-European organisations (such as the EEC and the EBU), national governments and, not least, broadcasters themselves.

NOTES

This article constitutes preliminary research for an ESRC project (1984–86) on regulatory policies for cable and satellite television in Western Europe.

1. See, for example, B. Wenham (ed.), *The Third Age of Broadcasting* (London: Faber, 1982); also J. Howkins, *New Technologies, New Policies* (London: British Film Institute, 1982).
2. Diana Green, 'Cable TV in France', *National Westminster Bank Review*, Summer 1984.
3. On 'policy communities' see J. Richardson (ed.), *Policy Styles in Western Europe* (London: Allen & Unwin, 1982); on 'policy networks' see H. Heclo, 'Issue Networks and the Executive Establishment', in A. King (ed.), *The New American Political System* (Washington, DC: American Enterprise Institute, 1978).

ABSTRACTS

Politics, Parties and the Media in Britain
Jean Seaton

The conventional view that the media have little or no political effect now needs to be re-assessed. It is not simply that voting behaviour appears to be changing rapidly, providing a new role for the press and broadcasting in Britain, particularly in establishing short-term moods and expectations. What is more important is that political institutions and forms of public life have already been radically altered by developments in media technology, and are likely to be changed even further in the future.

Proclaiming the Repubic: Broadcasting Policy and the Corporate State in Ireland
Desmond Bell

A review of current developments in broadcasting and communications policy in the Republic of Ireland reveals that a de-regulatory strategy has been a less significant aspect of government policy than in the UK or USA. Why is it that despite an ongoing crisis in public expenditure in Ireland and the increasing influence of neo-liberal economic thinking in political circles, 'public service' traditions of broadcasting remain relatively unchallenged? This chapter argues that the 'public service' tradition in Ireland, legitimised as it is by ideological concerns with national sovereignty and cultural identity, has not been effectively challenged in a political system with a markedly corporatist character.

France and the 'New Media'
Raymond Kuhn

The political debate on broadcasting in France still covers traditional issues such as financing, programming and control, with reference to the 'old media' of state radio and television. Increasingly, however, it is the 'new media' (*Canal plus*, cable and satellite) which are coming to dominate the political agenda on broadcasting. This article examines the debate on the 'new media' during the Mitterrand presidency, emphasising three aspects in particular: the importance of industrial policy considerations in their development; the present, and possible future, role of the state in the broadcasting field; and the ethos of broadcasting as a public service.

Political and Market Forces in Italian Broadcasting
Donald Sassoon

This article examines the development of the Italian state television service (RAI) since its inception in 1954, its control by the leading government party, the Christian Democrats (DC), and the 1975 legislation which transferred control to an all-party parliamentary committee. It analyses the subsequent carve-up of the RAI by the two principal coalition partners, the DC and the Socialists, and the Constitutional Court's decision to abolish the RAI's national monopoly, which opened up the way for the establishment of hundreds of private television stations. Finally, the article assesses the political and economic effects of this phenomenon, its likely impact on the 'information revolution' and the reactions of the main political parties.

Pluralism in the West German Media: The Press, Broadcasting and Cable
Arthur Williams

This article explores the implications of cable broadcasting plans in the Federal Republic of Germany. Developments in Luxembourg, Ludwigshafen and Munich, together with new and proposed legislation, are examined against the background of the existing broadcasting and press systems. The need for new opportunities to extend the plurality of opinion articulated in the public media is highlighted. While cable and related technologies hold out the promise of greater variety, progress in the Federal Republic is slow; the prospect of a significant boost to pluralism does not appear realistic in the foreseeable future. A potentially major obstacle to increased variety of opinion is identified as the involvement of publishing groups in private broadcasting.

Broadcasting and Politics in the Netherlands: From Pillar to Post
Kees Brants

The emergence of new electronic media has had a noticeable effect on political communication in the Netherlands which, for such a long time, has been determined by a pillarised political culture. This article examines changes within both the broadcasting and political systems. It shows how private interests seem to be benefiting from the development of the new media, while at the same time the political parties are losing their grip on the traditionally partisan broadcasting system.

Broadcasting in Spain: A History of Heavy-handed State Control
Esteban López-Escobar and Angel Faus-Belau

In this article the relationship between government and broadcasting in post-civil war Spain is explored, spanning the period of the Franco dictatorship, the transition to democracy and the election of the present Socialist government. The emphasis is on the overriding continuity of this relationship, despite changes of governing elites and broadcasting legislation. A liberalisation of broadcasting, whether in terms of the establishment of private competition for state television or in terms of a more impartial and balanced political output, has not taken place.

Greece: A Politically Controlled State Monopoly Broadcasting System
Dimitrios Katsoudas

This article covers the rise and development of Greek broadcasting over two clearly delineated periods: from its inception during the Second World War to the end of the Colonel's Dictatorship; and from the restoration of democracy to the present day. The arrangements for both periods are discussed, since they demonstrate admirably the strength of the political will for controlling broadcasting media. A practice of direct, or barely concealed control is evident in both periods, with even the democratic governments unable or unwilling to resist the temptation to manipulate radio and television for their own partisan ends. Despite promises in favour of change, the accession of PASOK power has done little to alter the prevailing tradition of government/broadcasting relations.

The Politics of Cable and Satellite Broadcasting: Some West European Comparisons
Kenneth Dyson

This article examines policy responses to the new technology of cable and satellite broadcasting in five West European countries: Great Britain, the Federal Republic of Germany, France, Ireland and the Netherlands – and in the European Community. Particular attention is given to the political problems of unified direction in the policy process and of conflict and cooperation over cross-national satellite broadcasting. The factors shaping policy processes are identified and analysed. The conclusions deal with the central characteristics of the policy process in this new field, and with the issues of policy priorities and of the relevance of new forms of European collaboration.